1233

Pope Gregory IX introduces the Inquisition as a further tool for persecuting heretics such as the Cathars, or Albigensians, in the south of France.

1261

The crusaders' Latin Kingdom is dissolved after Michael VIII Palaeologus inflicts a crushing defeat on the forces of Baldwin II, reclaiming Constantinople for the Greeks.

c.1250

A leader called Tariácuris, prince of the city of Tzintzuntán, succeeds in uniting the three Tarascan clans under his leadership.

c.1250

Xolotl unifies the Chichimec tribes under his leadership, and founds the cities of Xoloc and Tenayuca in the rich upland Valley of Mexico.

1250

from 1250

The first Mameluke sultan, Aybak, ascends the throne in Cairo, officially as co-regent with his new wife, Shajar.

1260

The Mamelukes defeat a Mongol army at the Battle of Ain Jalut, near Nazareth in Palestine. On the journey back to Cairo, Baybars I seizes power.

1250

Jalal ad-Din Rumi founds the Mevlevi Order of Whirling Dervishes.

1258

A Mongol army under Hulegu captures Baghdad, thereafter ruling as Il-khans in the former capital city of the Caliphate.

1260

Kublai Khan proclaims himself Great Khan, violating the elective principle laid down by Genghis.

c.1250

The Tahitians build the important cult centre of Taputaputea on Raiatea in the Society Islands.

EUROPE

1270

The St Gotthard Pass is opened and rapidly becomes the most important trade route across the Alps.

1278

Ottokar II, the Premyslid King of Bohemia, loses the Battle of the Marchfeld against the Habsburg Rudolf I, and with it his kingdom and his life.

AMERICA

1270

AFRICA

ASIA

1275

Marco Polo arrives at the court of Kublai Khan, at Cambaluc near Beijing.

12

For time, t help the J to repel an attempted invas armies of the Emperor of Ch Kublai Khan, inspiring the le Kamikaze – 'divine wind'.

OCEANIA

c.1291
The Swiss cantons of Uri, Schwyz and Unterwalden form an alliance to resist Habsburg rule.

1300
Construction of Rheims Cathedral is completed.

1309
Marienburg in what is now Poland becomes the seat of the Grand Master of the Teutonic Order.

c.1300
The Chancay civilisation loses its pre-eminence as the Chimú empire expands from its capital of Chan Chan. Both cultures will be overtaken by the Inca in the mid-15th century.

from 1300
Quinatzin founds a new Chichimec capital at Texcoco in Mexico and encourages other Chichimec tribes, including the Aztecs, to migrate south and settle in the region.

1290

1300
The sultanate of Kilwa, on an island off the coast of what is now Tanzania, enjoys its heyday is the trading hub of East Africa, shipping gold and ivory to the Middle and Far East.

c.1300
Thanks to lucrative commerce in gold and ivory, the city of Great Zimbabwe becomes the most important power in Southern Africa.

81
a second yphoons apanese ion by ina, jend of

1291
Acre, the last Christian bastion in the Middle East, is forced to surrender to Muslim forces commanded by the Mameluke Sultan Khalil.

1296
Ala ud-Din extends the rule of the Sultanate of Delhi across large parts of central India.

c.1300
In the wake of fierce power struggles, a secret male society dedicated to Oro, the god of war, emerges in the Society Islands.

1214

France's King Philip II (Augustus) wins the battle of Bouvines, consolidating the power of the French monarchy [b]oth at home and in [Eur]ope as a whole.

1215

The English barons force King John to sign the Magna Carta, acknowledging the rights of England's feudal aristocracy.

1218

French nobleman Simon de Montfort, father of the leader of the English barons, is killed fighting the Cathars of Toulouse.

1220

Frederick II, head of the Hohenstaufen dynasty, becomes Holy Roman Emperor.

1229

King Louis IX of France and Count Raymond VII of Toulouse sign the Treaty of Meaux to end the Cathar Wars.

1220

c.1231

Dunama Dubalemi becomes king of Kanem, a region of nomadic tribes centred on Lake Chad, and builds an enduring and powerful trading empire.

1235

Sundiata from the Keita clan defeats Sumanguru, the powerful Susu ruler, at the battle of Kirina and goes on to establish the Empire of Mali.

c.1222

After a bloody three-year campaign, the Mongols overrun the shahdom of Khwarizm.

...ering

...ir

...title

1238

Russia and Hungary collapse under the onslaught of the Golden Horde under Batu Khan. Batu rules his part of the Mongol Empire from the city of Sarai on the River Volga.

1249

With the capture of the Egyptian port of Damietta, Louis IX records the last great victory of the Christian crusaders.

c.1240

King Talatama of Tonga subjugates Samoa. As a result of ongoing conflict, he moves the Tongan capital from Heketa to a more sheltered site at Mu'a and fortifies its harbour.

1176
the Battle of Legnano, the north
an cities win an important
ry over Frederick Barbarossa in
struggle for independence.

1190
Death of
Frederick
Barbarossa.
His successors struggle
to build on the
successes of the great
Hohenstaufen Emperor.

1204
Under Venetian leadership,
the crusaders divert the Fourth
Crusade to plunder Constantinople
and found short-lived crusader
states in Asia Minor.

B
c
of
bo
Eur

1170
e Chancay and Chillon
ys that run down to the
of central Peru, several
ments and villages unite
n a strong political union,
h Chancay gains the
and.

1200
Nomadic tribes who
later became known
as the Tarascans found
three cities on the shores
of Lake Pátzcuara in western
Mexico. The tribes were all
followers of a fire cult.

1200

c.1180
Great Zimbabwe, the stone-
built capital of the Shona
kingdom, is developing into
a significant trading city.

c.1200
King Lalibela of Ethiopia
has eleven cross-shaped
Christian churches carved
into solid rock in the city
that is named after him.

1189
The largest
crusader
army ever
d in Europe – under the command of
rederick Barbarossa, Philip II (Augustus)
d the Lionheart – sets off on the Third
the Holy Land.

1206
Qutb ud-Din Aibak
founds the
Sultanate of Delhi,
the first Muslim
empire in India.

1206
At a Kuriltai – a gath
of the nomad clans –
the Mongolian chiefs
choose Temujin as the
leader, giving him the
Genghis Khan.

c.1200
The Tu'i Tonga
dynasty is at the
height of its
power in the
Tongan maritime
empire.

1314

At the Battle of Bannockburn, Robert the Bruce and his Scottish forces defeat the English under King Edward II.

1331

The new Serbian ruler Stefan Dusan begins to carve out a Serbian empire in the Balkans.

1339

At the Battle of Laupen the citizens of Berne and their allies from the Swiss cantons defeat a much larger and better equipped Habsburg army

c.1330

The heyday of the Ica-Chincha civilisation in Peru, a society renowned as traders and skilled craftspeople.

1310

c.1312

Mansa Musa comes to the throne in the fabulously wealthy Empire of Mali. He extends the empire in his 25-year reign, becoming the most important monarch of sub-saharan Africa, and greatly extends his own fame with a pilgrimage to Mecca.

1320

The Tughluq Dynasty assumes power in the Sultanate of Delhi.

c.1332

The Ethiopian emperor Amda Seyon inflicts a crushing defeat on Muslim invaders, consolidating Ethiopia's position as a Christian state.

1326

Sultan Osman I captures the Byzantine stronghold of Bursa, thus laying the foundations of the Ottoman Empire. Osman died shortly after the victory and was buried in the city he had just conquered.

THE AGE OF
KINGS AND KHANS

1154–1339

PUBLISHED BY THE READER'S DIGEST ASSOCIATION LIMITED
LONDON • NEW YORK • SYDNEY • MONTREAL

The land of Genghis Khan Herds graze peacefully around a nomadic encampment of traditional yurts on the Mongolian steppe. From a camp such as this Genghis emerged to build a fearsome mounted Mongolian army that carved out the biggest land empire the world has ever seen. At its greatest extent, it stretched from the Arabian Gulf to the South China Sea.

EUROPE

The Hohenstaufen dynasty

The Holy Roman Empire saw its heyday under the Hohenstaufen dynasty, with an empire stretching from Sicily to the Baltic Sea, taking in Italy as well as Germany.

Portrait of an emperor
Made in about the year 1160, this gilded bronze reliquary was cast in the likeness of the young Emperor Frederick I, known as Barbarossa. The Emperor presented it to his godfather, Count Otto von Cappenberg.

In October 1154 the Hohenstaufen ruler Frederick I crossed the Brenner Pass en route to Italy for his investiture as Holy Roman Emperor. He was the model of the chivalrous monarch: powerfully built, strikingly handsome and head of an aristocratic family from the Swabian region of southwest Germany. The chronicler Rahewin, co-author with Otto of Freising of *The Deeds of the Emperor Frederick*, described him thus: 'He has a fine figure. His eyes are clear and penetrating, his nose noble, his beard a reddish colour, while his delicate lips frame a mouth that is not excessively wide – indeed, his whole countenance is cheerful and merry.' The Italians gave him the nickname Barbarossa – 'Redbeard'.

A formidable Welf rival

Frederick was already Duke of Swabia when, in 1152, he was elected German king at the age of about 30. His journey south two years later was only possible because he had managed to reach a settlement with his ambitious cousin Henry the Lion, representing the rival Welf line, who agreed to accompany him to Italy. Ever since the Salian line of emperors had died out with Henry V in 1125, a bloody feud had raged between the Welfs and Hohenstaufens, Germany's two most powerful families, over who

pape le mj et dancence auenturee dicellm
tempe

De lempure frduit lefecond et du depofement
dicellui en lifforie des fedencive

Et hon adont ficomme u

should rule the empire. In part, Frederick had been chosen as king because he was the best compromise candidate to end the feud. Although a Hohenstaufen, he was also, through his mother Judith, half Welf, and so could act as the 'cornerstone that would bind the crumbling walls together', as Otto of Freising put it.

Through the exercise of subtle diplomacy, the new ruler did indeed manage to create a significant breathing space for the crisis-torn empire. The Welfs had been the more powerful of the two families, controlling the important German duchies of Bavaria and Saxony. They had lost Bavaria, however, under Conrad III, Frederick's uncle and immediate predecessor as emperor. Before setting off for Rome, Frederick promised to restore the duchy to Henry the Lion. Henry Jasomirgott of the Babenberg dynasty, who had been ruling it in the interim, was to be compensated with the newly created duchy of Austria.

Crowned by the Pope
The investiture of Emperor Frederick II by Honorious III in 1220. Like his grandfather Barbarossa before him, he travelled to Rome to receive the imperial crown. Both emperors' subsequent relations with the papacy were strained.

Hohenstaufen Empire

Hohenstaufen territory

● **Important cities and places**

Imperial image
Frederick II, Holy Roman Emperor, is depicted on this seal bearing the symbols of his authority. He is seated on a throne with the imperial crown on his head and the orb and sceptre in his hands.

Frederick put his plan into effect in 1156, but only succeeded in putting the conflict between Welfs and Hohenstaufens on hold. Both parties needed allies. In 1168 Henry the Lion married a daughter of King Henry II of England, forging a close link. Frederick Barbarossa turned to France and married the Burgundian princess Beatrix, who brought with her independent Burgundy as her dowry.

The downfall of Henry the Lion

The truce between the rival families did not last for long. By 1178, Henry – who resided in kingly splendour in his palace at Dankwarterode in modern Brunswick – had succeeded in alienating most of his Bavarian subjects through his autocratic rule. He had confiscated properties, revoked fiefs that he himself had granted, and forced the pagan Slavonic princes of Mecklenburg and Pomerania to be baptised. On the plus side, he had swelled ducal coffers by fostering trade and the development of towns, founding the port of Lübeck on Germany's Baltic coast and the great city of Munich, which began life as a small Bavarian market town collecting tolls at a crossing point over the River Isar. But Henry's powerful enemies had had enough.

Acting on accusations made by leading nobles, Frederick Barbarossa, in his role as Holy Roman Emperor, instituted legal proceedings against Henry the Lion that culminated in his being declared an outlaw and losing all his imperial fiefs, apart from some ancestral lands around Brunswick and Lüneburg in northern Germany. Henry himself went into exile in England. The Lion's fall was a personal triumph for Frederick Barbarossa, but it yielded little; Henry's principal vassals divided his lands up among themselves, leaving Frederick himself with nothing.

A troubled investiture

To strengthen his imperial authority, and replenish his treasury, Frederick had set his sights on Italy. But Italian politics would prove as difficult to manage as the rebellious Welfs at home. The very first meeting between Emperor and Pope, in 1155, had ended in acrimony. Barbarossa refused to pay the pontiff the courtesies that his predecessors had shown to the holy office, because he regarded such displays of reverence as demeaning. Deeply offended, the Pope then needed to be cajoled in lengthy negotiations before he agreed to Frederick's investiture as Holy Roman Emperor. This took place on June 18, 1155, but the citizens of Rome expressed their displeasure by storming the investiture banquet; the ensuing bloodbath left 800 people dead.

Frederick was to cross the Alps on five subsequent occasions. The cities of Lombardy had no intention of contributing to the imperial treasury without putting up a fight. Banding together under Milan's leadership in the Lombard League, they challenged their would-be ruler, with support from the papacy, which feared the growth of Barbarossa's power. The result was a bitter conflict, in the course of which the

Pope more than once excommunicated the Emperor, while Barbarossa retaliated by supporting anti-popes. A compromise between the two sides was eventually reached in 1183. The Emperor retained some influence in Italy, but was forced to recognise the privileges of the Lombard League cities, which won the right to manage their own affairs in return for the payment of a substantial cash sum.

Germany in the age of chivalry

The chief glories of the Hohenstaufen period lay less in its political achievements than in rising living standards and culture. The age of chivalry was at its height. This was the time of knightly tournaments, troubadours and courtly love. Middle High German literature reached a peak in the works of the lyric poet Walther von der Vogelweide (literally 'Walter from the Bird Meadow') and Wolfram von Eschenbach, epic poet and author of

Parzival, a classic version of the Holy Grail legend. Living standards improved for everyone. A warming climate combined with increases in the area and productivity of land under cultivation, thanks to forest clearances and the widespread use of the three-field system, meant that people were far better fed than in earlier times. Trade and cities flourished and expanded.

The general sense of well-being found expression in feasts and celebrations. At Whitsun in 1184, the Emperor organised a lavish festival to celebrate the investiture of his two sons, Henry and Frederick, as knights. Some 200,000 people made their way across the empire to Mainz, on the River Rhine. The Emperor's sons swore

The Emperor abroad
A manuscript illumination from the 15th century shows Frederick Barbarossa travelling with his retinue on the Third Crusade to the Holy Land. His men-at-arms carry banners emblazoned with the imperial eagle.

Bearers of the Gospels
This lectern from Freudenstadt in Bavaria is one of the few surviving ecclesiastical furnishings in the Swabian Romanesque style. Carved from willow and standing 120cm (4ft) high, it depicts the four Gospel writers, Matthew, Mark, Luke and John. Their symbols – respectively an angel, winged lion, ox and eagle – appear on the circular plinth that rests on their shoulders.

their knightly oaths clad in magnificent garments, before going on to display their military prowess in jousting tournaments. The choicest delicacies and finest wines graced the banquet that ended the festival, and the common people were entertained by fire-eaters, tightrope walkers, dancing bears and cockfights.

The Emperor drowns

While Germany as a whole prospered, the Emperor's own finances were slowly declining. Even so, exhibiting the knightly spirit of the times, Barbarossa embarked on the Third Crusade in 1189. He died en route attempting to swim the River Saleph (now the Göksu, in southern Turkey) on June 10 of the following year.

His son and heir, Henry VI, inherited an unstable empire. Four years before his accession, the 20-year-old Henry had tried to shore up the empire by marrying Constance of Sicily, a woman 11 years his senior. The match gave the Hohenstaufens a claim to the wealth not just of the island of Sicily but also of southern Italy, which Sicily's rulers controlled at that time. The reigning monarch, Constance's nephew William II, died heirless in 1189, but Henry's claim to the throne was contested by an anti-German party that installed William's half-brother, Count Tancred of Lecce, in his place. This embroiled Henry in a lengthy struggle for control of Sicily that distracted him from his other responsibilities.

When news of Barbarossa's death got abroad, Henry the Lion returned from exile in England to reclaim his former possessions in Saxony. Henry VI would no doubt have met the challenge head-on, but his commitments in Italy forced him to conclude a hasty peace with the rebellious Welf. He headed south for Apulia in the heel of Italy, stopping off en route in Rome for his investiture as Holy Roman Emperor. However, rebellion in Germany forced him to return home. He found uproar, with Saxony and the lands of the Lower Rhine in open revolt, supporting the Welf cause.

Then an unexpected stroke of luck came to the beleaguered Emperor's aid. England's King Richard the Lionheart had fallen into the hands of his arch-enemy, Duke Leopold of Austria, while returning from the Third Crusade, and Leopold duly delivered Richard up to Henry. This caused outrage, for crusaders were normally considered inviolate under the Truce of God intended to protect them from attack by fellow Christian rulers.

The Emperor was unmoved, for Richard could help him to extricate himself from the many problems he now faced. Richard was related both to Henry the Lion and to Tancred of Lecce, the Emperor's rival for the Sicilian throne. His arrest deprived the Welfs of their most important foreign ally and also dissolved the former alliance between England and Sicily. Henry demanded a ransom of 150,000 silver marks to free his hostage – a fabulous sum equivalent to 34 tonnes of pure silver. England raised the amount, with great difficulty, and Richard was finally sent home in 1194. As a condition of his release, he agreed in future to pay homage to Henry, making England, in theory at least, a vassal state of the Holy Roman Empire.

With this huge injection of English cash in his coffers, Henry was finally

TIME WITNESS

Richard the Lionheart captured

As a leader of the Third Crusade, King Richard I of England made many enemies, among them Duke Leopold of Austria. On the long journey home Richard wisely travelled incognito, adopting the pseudonym of 'Hugo the merchant'. When he halted outside Vienna, however, one of his companions foolishly paid for provisions with a Byzantine coin. The same attendant was later spotted wearing gloves bearing Richard's coat of arms, thereby blowing his master's cover. Richard was arrested and delivered to Leopold, who handed him over to Henry VI. He was held prisoner in a succession of Hohenstaufen castles until a heavy ransom was paid.

able to overrun Sicily and have himself crowned king in the cathedral of Palermo, the island's capital. The day after his coronation, the 40-year-old Constance gave birth to a longed-for heir, the future Emperor Frederick II.

Henry the Lion died seven months later, in August 1195, leaving Henry VI at the height of his power. He ruled over Germany, Sicily, Burgundy and most of Italy except the central Papal States. In addition, England, Poland,

Bohemia and Moravia all paid him homage, as did Armenia, Cyprus and the formerly Norman territories of Tunis and Tripoli in North Africa. His brother Philip of Swabia was engaged to a Byzantine princess, which could create an alliance with the Christian Eastern Empire.

Only one thing was missing for Henry to realise completely his imperial dreams. He wanted to change the system by which the Holy Roman Emperor was chosen, replacing election by a princely electoral college with a hereditary succession. In 1196, Henry presented his plans to the

Shrine of the Three Kings
In Frederick Barbarossa's reign, relics claimed to be those of the Magi who attended Christ's nativity were taken from Milan to Cologne in Germany. There, they were preserved in the cathedral in a magnificent reliquary shrine – one of the finest to survive from medieval times. The shrine (below and background) is in the form of a three-naved basilica, with portraits of apostles and prophets on its sides.

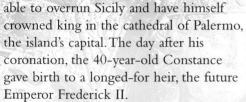

Mirror of the Saxons
Miniatures from a manuscript copy of the *Sachsenspiegel*, the most important German legal document of the High Middle Ages, show a knight dining and a coronation scene. The *Sachsenspiegel*, or Mirror of the Saxons, codified the common law in force in Saxony around the year 1220. Previously, the law had been passed down by word of mouth, but under the Hohenstaufen emperors attempts were made to codify and consolidate legal customs across the empire.

Fortress on a hill
The Hohenstaufen dynasty built many castles across Europe. This fortified tower stands in the German town of Bad Wimpfen, occupying a strategic vantage point above the River Neckar.

electors, who promptly them turned down, despite the many concessions he was offering in return. The most they were prepared to do was to elect his son Frederick as King of Germany. The Pope also opposed Henry's plan, fearing a Hohenstaufen encirclement of the Papal States. Henry's ambitions were on hold when he died of malaria in Palermo in 1197, aged just 32.

Henry's untimely death plunged the empire into crisis. Frederick II, his

elected successor as king of Germany, was only two years old and was living in Sicily. Frederick's mother Constance negotiated with the Pope to secure his future rule in her kingdom, in return renouncing any claim that Frederick might have on the Holy Roman Empire. Shortly before her own death, just a year after her husband in 1198, she named Pope Innocent III as Frederick's guardian.

North of the Alps in Germany, however, civil war broke out when two rival emperors were elected. Once again a Hohenstaufen candidate, Henry VI's brother Philip of Swabia, confronted a Welf – Otto of Poitou, a son of Henry the Lion. After 10 years of conflict Philip was murdered, and with English and papal support his rival was finally crowned Emperor Otto IV in 1209. Otto soon alienated the Pope, however, by launching an invasion of Sicily, once more threatening the long-term independence of the Papal States. In response Pope Innocent III conspired with rebellious German princes to depose Otto as German ruler in favour of Frederick. The Hohenstaufen prince, now turned 17, took the risk and accepted the candidacy.

The world's wonder

The 'child from Apulia', as he was known, arrived in Germany with little money and almost no retinue. Yet he was charming and spirited, and set out to win hearts and minds. Otto and his English allies were defeated at the Battle of Bouvines in 1214 by a coalition of Hohenstaufen and French forces. The following year Frederick II was crowned at Aachen.

The young Emperor was extraordinary, with a wide range of interests and a passion for new ideas. His contemporaries called him *Stupor mundi*, 'the Wonder of the World'. He spent most of his reign, which lasted until 1250, in southern Italy where he had grown up, making only two extended stays in Germany. The old Kingdom of Sicily was his power base, and he ruled it in a hands-on way, almost like a modern state, with the power of the feudal aristocracy severely restricted.

Early in his reign Frederick revoked concessions over property jurisdiction, customs dues and taxation that had been made to the barons, taking these areas back into royal hands. He relied on scholars with a background in law to administer the realm, and in 1224 established Europe's first state university at Naples to train them. His single greatest administrative achievement was the *Constitutions of Melfi*, issued in 1231, which comprehensively codified the constitutional law of the kingdom and gave the monarch huge power.

Frederick was fascinated with the world of Islam. He had Arab works translated into Latin and conversed with Muslim scholars. He enjoyed watching oriental dancers, and chose a bodyguard of Saracen warriors. Also following Islamic custom, Frederick had four wives and kept them in isolation, guarded by eunuchs.

BACKGROUND

A keen birdwatcher and the art of falconry

Frederick II was passionately interested in the sciences and conducted researches of his own in the field of ornithology. Towards the end of his life he published his findings in a book, *De arte venandi cum avibus – On the Art of Hunting with Birds*.

The Emperor's observations were surprisingly accurate for the time. He noted, for example, that cuckoos lay their eggs in other birds' nests. He was also interested in experimenting, having ostriches' eggs imported from Africa in order to find out whether they could be hatched in warm sand.

In the first part of his book, Frederick described the individual bird species and their behaviour, covering such subjects as their feeding, care for their broods, style of flight, and migratory habits. In the second part, he discussed the techniques of falconry, describing the various species of raptors and how to train them. For this section, he had birds of prey imported from all over the world, from Iceland to India. The numerous detailed drawings of birds in the book are also thought to be Frederick's own work.

An imperial bestseller
An illustration from Frederick II's treatise *On the Art of Hunting with Birds*, showing the Emperor with one of his beloved hunting falcons.

A widening breach with Rome

To secure his hold on Sicily, Frederick had assured Pope Innocent III that he would separate the crowns of Sicily and Germany. Yet he had himself been ruling both domains since Otto IV's defeat at Bouvines in 1214. In 1220, four years after the death of Innocent III, Frederick had his nine-year-old son elected King Henry VII of Germany, negating an earlier promise to give up the Kingdom of Sicily in his son's favour. To ensure that this was accepted, he granted many royal privileges to the German ecclesiastical princes. Placated by the concessions, Pope Honorius III – the ruler's one-time tutor – crowned him Holy Roman Emperor in Rome in November 1220. One of the conditions of the coronation was that Frederick would

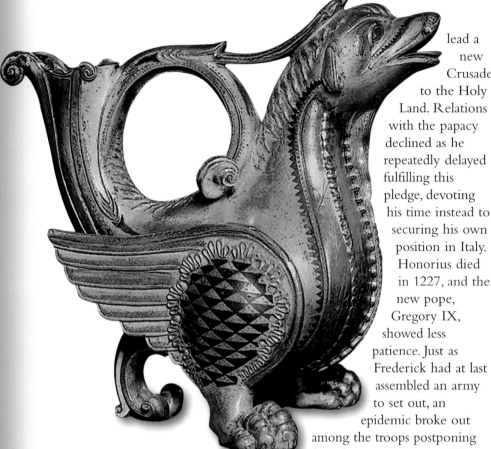

Winged water jug
Decorative bronze-casting was highly sophisticated during the Hohenstaufen period. This mythical beast is actually an ornate flagon.

lead a new Crusade to the Holy Land. Relations with the papacy declined as he repeatedly delayed fulfilling this pledge, devoting his time instead to securing his own position in Italy. Honorius died in 1227, and the new pope, Gregory IX, showed less patience. Just as Frederick had at last assembled an army to set out, an epidemic broke out among the troops postponing their departure. Gregory IX, angrily excommunicated Frederick, so when he did eventually depart the following year, he went as an outcast from the Church. He was successful in the Holy Land, negotiating a 10-year truce with the Sultan of Egypt and winning the return of Jerusalem, Bethlehem and other sites to Christian hands. But none of these achievements spared him from the vengeance of the Pope, who fomented rebellion in Sicily in his absence and delayed revoking the excommunication until 1230, a year after Frederick's return.

The Emperor also faced problems in Germany, where his son Henry VII had by now come of age. Henry sought to keep the autocratic imperial princes in check by promoting the interests of the cities and the lesser aristocracy. Frederick, however, sided with the princes. Needing their support to pursue his policies in Italy, he granted the secular princes the same rights that he had already bestowed on their ecclesiastical counterparts, according them virtually the status of independent rulers. Humiliated, Henry struck up an alliance with Frederick's arch-enemies, the cities of Lombardy. His father imprisoned him for high treason and Henry's brother, Conrad IV, took his place as King of Germany.

The bitter final years

In 1237 Frederick's feud with the papacy erupted once more when he tried to reassert imperial rights in northern Italy. The Lombard cities joined forces with the Pope to resist him, and Frederick found himself excommunicated for a second time. Gregory issued a papal bull accusing him of 'hurling spears of blasphemy against God's firmament and all the saints in heaven.' Frederick responded by calling the Pope a 'Pharisee annointed with the oil of evil'. In 1245 Frederick was formally stripped of his imperial title at the Synod of Lyons, and a rival was set up as anti-king in his place. One cardinal urged Frederick's subjects to 'show no mercy to this dastardly wretch … wipe out the name and the body, and all the seed and offspring of this Babylonian!' Frederick died suddenly in Apulia in 1250, with the conflict unresolved and the empire in disarray.

A sad end for a mighty dynasty

Conrad IV never managed to rescue the situation. He went to southern Italy to secure his position there, working with his half-brother Manfred, governor of Sicily. But before he could achieve his goal, he too died of malaria, in 1254 aged just 26.

Conrad was the last Hohenstaufen ruler. Civil war broke out on his death, and in 1268 his 15-year-old son Conradin attempted to claim his inheritance. He was defeated and handed over to Charles of Anjou, brother of the French king, who had accepted the Kingdom of Sicily in fee from the Pope. Charles had Conradin beheaded as a traitor in Naples, and with his death the imperial glory of the Hohenstaufens came to an ignoble end.

The Plantagenets and the Angevin empire

After promising beginnings, a long-running feud threatened time and again to tear apart the powerful Angevin dynasty and their realm straddling England and western France.

In December 1154, Eleanor of Aquitaine had every reason to feel satisfied. She had just become a queen for the second time. Once consort to the French king, she now graced the English throne. Even the hasty coronation ceremony in London's Westminster Abbey, conducted with little pomp before few guests, can have done little to lessen the pride that the 32-year-old beauty from southern France felt at the extraordinary marital coup she had accomplished.

Eleanor's story was the talk of the courts of Europe. From her father William, Duke of Aquitaine and Count of Poitiers, she inherited lands in southwestern France that were more extensive than those of the French king himself. Her marriage at the age of 15 to Louis, dauphin of France, was a great diplomatic triumph, for when her husband succeeded to the throne as Louis VII on his father's death just a month later, the couple found themselves ruling a united French realm.

A travelling king
The Angevin kings had no central seat of power. Instead, the court was constantly on the move. This fresco in a chapel at Chinon in France shows Henry II on horseback, followed by his wife Eleanor and the couple's third son, the future King Richard, 'the Lionheart'.

throne of England as Henry II on the death of his uncle, King Stephen. Once Eleanor's territories in southeastern France were added, the domain ruled by the royal couple stretched from the Scottish border to the Pyrenees. So the Angevin empire was born, taking its name from the House of Anjou to which Henry belonged. The ruling family took the name of Plantagenet from *plante genet*, French for sprig of broom, an emblem associated with Henry's father. The new Plantagenet dynasty which began with Henry II would rule England until 1399.

Becket's rise and fall
To force through his programme of administrative reform, Henry II called on the talents of able men of relatively humble birth. One such was Thomas Becket, who started his career as an accountant and rose to be Lord Chancellor. The two fell out when Henry appointed Thomas Archbishop of Canterbury and Becket transferred his allegiance from King to Church. They are shown in discussion on this enamelled reliquary.

Friends and rivals (background)
A 15th-century manuscript miniature by Jean Fouquet shows France's King Philip II (Augustus) with Richard, then the Duke of Aquitaine. Richard made common cause with Philip, against his own father Henry II, but the two fell out once Richard inherited Henry's crown and Richard spent the latter half of his reign at war with Philip.

Yet the match was less than satisfactory for the witty, worldly Eleanor. Her devout husband was only truly at ease in the company of churchmen. He had no interest in the arts or the courtly life that his wife adored. 'I have married a monk, not a man,' Eleanor used to complain. Louis finally had the marriage annulled in March 1152, ostensibly because Eleanor had borne him two daughters and not the son that he craved as his heir.

Twice a queen

Following feudal custom, Eleanor regained possession of her inheritance after the divorce. Just two months later she married Henry Plantagenet, the son of her husband's greatest rival, Geoffrey of Anjou. She was 30 years old at the time and Henry was 10 years her junior.

The union had important implications for the balance of power in western Europe. From his father, Henry had inherited Normandy and Brittany as well as the duchies of Anjou, Touraine and Maine in northeastern France. Two years after the marriage, he also acceded to the

The murder of Thomas Becket

The huge swathe of French land that Henry and Eleanor ruled inevitably brought them into conflict with Louis VII, and personal factors further inflamed their rivalry. Louis had renounced his wife for failing to produce a male heir, but in the first 15 years of marriage to Henry she bore no fewer than eight children, the last of them born when she was 45 years old. Among them were five sons: William, Henry, Richard, Geoffrey and John.

Henry and Eleanor were both strong-willed personalities, intelligent and politically astute, and they purposefully set about imposing their will on the lands they ruled, seeking to create an efficient state apparatus. Henry conducted successful military campaigns in north Wales and in Scotland; the first English intervention in Ireland also dated to his reign. Domestically, he devoted much of his energy to modernising the legal system, seeking to expand royal jurisdiction as a final court of appeal for the many feudal courts dispensing justice across his realm. He was particularly eager to restrict the power of the Church courts, which claimed exclusive rights to try those in ecclesiastical orders – perhaps a sixth of the male population at the time.

In pursuit of his goal Henry appointed Thomas Becket, one of his most trusted advisers, as Archbishop of Canterbury, only to see Becket transfer his loyalty from the state's to the Church's cause. The two clashed bitterly over the Constitutions of Clarendon, a legal code that substantially diminished the powers of the Church courts. The clash of wills led first to Becket's exile on the Continent for six years, and then to his assassination in Canterbury Cathedral when he finally returned to England. The outrage stirred by the murder forced Henry to revoke the Constitutions and to acknowledge Becket's status as a martyr. Becket was canonised in 1173, just three years after his death.

Rebellious sons

Meanwhile another clash was developing as Henry's own family rose against him. For the first 15 years of his marriage he lived happily with Eleanor, treating her as a close confidante and trusted advisor. Yet fidelity was never one of the king's virtues, and Eleanor was not a woman to be lightly scorned. Incensed by his enduring relationship with his English mistress Rosamund Clifford – the 'fair Rosamund' of legend – Eleanor turned against her husband and became his bitter enemy.

Henry's relationship with his sons was no less tense. He sought to defuse their ambitions by dividing his lands between them. William having died in infancy, the younger Henry was assigned England, Normandy, and the Angevin heartland of Anjou, and in 1170, at the age of 15, was given the title of co-regent with his father. Richard – the future Lionheart – received his mother's inheritance, the duchy of Aquitaine, while Geoffrey became Count of Brittany. The division left only scraps – the duchies of Mortain and Savoy, the recently conquered parts of Ireland – for the youngest, John, who grew up with the nickname 'John Lackland'.

Yet Henry was unwilling to hand over real power to his sons, taking care to keep government in his own hands. In 1173, fired up by their jealous mother, the teenagers rebelled, seeking immediate possession of the territories that had been

Murder in the cathedral
Infuriated by Thomas Becket's resistance to his plans after he had appointed him Archbishop of Canterbury, Henry mused aloud 'Who will rid me of this upstart priest?' Four of his knights took him at his word and slaughtered the Archbishop before the altar of his cathedral in 1170. Becket's last words were 'I am ready to die for my Lord'.

At the court of Henry II and Eleanor of Aquitaine

Eleanor was one of the principal sponsors of the Age of Chivalry. A devotee of courtly love poetry, troubadors and travelling players, she introduced a new style and polish to court life. She was a great patron of art and literature, and also spent many long hours playing chess.

Her husband, King Henry II, had a taste for traditional royal pursuits. He was a passionate lover of falconry and would even bring his favourite birds to the dinner table, where he fed them tasty morsels. However, he was also fluent in several languages and enjoyed conferring with court scribes and scholars.

The Norman poet known as Wace dedicated the first French version of the Arthurian legend to Eleanor and her husband. His *Roman de Brut* embellished the story on an epic scale, presenting Arthur as a paragon of chivalry and introducing the story of the Round Table.

The rituals of knighthood that Wace described had their real-life counterparts in the ceremonial tournaments that were a feature of the time. Early tournaments had arisen from the need to train men in the use of lances in mock battles that often turned into confused free-for-alls; injuries, and even deaths, were common occurrences. By Eleanor's day, the contests were regulated by an increasingly sophisticated code of conduct that turned them into magnificent spectacles combining courage and physical strength with pageantry and display.

Female poet
Little is known of Marie de France, the earliest recorded French woman poet, but she is thought to have been employed in the English court of Henry II and to have known Eleanor of Aquitaine. She is shown here in an author portrait from a 13th-century French manuscript.

earmarked for them. With Eleanor's assistance they forged alliances with several of Henry's fiercest rivals, among them King William I of Scotland. Eleanor even sought help from her ex-husband Louis VII. Already weakened by the scandal of Becket's murder, Henry now found his fortunes at a low ebb. He responded energetically, however, and by the summer of 1174 the revolt had collapsed and the Scots king had been taken prisoner. Henry pardoned his sons, saving his vengeance for Eleanor, whom he regarded as the ringleader of the rebellion. She spent the remaining 15 years of his reign as a prisoner, but outlived him and re-emerged after his death in 1189 to resume an active part in state affairs. She eventually died in 1204, aged 82, at the convent of Fontrevault in France, which she had endowed, having survived nine of her 10 children – all but the youngest, by then England's King John.

Long before then, the feud between Henry and his sons had been renewed. The younger Henry died on campaign in 1183 and Geoffrey three years later, trampled to death in a riding accident. The main beneficiary was Richard, Eleanor's favourite and a charismatic figure distinguished by his courage in combat. Even in his lifetime many legends grew up about the future Lionheart, who to medieval eyes seemed the very model of the chivalrous ruler. He made no secret of his desire for power, and resisted his father's attempts to prise Aquitaine from his grasp to provide an inheritance for his brother John.

Feast for the eyes
Decorated with enamelwork on a copper base, the medieval Balfour Ciborium held consecrated wafers for the Eucharist. It is now preserved in London's Victoria and Albert Museum.

An ignominious end

To further his ambitions, Richard forged an alliance with the new French king Philip II, who was happy to fan the flames of the Plantagenet family feud. With Richard's aid he attacked Henry's lands in France, meeting little resistance in taking the northern duchies of Anjou, Maine and Touraine. The ailing Henry conceded defeat in the Treaty of Azay-le-Rideau, in which he unwillingly recognised Richard as his sole heir. He died two days later, on July 7, 1189, aged 56.

Richard celebrated his accession the following September. The festivities were a highpoint of the Age of Chivalry, then in full bloom. Richard raised the institution of knighthood to new heights, surrounding himself with a coterie of warriors who engaged in tournaments and jousts at castles throughout his lands. He showed less interest in ruling England, spending only six months of his 10-year reign in the country.

Contention on Crusade

On coming to the throne, Richard set off as quickly as possible for the Holy Land in order to win back Jerusalem, which had fallen to Saladin's Muslim forces two years previously. He and Philip II of France, his one-time ally, set out in 1190 as joint leaders of the Third Crusade, but the two quickly fell out once more. Philip returned home the following year, allying himself against Richard with John Lackland (who had not accompanied his brother on campaign) and a dissident faction of the English nobility.

When Richard learned of the plot, he set off for England only to be captured on his return journey by the Holy Roman Emperor Henry VI. Eleanor and John managed to raise the enormous ransom demanded by the Emperor for Richard's release, but they caused huge popular resentment and brought England to the verge of bankruptcy. The troubles of the time gave rise to the legends of Robin Hood.

Death of a warrior

Richard finally returned to England in 1194 after a four-year absence. He took back the reins of power from his brother without bloodshed, then sailed for France within a month, never to return. He spent the last five years of his reign seeking to reclaim the lands lost to Philip II. In 1199 he was struck by a crossbow bolt while beseiging the castle of a rebel nobleman. He died a few days later of blood poisoning, aged 41, and control of the Angevin empire passed to John.

Family ties
The ruins of Castle Acre Priory stand in the village of the same name in Norfolk, England. The priory was built on land owned by the counts of Warenne, who were closely related to the English royal family. Isabel de Warenne married one of King Stephen's sons and then, after his death, wed a half-brother of Henry II.

The rise of the Italian city-states

Struggling to free themselves from the grip of the Holy Roman Emperors, the urban centres of northern Italy developed into strong independent city-states. At its peak Venice, the greatest of them all, controlled trade in the entire eastern Mediterranean region.

The year 1167 was a bad one for the Emperor Fredrick Barbarossa, and most of his problems stemmed from northern Italy. The expedition he led there had ended in disaster when the imperial army was cut down by plague, and he himself only just managed to escape an assassination attempt. The most powerful man in Europe had suffered the humiliation of being forced to flee to his German homeland, disguised as a peasant.

The root of Frederick's troubles was a new political alliance called the Lombard League. Milan, Mantua, Verona and other northern cities had banded together with papal support to present a united front against imperial rule. For centuries past, the prosperous cities of the region had paid only nominal allegiance to the Holy Roman Empire. Barbarossa had already led three previous expeditions to Italy to try to bring them into line.

Venice provided a role model for the Lombard cities in their struggle for independence. The rise of the lagoon port on Italy's Adriatic coast had begun in the 9th century. Back then, the Venetians were eager to rid themselves of their existing patron saint, Theodore of Euchaita, a Greek soldier martyred in Asia Minor in the 4th century. They replaced him with St Mark, one of the four Evangelists who had also founded the nearby episcopal see of Aquileia. Mark had gone on to serve as bishop of the Egyptian port of Alexandria, where he had endured a martyr's death; his mortal remains still lay there, in what had since become Muslim territory.

Accordingly, in 829, the Venetians dispatched an expedition across the Mediterranean to liberate the saint's relics

Oriental flair
Many Byzantine artists and architects worked in Venice in the course of the Middle Ages, and their crowning achievement was St Mark's Basilica, completed in 1071. Following the sack of Constantinople in 1204, the basilica was clad inside and out with marble panels brought back as part of the spoils.

Dante's politics

Chronic political instability and the violence and suffering that followed inspired the Italian poet Dante to write his political treatise *De Monarchia* ('Of the Monarchy') sometime early in the 14th century. In it he argued the case for imperial rule of the kind seen earlier under the Hohenstaufens.

Dante regarded the Emperor's authority as God-given – the secular equivalent of the jurisdiction over spiritual affairs vested in the Pope. His treatise, with its forthright assertion of imperial rights, made it highly controversial during the long struggles between Emperor and Pope. In 1329 it was burned on the Pope's orders, and in the 16th century it was placed on the Index of banned books, where it remained until Pope Leo XIII eventually ordered its removal from the list in 1897.

Of heaven and hell

The greatest poet of the Middle Ages, the Florentine Dante Alighieri (1265–1321), shown in a fresco in Orvieto cathedral. Dante's most famous work, *The Divine Comedy*, narrated a spiritual journey through Hell and Purgatory to Paradise.

and bring them back them to Venice. In honour of their new patron, they built a wooden church to receive the relics, but this structure went up in flames in 976. The campanile, or bell-tower, was spared from the conflagration, and survived for many centuries to become one of the city's most familiar landmarks.

The rise of Venice

The church itself was eventually replaced by another enduring symbol of Venice – the stone Basilica of St Mark that stands to this day. Soon after completion in 1073, the saint's relics were miraculously rediscovered, unharmed, within a column of the church, and the cult of St Mark began. The saint's symbol, a winged lion, became the city's own heraldic image. It still stands proudly on top of a granite column erected in 1180 in the small square in front of the Doges' Palace. Immediately next to it the Venetians built a shrine to their original patron, Theodore, no doubt seeking to make amends for his long neglect.

The Doge of Venice also had his residence in the heart of the city. The title derives from the Latin *dux* ('leader') and was originally used to designate the governor appointed to rule the region in the name of the Eastern Roman Empire. Over time the Doge, as the highest secular official in the city, came to wield almost unlimited power. The first stone Doges' Palace was built in the 12th century. When, early in the 14th century, that residence became too cramped for its increasingly grand occupants, the Venetians tore it down and embarked on the construction of the present palace.

By then the rise of Venice seemed unstoppable. The city had succeeded in disengaging itself from the jurisdiction of the Byzantine Empire without forfeiting any of the trading privileges it had always enjoyed. As far back as 1000, Venice had taken control of Istria and Dalmatia on the opposite side of the Adriatic. Thereafter it gained control of the most important eastern Mediterranean trade routes, assuring itself of dominance in the region for centuries to come. From 1099, when the forces of the First Crusade captured Jerusalem, the Holy Land also entered Venice's commercial sphere.

La Serenissima – 'the Most Serene Republic of Venice' – may have reigned supreme as queen of the seas, but it did not go unchallenged. Pisa and Genoa were both powerful maritime rivals. Since trade with the East was by far the most lucrative enterprise at the time, merchants from all over Italy attempted to gain a foothold in Constantinople, capital of the Byzantine Empire. Implacable rivalries set the individual city-states against one another, and for a time they threatened to bring Venice to her knees.

Commercial rivalries

Originally founded as a Byzantine outpost, Venice had a virtual monopoly of the eastern Mediterranean trade thanks to its position as part of the Byzantine Empire. That situation changed in 1171, when the Emperor in Constantinople also granted trading concessions to Venice's rivals Pisa and Genoa. When merchants from Venice attacked the Genoese colony in Constantinople, the Emperor responded by ordering the arrest of all Venetians resident in the city. Venice's entire future as a commercial power stood in jeopardy.

The crisis had a profound effect on the internal affairs of the city-state. Fearing that their trading empire was on the verge of collapse, the leading merchants withdrew decision-making powers from the People's Assembly, which had previously helped to steer the Republic's fortunes. Instead, they placed policy-making in the hands of a select committee that they considered better placed to protect the interests of Venice – and of themselves. Henceforth, the Grand Council – with an initial membership of 480 leading citizens, subsequently expanded to 900 – was charged with most of the responsibilities of government, and the powers of the People's Assembly were limited to declaring war and concluding peace treaties. The move gave control of the city to an oligarchy of rich merchants, who had the power to pass all laws and to elect the Doge.

The sack of Constantinople

In 1192, the Grand Council elected Enrico Dandolo as Doge, an unlikely candidate to turn the city's fortunes round, for he was 84 years old and almost blind when he took office. However, he was to lead La Serenissima to the zenith of her power and glory.

His chance came a few years later, when Pope Innocent III called for a new Crusade. Spotting an opening, Venice declared itself ready to transport the troops across the Mediterranean, in return for a sizeable cash sum and a half share of any booty taken.

When the crusaders assembled in the lagoon city in 1201 to launch this Fourth Crusade, it was obvious that the force was far smaller than expected. With the best will in the world, the crusaders could not hope to meet the transport costs that Venice had demanded. Doge Dandolo saw his opportunity. Against the wishes of the Pope, who later excommunicated the crusaders, Dandolo insisted that instead of heading for Jerusalem by way of Egypt, as originally planned, they should first attack the Christian city of Zara (now Zadar) on the Dalmatian coast, a former dependency that had been wrested from Venetian control.

Next on Dandolo's agenda was Constantinople itself. For years, Venetians had sought to revenge the humiliation

they had suffered in 1171. Now, wranglings over the Byzantine succession gave them an excuse to intervene. The crusaders had adopted the cause of one claimant to the Byzantine throne, and sailed to the Bosphorus to back his bid. With their support, the young prince was able to supplant his usurping uncle, coming to power as Emperor Alexius IV. Soon after, however, Alexius was killed by his own people, who saw him as a puppet

Money from trade
The wealth of the Italian city-states stemmed from the commercial activities of merchants like these, recorded transacting business in medieval manuscript illuminations. Venice, Milan and Florence ranked among the largest cities in western Europe in the 12th century, with only Paris and Córdoba to rival them.

Carnival in Venice

Carnivals are traditional in Italy, tracing their origins back to the Saturnalia, the winter solstice celebrations of ancient Rome. The first mention of Venice's famous carnival is in 1094. In the early days young men would parade through the city singing and masquerading, clothed in animal skins and wearing leaves in their hair, before ending with a gargantuan feast.

The carnival soon took on a political aspect as the one time in the year when individuals could briefly escape the watchful eye of the state, their identities protected by the masks that all revellers wore. On several occasions the Grand Council tried to ban the wearing of masks, supposedly to prevent crime, but to no avail.

Foreign artistry
The Church of San Zeno Maggiore in Verona is acclaimed as the most beautiful Romanesque building in northern Italy. Its 11th-century bronze reliefs show scenes from the Creation, including the expulsion of Adam and Eve from Eden.

of the foreign army. His successor quickly reneged on the promises Alexius had made to bear the crusaders' costs in return for their military backing.

Deprived of what they regarded as their just desserts, the crusaders fell on the Byzantine capital in April 1204, smashing their way into homes, churches and shops and helping themselves to whatever took their fancy. They set whole quarters of the city ablaze, and many priceless artworks and manuscripts went up in the flames.

Other treasures were taken back to Venice. Among them was the Quadriga – four bronze horses, Greek in origin and transported to Constantinople many centuries before from the Forum in ancient Rome – which went to adorn the main entrance to St Mark's Basilica. Finally sated, and having long since forgotten their original aim of liberating Jerusalem, the crusaders sailed home, laden with booty.

Mistress of the eastern Mediterranean

Venice profited hugely from the rape of Constantinople. In its wake the Republic seized three-eighths of the territory of the Byzantine Empire, including the islands of Crete and Rhodes as well as the Euboean peninsula on the Greek mainland. It also won a monopoly of trade with the city, along with control over all the straits in the area and numerous bases from which to guard the sea-lanes. La Serenissima emerged from the episode as the unchallenged mistress of the eastern Mediterranean.

Venice's triumph made it the richest city in Europe in the 13th century, but its success only increased the jealousy of its Italian rivals, notably Genoa, and their time was soon to come.

Venice's position depended to a large extent on the survival of the Latin Kingdom, the crusader state set up in Constantinople to rule over the remnants of the Byzantine realm. In 1261 the Latin Kingdom collapsed when Byzantine forces managed to retake their city. Their leader Michael Paleologus went on to rule over a revived Byzantine Empire as Michael VIII. He had relied on Genoese support in his rise to power, and once in office he proceeded to favour merchants from Genoa over the Venetians.

Yet even though Genoa thrived in the wake of this coup, it never managed to catch up economically with Venice. One reason lay in the different political structures of the two city-states. In Venice, the tightly-knit oligarchy that controlled the Grand Council took care to pull together, cooperating to further the best interests of the city. In contrast, Genoa's ruling families were hopelessly at odds with one another and often engaged in bloody vendettas.

Milan and the Lombard League

In the course of the 13th century it was Milan – first under the rule of the noble della Torre family and then, from 1277 on, under the Viscontis – that rose to become the second-most powerful city in northern Italy after Venice. Its progress was not untroubled. In the preceding century it had led resistance to the Holy Roman Emperor and in 1162 had borne the brunt of Barbarossa's fury when his troops almost razed it to the ground.

The atrocity was intended to make an example of Milan and to deter other North Italian centres from following its disruptive example. In fact it had quite the opposite effect. The Milanese rebuilt their shattered city and just five years later they were leading lights in the formation of the Lombard League, which succeeded in sending Barbarossa packing from northern Italy. A few years later, in 1176, they chalked up another triumph over the Emperor at the Battle of Legnano.

Following that victory, Frederick was forced to recognise the *de facto* autonomy of the northern Italian cities at the Peace of Constance in 1183. The emperor retained only nominal suzerainty and some limited political and judicial powers, along with the right to exact a modest contribution to the Empire's military expenses that made little impression on the city-states' growing wealth.

A golden age of urban growth

In the 13th century, Milan became the wealthiest and most powerful of all the cities of the Po Valley. It owed its pre-eminence partly to its situation at the meeting point of several major trade routes, a position strengthened from about 1270 by the opening of the St Gotthard Pass, the most important trans-Alpine link with German lands. Milan's artisans also played a key role in creating the city's prosperity. For much of the Middle Ages the city's name was synonymous with the manufacture of arms, and its textile industry was also internationally celebrated. In mid-century, however, power shifted decisively away from popular elected bodies to the so-called Signoria. Henceforth, as in Venice, authority lay exclusively in the hands of leading aristocratic families.

By 1300 the cities of northern Italy had pioneered a sophisticated, cosmopolitan way of life that contrasted markedly with the rural feudalism of the rest of Europe. Their populations were growing fast and were, for the most part, prosperous and well-fed. One visitor to Venice noted with amazement that the citizens neither ploughed nor sowed, yet could buy wine and corn in abundance. Then things changed for the worse. A succession of rainy summers brought failed harvests to the surrounding countryside, while even in better years the exhausted soil produced diminishing yields. Venice and Genoa were able to import food, but not enough to meet the growing need. Then, in 1348, growing hardship turned to calamity when the Black Death struck, carrying off three-quarters of the population of Venice alone. Yet the cities would rise quickly from the ashes, for the glories of the Italian Renaissance still lay ahead.

Master of war
In the later Middle Ages, the Italian city-states turned increasingly to foreign mercenaries to conduct their almost incessant wars. Troops usually came under the command of a *condottiere* ('commander'), for whom warfare was entirely a commercial matter. This image from a fresco in Siena shows Condottiere Guidoriccio da Fogliano.

The struggle for Balkan supremacy

Casting off Byzantine rule in the 1180s, the Bulgars built up a second Bulgarian Empire, only to be challenged in the 14th century by a great Serbian king, Stefan Dusan. Soon after, both fell to the rising might of the Ottoman Turks.

O riginally a Turkic people, the Bulgars first arrived in the Balkans in the 7th century. They imposed their rule on the Slavs already living in the area, and took advantage of the weakness of the Byzantine Empire at the time to create an empire of their own that stretched from the Black Sea to the Adriatic. In time, the Bulgar and Slav populations mingled, and from 864 onwards, this mixed Bulgarian people accepted the Orthodox Christian religion and much of the culture of a resurgent Byzantium. This first Bulgarian Empire collapsed in 1014 in the face of a furious onslaught by the Byzantine Emperor Basil II Bulgaroctonus, 'Basil the Bulgar-slayer', who compounded military victory by ordering the blinding of almost 14,000 Bulgarian soldiers. In the wake of his triumph, the entire Balkan peninsula once more became a Byzantine province.

Byzantine power diminished in the course of the 12th century, however, and in 1185 discontent at the harshness of Byzantine rule erupted in a rebellion that quickly spread across the eastern Balkans. The leaders were two brothers, Ivan and Peter Asen. Initially defeated by Byzantine forces, they turned for help to the Turkic Cuman people north of the Danube, and with their aid forced the Byzantine Emperor to come to terms. By 1188 they had accepted a truce that left them in possession of Bulgaria north of the Balkan mountains. The Asens established a capital at Türnovo, in their home region. Set on a ridge, the town was protected by the gorge of the River Yantra; to the south the Balkan range formed a natural barrier against invasion.

The brothers' ambitions were still far from satisfied. Having freed northern Bulgaria from the Byzantine yoke, they turned their attention toward Thrace. Emperor Isaac II Angelus did what he could, but failed to halt the rebels' advance. After further defeats, Isaac was deposed and blinded on the orders of his brother, Alexius III, who subsequently agreed to terms with the rebels.

One empire, three seas

By 1201, when a truce was finally called, the Bulgarians had managed to wrest much of Macedonia and the cities on Bulgaria's Black Sea coast from Byzantine control. By this time their ruler was a third Asen brother, Kalojan. A skilful diplomat as well as a gifted

Power centre (background)
The capital of the Bulgarian Empire from 1186 to 1393, Türnovo is situated on three hills above the River Yantra, a tributary of the Danube.

Ring of Serbian unity
The reign of Stefan Nemanjic, founder of Serbia's Nemanjic dynasty, was characterised by piety as well as power politics. Stefan adopted the Orthodox version of Christianity for his kingdom. He ended his days in a monastery on Mount Athos that had been founded by his son, St Sava.

military commander, Kalojan established friendly relations with the Roman Catholic Church, seeking to strengthen Bulgaria's international standing while further distancing himself from Byzantium. In 1204, a papal legate sent by Innocent III crowned Kalojan King of the Bulgars, and at the same time recognised the authority of the Bishop of Türnovo as primate of the Bulgarian church.

The situation changed radically when, also in 1204, Constantinople fell to the forces of the Fourth Crusade. The Byzantine Empire gave way to the Latin Kingdom of the Franks, who soon laid claim to Bulgarian lands. Despite the crusaders' fearsome military reputation, Kalojan humbled them at the Battle of Adrianople in 1205, taking captive their ruler, Baldwin I. In the wake of the victory, Kalojan's forces overran much of Thrace and Macedonia, decimating the native Greek population. Two years later, Kalojan fell victim to a palace conspiracy, and his nephew Boril, who replaced him, had less success against the Franks.

The situation improved again under Boril's successor, Ivan Asen II, under whom the empire reached its greatest power and extent. He met the challenge presented by Theodore Comnenus, the Byzantine ruler of Epirus, defeating and capturing Theodore when his forces invaded Bulgarian territory. Over the next 11 years Ivan Asen broke with Rome, restoring the independence of the Bulgarian Church, and further extended the lands under his control at the expense of the Franks of Constantinople. By the end of his reign, Macedonia, Albania and the entire region between Gallipoli and Mount Olympus, as well as a large part of Thrace, belonged to the Bulgars. Their empire now bordered on three seas – the Black Sea, the Aegean, and the Adriatic.

Invasion and revolt

Disaster struck shortly after Ivan Asen's death in 1241. The Mongol horde that was ravaging central Europe at the time swept through Bulgarian lands, leaving devastation in their wake and enforcing the payment of a massive annual tribute that continued to be paid until the end of the century. The Bulgarian economy never entirely recovered from the shock.

The Mongol irruption also weakened the monarchy, emboldening the boyars (leading nobles) and contributing to a series of succession crises that saw four rulers on the throne in the course of the

Imperial family
Ivan Alexander – shown in this miniature painting with his Jewish wife Theodora and his sons Ivan Sisman and Ivan Asen – ruled Bulgaria from 1331 to 1371. His long reign was a time of decline during which his empire felt the full impact of the Ottoman onslaught.

next 17 years. One unsuccessful claimant, Jakov Svetoslav, seceded from the empire, declaring himself the independent king of northwestern Bulgaria. At the same time, Byzantium succeeded in reconquering much of Thrace and Macedonia, while in the north of the country the Mongol Tatars laid waste to large tracts of land.

Provoked by the hardships that the incessant conflicts brought upon them, Bulgaria's farmers and labourers rose up in the largest peasants' revolt in the region in all the Middle Ages. The rebels captured Türnovo in 1278 and installed a onetime swineherd, Ivailo, as the new ruler. Ivailo married his predecessor's widow to bolster his claim to the throne, but held power for less than three years.

Supreme ruler
The Serbian Emperor, Stefan Dusan, was one of the most imposing personalities of the Balkans in the Middle Ages. This wall-painting of him was made in 1347.

Serbia's Nemanjíc dynasty

The weakened Bulgarian Empire was in no state to meet the new challenge of the 14th century – the rising power of Serbia under the re-emergence of a dynamic Nemanjíc dynasty. The Serbs had originally come to the Balkans from beyond the Carpathian Mountains in the 7th century at the invitation of Byzantine Emperor Heraclius, who wanted a counterweight to the troublesome Avar peoples. Mingling with the existing Slav population, they soon found a new home in the region known to this day as Serbia. Unlike their neighbours, the Croats, who opted for Catholic Christianity, the Serbs chose the Orthodox faith, forming enduring links with the Byzantine cultural sphere, and for almost five centuries they preserved a distinct national identity under the leadership of elected *zupani* (lords) as tributaries of the Byzantine Empire.

The situation changed after 1165 when Stefan Nemanjíc came to power as Grand Zupan. Although still formally a vassal of Byzantium, Stefan set about building an autonomous kingdom along the shores of the Adriatic Sea. A champion of the Orthodox faith, he persecuted the Bogomils, an austere heretical sect that preached that the physical world was the creation of the devil. Before retiring to a monastery on Mount Athos in 1196, he had won recognition from Constantinople as the ruler of an independent state.

Stefan's immediate successors continued his policies with signal success. His eldest son, Stefan II, first married a daughter of the Byzantine Emperor, and then a granddaughter of the Doge of Venice. His youngest son Rastko, who had taken monastic vows under the name of Sava, became Bishop of Studenica, in which capacity he fought heresy, founded churches and monasteries, and ultimately wrested full autonomy for the Serbian Church from the Byzantine Emperor, Theodorus I Lascaris. As first primate of the Serbian Orthodox Church, he played a key role in defining the ecclesiastical and cultural life of his people and is revered to this day as St Sava.

In the mid-13th century Urosh I, a grandson of Stefan Nemanjíc, extended Serbia's sovereignty to take in parts of Macedonia. Rich mineral deposits in the area contributed to an economic boom. Another Serbian king, Milutin, made strenuous efforts to introduce Byzantine customs into his court, reorganising the state administration along Byzantine lines, adopting Constantinople's tax system, and turning Serbia into a feudal state. Even so, contemporaries continued to regard Serbia as a barbarian state.

The brief Serbian Empire

Stefan Dusan showed no subservience to Byzantium when he came to power in 1331, having deposed his father, with whom he had previously served as co-regent. In the course of a 24-year reign he built a Serbian Empire stretching south from the Danube, deep into what is now Greece. Most of his gains were made at the expense of the Byzantines, although as a young man he also won an important victory over the Bulgarians. After gaining the Serbian throne, he married a sister of the new Bulgarian ruler, Ivan Alexander, and peace between the two powers lasted for the rest of his reign.

Stefan Dusan left his mark on Serbia in other fields besides military conquest. He commissioned a legal code that remained in force as long as the Serbian state survived. He also set up an independent Serbian patriarchate – an act for which he was later denounced by the Greek patriarch of Constantinople.

Ottoman onslaught

Stefan Dusan's empire did not long survive his death in 1355. He was succeeded by his son, Urosh V, who was unable to hold the conquered lands together. Powerful vassal rulers on the empire's fringes

seized their chance to secede from Serbian rule, and within 15 years of Stefan's death the Serbian realm was smaller than it had been before he set out on his conquests.

New conquerors played a crucial part in the decline of both the Bulgarian and Serbian empires. In 1354 the Ottoman Turks established a presence in Europe by taking control of Gallipoli. They used the peninsula as a bridgehead to launch further conquests, moving westward across Thrace and taking Adrianople (modern Edírne) in 1361. In 1389 the decisive Battle of Kosovo confirmed their hold over the Balkans, and by the end of the century, Bulgarians and Serbs alike were vassals of the sultan.

Dynastic table
The Nemanjíc family tree is displayed on a wall of the monastery church at Gracanica, near Pristina, the capital of Kosovo.

Bulgarian monastery
Founded in the 10th century, the Orthodox monastery of Rila played a significant part in the religious life of Bulgaria. The complex is now a UNESCO World Heritage site.

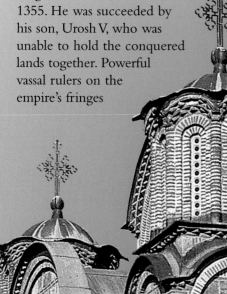

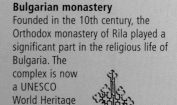

The golden age of Bohemia

In the 13th century, skilful diplomacy and political marriages nurtured a final flowering of Bohemia's long-lasting Premyslid dynasty.

Famous ancestor
Ottokar I laid the foundations for Premyslid greatness. His tomb was the work of a German mason, Peter Parler, also credited with the statues on Prague's famous Charles Bridge.

Cross of Ottokar (background)
Ottokar II commissioned this splendid reliquary cross of gold, studded with amethysts, rubies and sapphires. It is now in a museum in Regensburg, Germany.

Ottokar I, the first Premyslid to be crowned King of Bohemia, took an important step toward securing his kingdom's future before his death in 1230. He arranged the marriage of his son Wenceslas to Kunigunde, daughter of the Holy Roman Emperor. So the Premyslids became imperial electors, gaining a seat on the council that chose future emperors.

The Bohemian *Chronicle of Cosmas of Prague* recounts the family's rise to power. The Prague line of the Premyslid dynasty pursued its political goals with great determination. Their aim was to establish control over an enlarged kingdom made up of the duchies of Bohemia (now the western Czech Republic), Moravia (the republic's eastern part) and the Czech parts of Silesia (today, mostly in southern Poland). The rulers were sometimes less than scrupulous in their methods – political skullduggery, even assassination, were accepted ways of neutralising troublesome opponents. In addition, the Premyslids fostered good relations with neighbouring Poland, Hungary and the Holy Roman Empire, using marriage as a favourite diplomatic tool to link themselves with the leading aristocratic families of eastern Europe.

The policy of aggrandisment paid off in the 12th century, when the Premyslids won a place among the inner circle of the Emperor's leading allies. As his reward, in 1198 Duke Ottokar was granted the title of King of Bohemia by Emperor Philip.

When Frederick II confirmed the grant in a Golden Bull (a sealed edict) issued from his court in Sicily in 1212, Bohemia was assured of its new status. It still remained within the Holy Roman Empire and its ruler continued to recognise the overall power of the Emperor, but it was now an autonomous kingdom.

A booming economy under Wenceslas

Wenceslas I – who succeeded Ottakar in 1230 and reigned to 1253 – made further advances along the path his father had set. He encouraged Germans to settle in the kingdom, creating a counterweight to the over-mighty local aristocracy and giving fresh impetus to agriculture and mining.

Previously Bohemia had lagged behind the rest of eastern Europe in founding monasteries and the development of cities. Now the merchants, craftsmen, miners, priests, monks and farmers who came to Bohemia helped to usher in a golden age. Soon new towns, monastic foundations and industrial settlements sprang up across the country. German immigrants ran silver mines at Jihlava, Kutná Hora and other sites. Wenceslas established a fresh administrative framework for the kingdom, while his reorganisation of the law gave it one of the most modern legal systems in central Europe.

For all his many successes, Wenceslas had to endure a period of serious crisis in 1241, when his lands were invaded by

Batu Khan's Mongol horde, which was ravaging central Europe at the time. The Mongols swept through Moravia like a whirlwind, spilling blood, committing atrocities and spreading death and destruction in their wake.

German immigration to Bohemia reached its peak under Wenceslas's son, Ottokar II, who brought many of his father's projects to fruition. Yet during Wenceslas's lifetime, relations between the two were strained. The young Ottokar conspired against his father with rebel Bohemian nobles; civil war was prevented only by the last-minute intervention of Ottokar's aunt Agnes, Wenceslas's sister.

Agnes of Bohemia, who was later canonised, was one of the country's most devout noblewomen, and she acted as a peacemaker throughout her career. She showed great political far-sightedness, including prophesying the downfall of the Premyslids several decades before it occurred. According to legend, Agnes had a vision that Ottokar would bring misfortune on the land. As it turned out, the quick-tempered ruler did indeed provoke a situation that almost cost his son, Wenceslas II, the crown.

Marital politics

Following his father's example, shortly before his death, in 1253, Wenceslas I arranged his son's marriage to Margaret of Austria, who was almost 30 years Ottakar's senior. The Premyslids thereby gained control of Austria during Margaret's lifetime, and quickly revealed ambitions to establish a hereditary right to the Austrian crown. Yet the one thing that the 50-year-old Margaret could not give her husband was the son and heir he needed to make good his claim. So Ottokar asked the Pope to recognise his illegitimate son, by one of Margaret's maids, as his rightful successor.

A cultured king
Wenceslas II was a great patron of the arts at his twin courts of Prague and Kraków. A poet in his own right, he surrounded himself with the leading politicians, troubadours and artists of the day.

The Pope refused and Margaret sued for divorce. Ottokar then married Kunigunde von Machow, grand-daughter of the King of Hungary, in an attempt to establish a claim to the Hungarian crown.

Ottokar also tried to extend his kingdom by military means, and his campaigns succeeded, briefly, in making Bohemia the hub of a central European empire. By the early 1270s, he ruled over a realm that stretched from the Adriatic to the Baltic, taking in Austria, Styria, Eger, Carinthia and Carniola as well as Bohemia itself – a kingdom that suggested the shape of the future Habsburg Empire.

Ottokar's semi-imperial status enabled him to engage in power politics on a scale unknown to earlier Premyslid rulers. Known as the 'King of Iron and Gold' for his wealth and power, he championed the Christian cause in his lands by founding monasteries and also supported the Knights of the Teutonic Order in two Crusades against the heathen Prussians. In recognition of his contribution, the city of Königsberg – literally 'King's Town', now known as Kaliningrad – was named in his honour in 1255. He maintained two separate courts, one in Prague and the other in Vienna, both in magnificent style. The two capitals became magnets for artists and craftsmen from across Europe, and Prague won a reputation for poetry, attracting poets and troubadours from many parts of Germany.

Disaster at the Marchfeld

Eventually Ottokar overreached himself. The established noble families of Germany regarded him as an upstart, and none more so than the German imperial princes. Buoyed up by a false sense of his own power, Ottokar committed a fatal error that played into their hands. Having failed to secure his own election as German king, he refused to pay homage to Rudolf I Habsburg, the man who had secured the crown. In 1274, Rudolf duly outlawed him within the imperial lands, barring him from playing any part in the electors' council and declaring all his acquisitions void. Ottokar was not only disgraced, but was forced to give up Austria, Styria and Carinthia after a combined challenge from Rudolf, Hungary and some of his own Bohemian nobility.

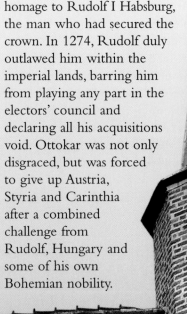

Sojourn in Poland
For a brief period at the end of the 13th century, the principality of Lesser Poland, with its capital of Kraków, came under the rule of the Premyslid kings. The town wall surrounding the later residence of the Polish kings dates from this period.

Ottakar made one last, vain attempt to regain the lost territories, but paid for it with his life. On August 26, 1278, around 30,000 heavily armoured knights faced one another on the Marchfeld, the plain east of Vienna, in one of the great setpiece battles of the Middle Ages. Initially, it seemed that Ottokar's forces would prevail, but Rudolf had concealed a reserve of 60 knights in vineyards bordering the battlefield. When the Bohemian cavalry was exhausted after three hours' combat in heavy armour, the Habsburg king unleashed his fresh troops on them. Ottokar died in the carnage that followed, along with 12,000 of his men.

A final flowering

Defeat at the Marchfeld had a devastating effect on the Bohemian national psyche. Ottokar's heir, Wenceslas II, was just 7 years old at the time. During his minority Bohemia was effectively ruled by his uncle, Margrave Otto IV of Brandenburg, who kept his royal ward a virtual prisoner in his home duchy. The nobility exploited the power vacuum by occupying royal lands and spreading rapine and pillage. Wenceslas is said to have been harshly treated in his confinement, being forced to live like a monk. Cold and half-starved, the poor boy was frightened by the slightest sound.

To prevent the kingdom from descending into total anarchy, Bohemia's leading nobles eventually clubbed together to buy Wenceslas's freedom. He returned to Prague in 1283, and despite his upbringing he blossomed into an effective monarch. In 1285 he married Guta, a daughter of Rudolf of Habsburg. There was no longer any question

of reclaiming the lands Bohemia had lost to the south and west, so Wenceslas turned his attention instead to Poland and the north. When Guta died giving birth to a daughter, he chose a Polish princess named Richeza as his second wife, and in 1289 she bore him a son, the future Wenceslas III. In 1290, he inherited the principality of Kraków, and in the following year conquered Upper Silesia, winning for himself the title of Prince of Poland. Nine years later, in 1300, he was crowned King of Poland in Gniezo, near the modern city of Poznan. The following year Wenceslas nominated his son, then aged 12, to the vacant throne of Hungary. The mistreated youth had become the creator of a new Premyslid kingdom, this one stretching from the Baltic to Lake Balaton in Hungary.

When Wenceslas II died of tuberculosis in 1305 and the younger Wenceslas acceded to his father's Bohemian throne, treaty obligations required him to cede the Hungarian crown to Rudolf's son, the Habsburg Emperor Albert I. Wenceslas III decided to contest the arrangement. Before he could assert his authority, however, he was murdered by a Thuringian knight while travelling to Poland on August 4, 1306. He left no heir, and the kingdom of Bohemia passed out of Premyslid hands into those of their longtime adversaries, the Habsburgs.

A pious noblewoman
Manuscript illuminations show scenes from the life of St Hedwig, patron saint of Kraków and other Silesian cities. As Duchess of Silesia, Hedwig became famous for her piety and charitable works. She lost her husband and one of her sons during the Mongol invasion of 1241.

The Latin Kingdom of the crusaders

The sack of Constantinople by fellow-Christian crusaders was one of the great tragedies of the Middle Ages. Latins and Greeks fought over the city for the next 50 years.

The fall of Constantinople
The crusaders launch their assault on the Byzantine capital (right). They attacked from the seaward side of the city, where the defences were less sturdy.

Spoils of war
Many works of art looted from Constantinople were taken to Venice. Among them was the Quadriga – a sculptural group of four gilded bronze horses which was displayed over the door to St Mark's Basilica. The restored original is now in the museum and a replica is on the Basilica's roof.

An overwhelming catastrophe struck Constantinople, capital of the Byzantine Empire, in 1204. For centuries the city had withstood assaults by Arabs and Avars, Bulgars and Vikings. But now the supposedly impregnable walls were stormed by western European crusaders, known to the Greek-speaking Byzantines as 'Latins' or 'Franks'. The city's defences soon crumbled as it was engulfed in flames, and a furious mob of soldiers rampaged through the streets, lusting for blood and booty. The orgy of murder and plundering lasted for

several days, as the conquering army slaughtered untold thousands of people and amassed huge spoils.

The tragedy was set in train when Pope Innocent III announced a Fourth Crusade in 1199. His call was answered by leading noblemen from northern France, among them Count Theobald of Champagne and Baldwin of Flanders, later joined by Boniface of Montferrat in northern Italy. The crusaders were to assemble in Venice, which would provide ships to transport them, ostensibly to the Holy Land. The leaders of the Crusade, however, in collusion with the Venetians, had decided to go by way of Egypt, which offered easier pickings than a direct assault on the Levantine coast.

Crusade diverted

Things started to go wrong when only 10,000 crusaders – a third of the anticipated number – showed up in Venice. They quickly realised that they could not afford to pay Venice the price that they had agreed for transportation. Venice, however, had an agenda of its own – it wanted to recover the city of Zara (now the Croatian port of Zadar) on the eastern side of the Adriatic, which had been prised from Venetian control by the King of Hungary. Enrico Dandolo, the nonagenarian Doge of Venice, agreed to supply the ships

for a reduced sum, but only if the crusaders agreed to win back Zara to Venetian rule. Eager for booty as well as glory, the crusaders were happy to oblige. Sickened by the cynicism of the move, Pope Innocent not only condemned the attack but also excommunicated all those who took part.

Regardless of papal disapproval, and acting very much like a mercenary army, the crusaders were happy to be diverted again. This time they took up the cause of Alexius, a dispossessed Byzantine prince, who offered them huge sums of money if they would help him to uphold his claim to the imperial throne. The Venetians saw the potential of having a friendly ruler in Constantinople, and so the force that originally gathered to liberate the Holy Land ended up at the gates of Christian Constantinople.

Initially, the crusaders successfully established Alexius on the Byzantine throne, but this caused massive discontent within the empire, and when Alexius imposed taxes in order to pay off his armed helpers, anger boiled over in an insurrection in which Alexius was killed. His successor refused to pay the crusaders and demanded that they left his lands. Cheated of what they regarded as their legitimate rewards, the crusaders reacted with blind fury, and in 1204, the violent sacking of Constantinople ensued.

The crusader emperor

In western Christendom, where the Byzantines were regarded as heretics for rejecting Catholicism in favour of the Orthodox faith, there was rejoicing when news came of their defeat. Only a few voices were raised in protest at crusaders attacking fellow Christians.

Meanwhile, in Constantinople itself, the victorious crusaders chose Count Baldwin of Flanders as the first ruler of a new Latin Kingdom. He accepted the crown in a ceremony at the Church of St Sophia, then paid off his fellow crusaders by granting fiefs over Byzantine land to some 600 of the leading noblemen. For his own portion, he took the imperial palace, an entire district of the city of Constantinople and a quarter of the former Byzantine Empire, including Thrace, northwest Asia Minor and the islands of Lesbos, Chios and Samos. His powers as emperor were limited by various civil and military ordinances that made him first among equals rather than the autocratic ruler of all he surveyed.

Dividing the spoils

Boniface of Montferrat had been the other principal contender for the imperial title. As consolation for failing to win the prize, the imperial council granted him, with Baldwin's grudging agreement, a kingdom in central Greece with its capital at Thessalonica. He bought Venice's acceptance of the deal by granting it the island of Crete, which had originally been apportioned to him.

As King of Thessalonica, Boniface claimed suzerainty over the duchy of Athens and the principality of Achaea on the Peloponnese, awarding them to vassal rulers. Achaea was divided into 12 separate baronetcies whose rulers took over and extended existing Byzantine strongholds and also built new fortresses at strategically important locations. In the years that followed, the principality became a miniature replica of the French feudal system, an island of western knighthood in a Greek-speaking world.

The Venetians benefited most from the fall of Constantinople. They received three-eighths of the former territory of the Byzantine Empire, mostly in the form of islands or strips of coastal land, giving them a maritime empire in the Eastern Mediterranean that was to last far longer than the Latin Kingdom itself. Here they introduced large-scale cultivation of cereals, vines, and cane sugar. A Venetian also took the office of Patriarch of Constantinople, supervising a new, Catholic hierarchy of bishops mainly brought in from Italy and France.

Crusader castle (background) With the establishment of the Latin Kingdom, the French knight and chronicler Geoffroy de Villehardouin became Prince of Achaea in the Peloponnese peninsula of Greece. His son William II constructed this castle near the Church of St Sophia in Mistra.

The Greek backlash

All of this fanned the flames of resistance among the Greek population. Three new Greek states, all ruled by members of the former imperial dynasty, arose on the fringes of the empire in regions that had not been conquered by the Latins. In northwest Greece and what is now Albania, Michael I Angelus established the kingdom of Epirus, and in western Asia Minor, Theodore Lascaris founded the kingdom of Nicaea.

Within a year, Constantinople's new Latin rulers were in conflict not just with the Thracian nobles they had supplanted but also with the neighbouring Bulgarian empire. Baldwin rashly laid claim to parts of the Emperor's territory, and the Latin patriarch also insisted that he should have sovereignty over the Bulgarian Orthodox Church. In response, in 1205, the Bulgarian Emperor Kalojan with the aid of the Greek nobility annihilated a Latin army at the Battle of Adrianople. Baldwin ended his days a Bulgarian prisoner.

In the wake of the battle, the Greek kingdoms of Epirus and Nicaea took the initiative in the struggle against the Latins, who were now led by Baldwin's brother Henry. Theodore Ducas, the heir to Michael Angelus as ruler of Epirus, took Henry's successor captive in 1217, and then in 1222 conquered the weakened Latin kingdom of Thessalonica, bestowing on himself the grand title of Emperor of the West.

Allies turn rivals

As Latin power weakened, the other powers in the region fell out with one another. The success of Epirus aroused the hostility not just of the Nicaeans but also of the Bulgars, who defeated and captured Theodore in 1230, reducing his kingdom to a rump state centred around Thessalonica. Meanwhile, across the Bosphorus in Asia Minor, the kingdom of Nicaea was making inroads on the weakened Latin Kingdom. Under the capable rule of John III Vatzates, who reigned from 1222 to 1254, the Nicaeans reduced the Latin realm to little more than the city of Constantinople itself. John then directed his attention to Epirus, taking Thessalonica in 1244 and subsequently forcing its ruler to recognise his sovereignty.

Byzantium resurgent

Meanwhile, Baldwin II had come to the throne in Constantinople, but was so short of money that he was forced to sell the city's most famous religious relic, the crown of thorns said to have been worn by Christ on the cross, to King Louis IX of France. Such desperate measures could only delay the day of reckoning.

The man who finally won Constantinople back for the Greeks was Michael VIII Paleologus of Nicaea. In 1259, at the head of a force that included Turkish archers and Latin mercenaries alongside Greeks in its ranks, he routed a Latin army at Pelagonia in western Macedonia. Two years later, in 1261, a Greek army took advantage of the temporary absence of the Venetian fleet to retake Constantinople itself. Baldwin and the remaining Latin defenders fled, and Michael entered the city to the joy of the populace, ending Latin rule and restoring Byzantine control.

Scourge of the Byzantines
Doge Enrico Dandolo of Venice – seen in this manuscript illumination kneeling at Baldwin I's coronation as Latin emperor – has often been blamed for diverting the Fourth Crusade to Byzantium from its original target of the Holy Land. In fact, a number of circumstances came together to bring about the catastrophe.

BACKGROUND

Plundering Constantinople

The crusaders caused widespread devastation when they took Constantinople. They particularly targeted art treasures, doing such massive damage that the city's fabric and heritage never fully recovered. As well as gold and jewellery, they also looted holy relics, along with the precious reliquaries that contained them. Among those taken were supposed fragments of the True Cross and body parts of various saints including the heads of John the Baptist and St Anne.

The Venetians particularly sought out the masterpieces of classical antiquity that Constantinople had inherited from its days as capital of the Eastern Roman Empire. They seem to have been swayed not just by the material worth of the pieces and their outstanding historical value but also by a conscious desire to see Venice take over Constantinople's mantle as the true successor of ancient Rome.

The persecution of the Albigensians

The Albigensians, or Cathars, of southern France represented a radical challenge to the Roman Catholic Church, which launched a merciless military Crusade to exterminate the sect.

A fateful incident occurred in southern France in 1208. While attempting to serve notice of excommunication on the powerful Count of Toulouse, the papal legate Pierre de Castelnau was set upon and murdered by a number of men with close connections to the Count and the Cathars. With this act, a religious dispute that had already caused bitter disagreement turned violent.

Pope Innocent III launched a Crusade against the heretics that raged for five years. When it was over, the remaining Cathars took refuge in their most inaccessible fortresses in southwestern France, but almost all were eventually forced out and slaughtered.

The devil's work

The Cathars – from the Greek *katharoi*, 'the pure' – referred to themselves as 'good Christians', 'good men' or 'good women'. One of their main centres was at Albi in the south of France, from which they also became known as Albigensians. Even though they regarded themselves as Christians, the faith that they adhered to had ceased to have much in common with orthodox Catholic Christianity.

The roots of Catharism stretch far back to the first centuries AD. Its tenets were based on the concepts of Gnosticism, which had originated in the Near East, and of Persian Manichaeism, which looked on the material world as the realm of Satan.

Last bastion
The Cathars barricaded themselves in inaccessible mountain fortresses such as the castle of Montségur in the Pyrenees. Yet even these defensive strongholds were captured, one by one.

In various guises, these traditions endured for centuries, first in the Byzantine Empire and from the 12th century on in southern France, having arrived by way of Italy and the Rhineland.

A quest for spiritual perfection

The Cathars identified the Old Testament god Jehovah – the creator of the world – with Satan. They believed that the true, benevolent God existed far above the material universe. From his high vantage point he sent Jesus, seen by the Cathars as a good angel, down to Earth to reveal the possibility of salvation to its inhabitants.

Mankind could only reach this goal by gradually dissociating itself from the physical world, for only then would people's captive souls be able to return to the light. Accordingly, the most devout Cathars lived as monks, rejecting both procreation and marriage. Furthermore, there was no place in their worldview for the Church and its sacraments, for military service, or for Hell. In their communion, the Cathars drew a distinction between the *perfecti* ('perfect ones') and the 'believers'. Believers could graduate to perfect status by undergoing a ceremony of initiation, the *consolamentum*, in which

A terrible death
Adherents of the Cathar faith who refused, under torture, to publicly recant their beliefs were either condemned to long imprisonment or to death. Executions of heretics were mostly carried out by burning at the stake.

they agreed to lead an exemplary life. Individuals who had already distinguished themselves on the path to perfection were assigned leadership roles in the various Cathar communities.

The spread of Cathar beliefs

To the Catholic Church, such notions were deeply heretical. They attacked the very foundations of Catholic belief by calling into question essential tenets of faith, as well as the Church's role as the vehicle of salvation. Yet the Cathar religion spread quickly among both the people and the petty nobility of southern France, causing a Christian chronicler of the time to write: 'So powerful was the Albigensian heresy that it swiftly infected around 1000 towns, and if it had not been checked by the swords of the faithful, I honestly believe that it would have corrupted the whole of Europe.'

One reason for the popularity of the Cathars lay in the increasing worldliness of the established Church, seen in the ostentatious wealth of its prelates as well as in accusations of corruption and immorality. Another important factor was that the Cathars enjoyed the protection of the powerful Counts of Toulouse who, along with other noblemen, looked favourably on the sect to counter the growing secular power of the Church, which threatened their own authority. As one magnate explained to the Bishop of Toulouse: 'The Cathars are our relatives, and they live decent lives. Why should we persecute them?' So, for a time, the Cathars were able to operate with impunity, even challenging Catholic spokesmen to public debates.

The launching of the crusade

After the murder of the papal legate, when Innocent III proclaimed his crusade against the heretics, everything changed. Driven less by religious zeal than by the prospect of acquiring land and riches, many noblemen from northern France heeded the call, among them the counts of Nevers and Champagne. France's King Philip II Augustus, however, remained aloof from the enterprise.

In 1209, a large army assembled at Lyons and marched south. Taking the city of Béziers, it unleashed a bloodbath on the inhabitants. Asked how the crusaders could distinguish Cathar from Catholic, Abbot Arnaud Amaury of Cîteaux is said to have replied: 'Kill them all. God will recognise his own!' But even when given the chance to recant, many Cathars chose death rather than abandon their cause.

There were similar scenes when the town of Minèrve fell to the crusaders. Abbot Amaury offered to spare the lives of citizens willing to give up their faith, telling fellow-crusaders who expostulated at such clemency, 'Don't worry. I don't imagine that many will accept.' And so it turned out: 140 Cathars chose to throw themselves into the flames rather than recant. Soon afterwards Carcassonne was besieged and swiftly capitulated.

The French nobleman Simon de Montfort subsequently took charge of the campaign. It was conducted with the

Heresy hunter
The French nobleman Simon de Montfort, shown on this seal hunting with horn and hounds, led the Pope's crusade against the Cathars. His son of the same name moved to England in 1229, and was to play a significant role in English history as the leader of the Barons' Revolt against Henry III.

utmost brutality, and mercy was rarely shown. Both sides gave no quarter, even dismembering the bodies of the dead. On one occasion, Simon de Montfort had the eyes of 100 prisoners put out, leaving one man with a single eye to lead the others into captivity. After the capture of Lavaur in 1211, Montfort had the throats of 80 Cathar knights cut and condemned 400 heretics to be burned to death.

Changing fortunes of war

Count Raymond VI of Toulouse claimed to be a good Catholic despite his Cathar sympathies, but seeing the massacres and looting that the crusaders were inflicting on his lands, he finally committed himself to the Cathar cause. He was supported by the counts of Foix, who were themselves Cathars. Although Raymond managed to break the siege of Toulouse in 1211, he was defeated by a crusader army two years later at the Battle of Muret.

Meanwhile the Catholic curia took up the fight against the Cathars on another front. In 1215, the 4th Lateran Council passed resolutions condemning the heretics and threatening any nobleman who failed to hunt them down in his lands with seizure of his property.

In the wake of the council, Count Raymond was stripped of his title, which was granted instead to Simon de Montfort. This prize was not enough to sate de Montfort's ambition; rather, it encouraged him to seek to extend his sovereignty across all of southern France. He suffered a setback, however, at Tarascon, sparking a revolt in Toulouse. Although de Montfort succeeded in crushing the uprising, he was forced to embark on a fresh campaign to shore up his weakened position. Raymond was subsequently able to exploit his absence to win back his old capital.

Death of de Montfort

As expected, de Montfort returned to Toulouse, where he met his end at the hands of a woman while besieging the city in 1218. Legend has it that all hands were called up in the town's defence, and de Montfort was struck by a missile from a catapult fired by one of the female defenders.

Leadership of the crusading army passed to de Montfort's eldest son, Amaury, who lacked his father's outstanding military skills. Over the next few years Raymond and his son Raymond VII, who succeeded him in 1222, managed to reconquer most of their hereditary lands.

Franciscan inquisitors
Painted in oil on wood, St Francis of Assissi is seen preaching to the birds. From 1236 on, friars from the recently founded Franciscan Order joined Dominicans on the Inquisition tribunals directed against the Cathars.

BACKGROUND

The Dominicans – the Lord's enforcers

In 1215, a Spanish monk named Dominic founded a mendicant brotherhood in Toulouse with the express aim of fighting the Cathars. The Dominican Order he set up rapidly became one of the Catholic Church's most important weapons against the heretics.

Dominic's main concern was to win the diocese of Toulouse, a stronghold of the Cathar faith, back to the Catholic cause. The monks who took up the challenge prepared themselves through intensive study and a practical education designed to enable them 'to preach the gospel of truth through evangelical poverty'. They also wrote tracts attacking the heresy. By such means they succeeded in converting many Cathars and prevented wavering Catholics from leaving the fold.

After 1223, Pope Honorius III gave the Dominicans the responsibility of implementing the Inquisition in the Cathar lands.

They met with such bitter resistance at first that they were forced to withdraw from Toulouse and Carcassonne for several months. The Dominican inquisitor, Guillaume Arnault, was even assassinated in Avignon in 1242.

In England, the Dominicans became known as Black Friars from the black coat and hood that they wore when preaching.

The Church's troops
This 13th century altarpiece shows St Dominic, founder of the Dominicans, with his fellow friars.

After 1224 the balance swung back again in favour of the crusaders, when the new King of France, Louis VIII, took their side. Louis renewed the assault on the south, conquering Avignon but holding back from besieging Toulouse.

Louis died in 1226, just three years after taking the throne, but by that time the forces lined up against Raymond VII were too strong to resist, and the Count was forced to negotiate with his enemies, concluding the Treaty of Meaux with Louis' successor, Louis IX, in 1229. The compact recognised Raymond's sovereignty in Toulouse itself, but required him to cede all his lands to the east to the crown. Even more significantly, he also had to agree to give his daughter in marriage to Louis's brother Alphonse, an arrangement designed to ensure that his lands would one day pass to the crown through inheritance.

The end of the Albigensians

The Albigensian war was finally over, but the task of eradicating Catharism still had some way to go. From 1233 onwards, Pope Gregory IX entrusted the job of rooting out heresy to the Inquisition, a new institution specifically set up for the purpose. Many Cathars were burned at the stake for refusing to renounce their beliefs, sparking uprisings in Toulouse, Albi and Narbonne that were brutally suppressed. Surviving Cathars found refuge among the largely sympathetic population: when one citizen of Toulouse informed on the heretics, he was later found strangled in his bed.

The Cathars struggled on in face of persecution for another decade, but their ultimate fate was sealed. They made their last stand in the mountain fastness of Montségur in the Pyrenees. They held out there for 10 months but were forced to surrender in March 1244 after the besiegers staged a surprise assault, scaling the heights overnight to take up position before the gates of the castle. The lives of believers were spared, but the *perfecti* sheltering within the walls were burned at the stake at the foot of the castle rock.

The fall of Montségur broke the backbone of the movement. For something over 100 years thereafter, Catharism survived in isolated pockets in southern France, northern Spain and Italy, but eventually these last vestiges, too, were wiped out.

Expulsion of the Cathars
After the fall of Carcassonne, a Cathar stronghold, Simon de Montfort expelled all suspected heretics from the city. The expulsion is recorded in this 14th-century manuscript illumination.

The growing might of the French kings

Within the space of a century a woman, a saint and an unscrupulous egotist took France to the pinnacle of power in Europe. The nation's rise began with a battle in the provinces.

The Battle of Bouvines was fought near Lille in northern France on July 27, 1214, and marked the rise of France to the position of a great power. From a French point of view, the news from the battlefield was thrilling: the King was safe and so was the Crown Prince, the future King Louis VIII. The Welfs and Flemings had been beaten, and the English army, which had not even reached the battlefield, was retreating in disarray.

The battle's aftermath marked a major shift in the balance of power between major European players. Germany's imperial princes were left hopelessly at odds with one another, while England had suffered a crushing defeat and was wracked by unrest at home. In contrast Philip II of France, already Europe's elder statesman after almost 35 years on the throne, emerged from the conflict stronger than ever; in the wake of the victory chroniclers would name him Philip Augustus ('the Majestic').

Philip's last years

Now, in the autumn of his reign, Philip set about reorganising the internal affairs of the nation. He centralised the administration by introducing crown agents called *baillis* (bailies), adopting a model that the Normans had employed successfully in England and Sicily. The King adapted the system to his own purposes by giving each of these travelling magistrates responsibility for a specified district, known as a baillage, overseeing the activities of the administration within its bounds.

Philip Augustus also took steps to encourage more wealth creation and to foster the dawning sense of French nationhood, giving his patronage to cities, trade and learning. The University of Paris had its origins in cathedral schools, and from the turn of the 13th century

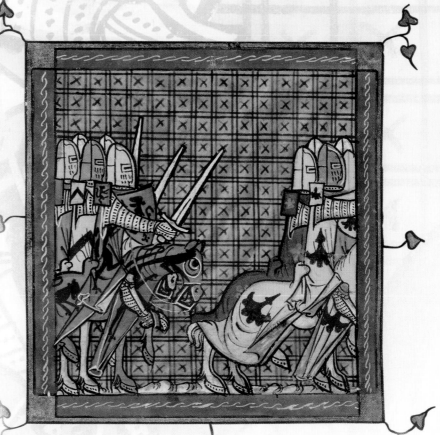

Decisive encounter
Fought in 1214, the Battle of Bouvines brought about the downfall and deposition of the Holy Roman Emperor, Otto. It also sparked major unrest in England, while it catapulted France, the victors, to the forefront of European power politics. This 14th-century manuscript illustration shows the flight of Otto's imperial army.

onwards scholars and teachers were given immunity from prosecution by the state, a measure that guaranteed academic freedom, and statutes were drawn up to govern their administration.

The university was organised into four faculties, devoted respectively to theology, medicine, ecclesiastical law and the liberal arts. This last discipline covered seven separate subjects, divided into two consecutive courses. The first was the trivium, comprising Latin grammar, rhetoric and logic, which took two years. The next three were given over to the quadrivium, which covered music, arithmetic, geometry and astronomy. Dedicated scholars could then go on to complete a doctorate in their specialist field of study, which required at least another six years' work. The earliest age at which a student could qualify for a doctor's degree was 35.

The Church, monastic orders and private patrons all founded and maintained colleges for hard-up students, providing accommodation as well as teaching facilities. Colleges were mostly situated on the left bank of the River Seine near the Cathedral of Notre Dame, and Parisians came to call the university district the Latin Quarter, because that was the language normally spoken by the students, even outside classes. Teaching began at 4.00 each morning and finally ended with evening prayers at 9.00.

A widow in charge

Blanche of Castile, Philips' daughter-in-law and wife to the Crown Prince, spent her married life in the sheltered yet boisterous atmosphere of the French court. She had

Troubled see
Pope Boniface VIII deposed his predecessor Celestine V, but lost a power struggle with France's King Philip IV. This 13th-century statue of Boniface is now in Florence.

been married at the age of 12 in a ceremony arranged by her grandmother, Eleanor of Aquitaine. She gave birth to her second child (the first to survive to adulthood) in the same year as the Battle of Bouvines. The future Louis IX was to have plenty of siblings, for Blanche bore eight more sons and daughters over the next 12 years. The last was Charles, born in 1226, who as Charles of Anjou would many years later deliver the coup de grâce to the Hohenstaufen dynasty of Holy Roman Emperors.

On the death of Philip Augustus in 1223, Blanche, now aged 35, became Queen of France alongside her husband, the new King Louis VIII. Just three years later Louis was dead, struck down by dysentery, leaving the reins of government in Blanche's hands as regent for 12-year-old Louis IX. She quickly showed a talent and taste for power. She put down a dangerous revolt of the nobility and displayed great political adroitness in extending the power of the French crown in southern France, where she fiercely prosecuted the Cathar war she had inherited from her husband. The sect, which drew its beliefs partly from ancient Gnostic traditions, had become firmly entrenched in the Midi in the previous century. It was tolerated or even actively supported by many local nobles who saw it as a useful counterweight to the growing power of the Catholic Church.

The Cathars' growing influence provoked Pope Innocent III to intervene at the start of the 13th century. He ruled that the Cathars, also known as Albigensians, after the town of Albi, were heretics and proclaimed a

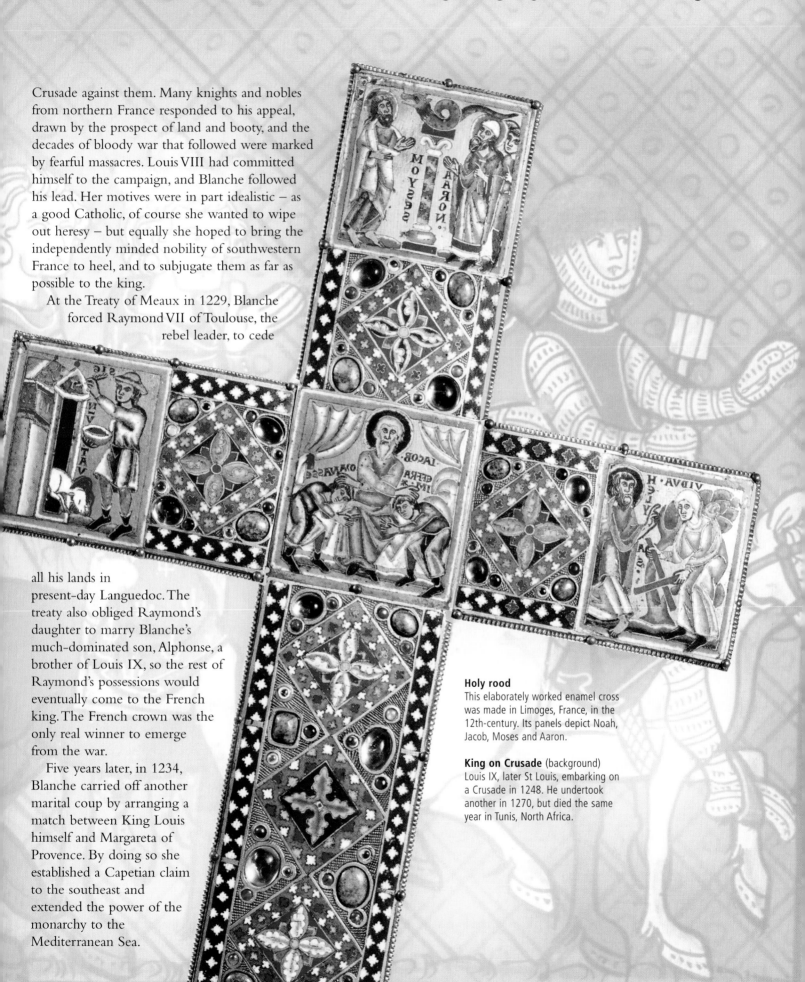

Crusade against them. Many knights and nobles from northern France responded to his appeal, drawn by the prospect of land and booty, and the decades of bloody war that followed were marked by fearful massacres. Louis VIII had committed himself to the campaign, and Blanche followed his lead. Her motives were in part idealistic – as a good Catholic, of course she wanted to wipe out heresy – but equally she hoped to bring the independently minded nobility of southwestern France to heel, and to subjugate them as far as possible to the king.

At the Treaty of Meaux in 1229, Blanche forced Raymond VII of Toulouse, the rebel leader, to cede all his lands in present-day Languedoc. The treaty also obliged Raymond's daughter to marry Blanche's much-dominated son, Alphonse, a brother of Louis IX, so the rest of Raymond's possessions would eventually come to the French king. The French crown was the only real winner to emerge from the war.

Five years later, in 1234, Blanche carried off another marital coup by arranging a match between King Louis himself and Margareta of Provence. By doing so she established a Capetian claim to the southeast and extended the power of the monarchy to the Mediterranean Sea.

Holy rood
This elaborately worked enamel cross was made in Limoges, France, in the 12th-century. Its panels depict Noah, Jacob, Moses and Aaron.

King on Crusade (background)
Louis IX, later St Louis, embarking on a Crusade in 1248. He undertook another in 1270, but died the same year in Tunis, North Africa.

Royal wedding
A manuscript illumination shows Philip IV of France marrying Johanna of Navarre on August 16, 1284. Besides the Spanish kingdom of Navarre, her dowry included the French duchies of Brie and Champagne.

A jealous mother

Even after his marriage Blanche kept a jealous eye on her son, forbidding him any contact with his wife in daylight hours and only permitting him to join her in the evening, shortly before bedtime. Even then the couple had to be on their guard. At their favourite residence at Pontoise north of Paris, the king's chambers were located above those of his wife, and the two sets of rooms were linked by a spiral staircase. Whenever Blanche approached the suite, a guard would knock on the queen's door, warning Louis to hurry back to his own chambers.

Although Blanche's regency officially ended in 1234 when Louis reached the age of 20, she remained in effective control of the state until her death 18 years later. As such, she was instrumental in the final submission of Toulouse and Aquitaine in 1243, following the failure of an expedition sent by their ally Henry III of England. Her role increased in 1248, when Louis took the cross and set off on Crusade, only to be captured by Muslim forces while campaigning in Egypt. Ransomed for a huge sum, he continued

to direct operations from the crusader stronghold of Acre, finally returning to France on receiving news of Blanche's death in 1252.

France's sainted king

It took Louis two years to get back to France. Only then, at the age of 40, did he take full personal control of his kingdom. He continued his mother's policies of extending the power of the crown in the south, seeking to resolve disputes peacefully. For example, he managed to persuade the ruler of the Spanish kingdom of Aragon to renounce his claims to the Duchy of Toulouse by waiving his own rights to the duchies of Roussillon and Barcelona and granting him Montpellier in compensation. His greatest success came in negotiations with England's King Henry III, who agreed to accept the French king's suzerainty over the lands he had inherited in Gascony and Aquitaine, agreeing to swear allegiance to Louis as his feudal lord.

Louis also introduced important internal reforms. The *parlement* or high court developed in his reign as an offshoot of the council that advised the King on judicial matters. Initially membership was limited to clergymen, nobles and knights, but in time legal specialists were co-opted as permanent members. These *maîtres* (magistrates) were scholars who had studied Roman and ecclesiastical law, and by the end of Louis's reign they were setting up investigations and dealing with complaints brought by vassals against their lords. Louis banned judicial duels and trial by combat, which had previously legitimised might as right and ensured justice only for the strongest.

By the end of his reign Louis IX was venerated by his subjects with almost religious fervour. Even as a child he had a saintly side to his character, and the high principles he adopted in his youth continued to guide him for the rest of his life. He combined military bravery, a sense of justice, charity towards the poor and devout religious faith. His piety not only led him to set out twice on Crusade but was also evident in his secular dealings, winning him an international reputation as an honest broker in many political disputes. One of his best-known judgments settled a bitter conflict over the succession in Flanders, and he was also consulted in the course of England's Barons' War.

In his final years Louis' thoughts turned increasingly to religion, and in 1270 he took the cross once again. He got only as far as Tunis on the North African coast before he was carried off by the plague. Death on Crusade added the crown of martyrdom to his saintly reputation, and he was formally canonised as St Louis in 1297, just 27 years after his death.

King against Pope

Louis's immediate successor, Philip III 'the Bold', achieved little in the course of a 15-year reign. The same could hardly be said of his son and heir, Philip IV 'the Fair', a handsome but ruthless monarch who remorselessly advanced the interests of the crown over the power of the feudal lords, the claims of the Catholic Church and the pretensions of the Holy Roman Emperor.

Unlike his grandfather, St Louis, Philip cared only for power – both his own and the crown's. The strong religious impulses that permeated the royal and aristocratic houses of Europe at that time left no mark on him whatsoever. He took the view that religion should be strictly subordinate to the demands of the state. Ironically, he was the first French ruler to style himself 'Most Christian King', and he employed an army of lawyers to produce pamphlets supporting his claim to be the true champion of the Church, thereby implicitly contradicting the rival claims of the Holy Roman Emperor and the Pope. He was a stubborn man,

and instinctively identified his own interests with those of the Christian faith. It was only a matter of time before a clash occurred with the Holy See.

In 1301 the King ordered the arrest of a papal legate, the Bishop of Pamiers (in southeastern France), on charges of treason. Pope Boniface VIII reacted

Coronation seat
The Capetian kings settled on Rheims Cathedral as the site of future coronations while it was still under construction. Louis VIII and Blanche of Castile were the first royal couple to be crowned there, in 1223. The building was not completed until 1300.

furiously, issuing a series of papal bulls asserting the primacy of Church authority over secular power. Philip's jurists countered with the claim that the King was entitled to depose even the Pope if he proved unworthy of his high office.

Boniface took steps to excommunicate Philip, who responded by sending a representative to the Pope's residence at Anagni, in the hills above Rome. The envoy burst in on the Pope and threatened his life, holding him prisoner for two days. Traumatised by his ordeal, Boniface died a month later.

The Archbishop of Bordeaux was chosen as Boniface's next-but-one successor, taking the title of Clement V. Under pressure from Philip, Clement

Strong cities
A miniature from a 14th-century French manuscript shows a bishop blessing the June Market in Paris. The 13th century saw France's capital and other towns flourish as centres of trade and learning.

chose to take up residence outside Italy, in the border region of France. Then, in 1309, he established his seat at Avignon rather than Rome, so instigating the 60-year 'Babylonian captivity' of the papacy.

The last Capetians

In keeping with his generally secular nature, Philip showed little interest in the Crusades that had so preoccupied his predecessors. Acre, the last Christian stronghold in Outremer, finally fell to Islamic forces during the course of his reign. Its fall deprived the Knights Templars, originally founded to protect Chistian pilgrims visiting the Holy Land, of their principle reason for existence. Jealous of their wealth and power, which

he saw as a possible threat to royal authority, Philip decided to destroy the order. He denounced the Templars as heretics, seized and tortured their leaders and had more than 50 individuals, including the last Grand Master, burned at the stake.

Soon afterwards Philip himself died. His legacy included a well-stocked treasury, a monarchy vastly strengthened in relation to its vassals, and a papal curia that was wholly dependent upon the French crown. Yet the dynasty that he had sought to aggrandise hardly benefited from his efforts at all. He was succeeded by three of his sons – Louis X, Philip V and Charles IV – all of whom reigned briefly and died without leaving male heirs.

On Charles IV's death, in 1328, the Capetian line of kings died out, to be replaced by the collateral line of the House of Valois.

England's kings and barons vie for power

Amid the bitter conflicts that divided Crown and aristocracy in 13th-century England, an institution arose that was to have crucial long-term political significance – Parliament.

The scene that played out on the island of Runnymede in the River Thames on June 19, 1215, would cast a long shadow. On one side sat King John, 48 years old, an energetic but unpopular ruler whose political machinations had recently collapsed in ruins. Opposite him stood leading barons of the realm who had forced the financially embarrassed monarch to the negotiating table against his will. The immediate bone of contention was a document, drawn up in Latin by the rebel barons, to which John had finally agreed to set his seal. History would know it as Magna Carta, the Great Charter, and even though it concerned itself mostly with the rights and privileges of the feudal aristocracy, it would come in time to be seen as the cornerstone of the nation's political liberties.

An ill-starred reign

Under John's rule, England reached a turning point. The upper ranks of the nobility rebelled against royal autocracy and demanded the rights they considered themselves entitled to by tradition and custom, and that had been respected by earlier Plantagenet kings. The conflict began in John's reign and would eventually, under his successors Henry III and Edward I, provide a political voice for the petty nobility and wealthy town merchants, too, through the institution of Parliament.

Another recurrent theme of the 13th century would be the attempts made by the English Crown to extend its power throughout Britain. While John had little success in this respect, the warrior Edward would succeed in subduing Wales, although even he was hard pushed to make lasting roads into Scotland.

The chain of events that brought King John to the point of having to make concessions to his own subjects was a lengthy one. Born the youngest son of Henry II and Eleanor of Aquitaine,

Magna Carta (background)
The Great Charter was drawn up to address baronial grievances with the King. It comprised 61 clauses detailing relations between the Crown, the nobility and the Church, and is sometimes seen as a pioneering example of a written constitution.

Royal seal
The great seal of King John, which was appended to Magna Carta to signify royal assent, portrays the monarch as a knight on horseback. In medieval times, seals acted as signatures, guaranteeing that documents had legal force.

John had been nicknamed 'Lackland' in his youth because most of the lands available for royal inheritance were allotted to his elder brothers, leaving only scraps for him. Yet when he finally came to the throne in 1199, on the death of his brother, Richard the Lionheart, he found himself in charge of the most powerful kingdom in the West. The domains of the Angevin empire that his father and mother created straddled England and western France, stretching from the Scottish border and Irish Sea to the Pyrenees. John spent the first four years of his reign in his French territories, only visiting England for three weeks at the time of his coronation.

Three great crises marked John's reign, and he came out the loser from all of them. The first involved his French lands. A local dispute in Poitou escalated when John married the promised bride of a local nobleman. Outraged, the jilted suitor appealed to King Philip II of France, his overlord, who in turn summoned John as his feudal vassal to answer the charges. When John refused to comply, Philip had the excuse he needed to invade. After a seven-month siege in 1204, he took John's principal stronghold, Chateau Gaillard on the River Seine. By the following year all of John's possessions north of the River Loire – Normandy, Maine, Touraine, Anjou – had fallen to the French king. At a stroke, John had lost the wealthiest part of his empire. An attempt to regain the lands later in his reign failed miserably when Philip crushingly defeated John's ally, the Holy Roman Emperor Otto IV, at the Battle of Bouvines in 1214.

Conflict with the papacy

John's troubled relationship with the papacy provided the second crisis. He refused to accept the Pope's nominee, Stephen Langton, as Archbishop of Canterbury, insisting on his own right to select the primate of England. The climax

Fortress town
Edward I had Caernarfon Castle built as the seat of royal administration for the conquered principality of Wales. His son Edward II, the first Prince of Wales, was born in the stronghold.

came in 1209 when Pope Innocent III excommunicated John and placed the whole kingdom under an interdict that prevented Mass from being celebrated anywhere in the realm. The conflict was only settled in 1213 when John backed down, agreeing to accept Langton and, in future, to pay an annual tribute to the Pope in Rome.

John's troubles with the Church and the disastrous foreign expedition that ended at Bouvines (at which John and his army were not even present) set the scene for the culminating confrontation with the barons. They had grown used to absentee kings in the days of the Angevin Empire, but with the loss of the northern French lands John was now rarely out of England. There he devoted much of his energy to finding new ways to raise revenue, most of which went to pay for further foreign adventures.

In 1215 the discontent of the barons escalated into violent confrontation. The rebels upbraided the king with imposing ever higher taxes, with arbitrarily revoking fiefs and with extorting huge sums from the Church while the see of Canterbury stood vacant. John made matters worse by his penchant for foreign advisers, and also by his habit of holding the children of leading noblemen hostage as a guarantee of their parents' good conduct.

The road to Magna Carta

In December 1214, John's enemies gave him a deadline of the following Easter to guarantee the full restoration of their traditional rights. When the date passed and the King looked to the Continent for mercenary troops with which to crush the rebels, the barons rose up, seizing cities and castles. London opened its gates to them, shutting John out.

In desperation, John offered to abide by the decision of a court of arbitration under papal direction. But the barons no longer wanted any part of such a deal. Instead, they drew up a document listing their grievances over the abuse of royal

power and wrested the Magna Carta treaty from him clause by clause. With a heavy heart John agreed at Runnymede to abide by its terms. The barons had won.

Even so, the concessions failed to prevent England from spiralling further into civil war. John turned for support to the Pope, who obliged him by declaring Magna Carta null and void, since the King had not given his consent freely.

Meanwhile the rebel barons were still up in arms, and they turned to John's old enemy, King Philip of France, for help. He sent his son and heir, the future Louis IX, at the head of an expeditionary force that landed on the east coast of England.

King and Parliament
Edward I set the precedent of summoning regular parliaments to approve his actions, particularly in raising taxes to finance his wars. Although the members were mostly selected, not elected, the King's initiative set England on a path that would eventually lead to representative democracy. This pen on parchment drawing of Edward was done in the 13th century.

Charter of liberties

John fought back energetically, but the situation was still in the balance when he was struck down by dysentery and died. Monastic chroniclers, who hated John for his contemptuous treatment of the Church, would later claim that his death was the result of gluttony, brought on by a surfeit of peaches and cider, seeking to draw a moral from his sudden demise. A few days earlier he had lost much of his baggage train, including some of the royal treasury, when the wagons got caught by the incoming tide while crossing a river at the landward end of the Wash. Bad luck dogged him to the end.

John's reign ended in chaos and civil war, and he went down in history as England's most hated king. Yet he left the nation an enduring legacy in Magna Carta, which still stands as the foundation stone of English constitutional law. Its chief provision was to guarantee all the monarch's subjects freedom from arbitrary arrest or punishment: henceforth, no-one could be held in custody without being

An inglorious end
Edward II's tomb lies in Gloucester Cathedral. At the end of his reign he was deposed by forces gathered against him by his wife Isabella. Forced to abdicate in favour of his son Edward III, he was murdered in Berkeley Castle.

The mill and the plough

The Domesday Book, compiled in the 11th century after the Norman conquest of England, listed 5624 mills across the length and breadth of the country. The inventory was taken at a time when the number of watermills was growing rapidly, both in England and on the Continent, as a result of the invention of the camshaft. Other technological advances were also taking place. The vertically aligned water wheel was being supplanted in the milling of cereals by the horizontal mill-wheel, which was small enough for individual farmers to install.

Windmills were also being widely introduced. The classic mill, with a vertical axle turned by sails, was introduced to Europe by returning crusaders who had learned its design from the Arabs. It evolved into the post-mill, with a horizontal axle, and the smock-mill, with a revolving top. From the 13th century onwards – initially in southwest France, Normandy and northern Italy, and later in Moravia and Swabia – mill technology was used to power drop-hammers in the manufacture of iron.

In agriculture, farmers benefited from new ploughing technology. Ploughs were now equipped with a coulter – a vertical blade in front of the ploughshare – to cut the turf, an iron ploughshare to excavate the soil, and a wooden mould-board to turn the sod, as well as a handle to guide the plough and set the depth of the furrow. Teams of six or even eight oxen drew large ploughs. Because ordinary farmers seldom owned so many oxen, they would band together to do the ploughing.

Harnessing water power
Applying the new mill technology, engineers in central Europe began to build tide-mills from the 13th century onward.
Background: A peasant tills the land in a marginal illustration from the Luttrell Psalter.

given a fair trial. Magna Carta also secured the freedom of the Church from royal interference, imposed norms for the administration of justice, established the principle of baronial scrutiny over royal jurisdiction, and even contained the first attempts to limit the monarch's political freedom of action.

Other aims of the charter were to get the royal courts to deliver prompt and efficient justice, to limit the power of the monarchy to impose extraordinary taxes, and to guarantee freedom of movement for trade goods. Finally, it established a tribunal of 25 barons to supervise compliance with the terms of the charter. Contemporaries were well aware of Magna Carta's significance in limiting royal powers, as is shown by the fact that later monarchs were several times forced to reissue it when their subjects again felt that their rights were under threat.

Barons in charge

The fact that John's son and successor Henry III was only 9 years old at his accession might have threatened more chaos, but in fact the kingdom entered a time of consolidation. A regency council composed of high royal officials and barons took over the government, under the competent leadership first of William Marshal, Earl of Pembroke, and then of Hubert de Burgh. Over the next 11 years the council set about implementing the provisions of Magna Carta, which was twice reissued, and the French invasion force went home. They managed to restore internal peace and security, subduing the rebel nobility and putting the country's administration and legal system on a sound footing. By collaborating with the papacy in their foreign policy, they also maintained peace with their neighbours, notably France.

The growth of the administrative and legal system at this time created an increasing demand for the services of laymen who could read and write. These people received their education at grammar schools, which spread across the country in the course of the 12th and 13th centuries, either developing from existing cathedral schools or being founded by masters who had taught in them. At the same time, centres of higher learning were developing at Oxford and Cambridge. Oxford was already attracting students in significant numbers in the 12th century, and it entered a new, settled phase with the foundation of University College in 1249. Cambridge benefited from the migration of a large group of Oxford students in 1209.

Growing nationalism

The times changed once more in 1227, when Henry III began to rule in his own right. Politically, his reign was a failure, marked by abortive foreign campaigns to regain Aquitaine and Poitou, as well as a costly attempt to place his brother Richard of Cornwall on the German imperial throne, that proved as unpopular as they were expensive. Throughout Henry's reign the barons chafed against his

Gothic splendour
Built between the 11th and 14th centuries, Lincoln Cathedral stands witness to the prosperity, technical expertise and religious fervour of England and much of Europe in the High Middle Ages.

reliance on foreign advisors, which only increased after his marriage in 1236 to Eleanor of Provence, a sister of the French queen. In ecclesiastical matters, Henry devoted himself to the papal cause, again alienating the growing nationalism of his subjects. English churchmen began to resent the appointment of absentee Italians to English bishoprics and the constant outflow of cash to Rome.

The Provisions of Oxford

The political tensions of Henry's reign came to a head in a disastrous attempt to secure the throne of the Italian kingdom of Naples and Sicily for his second son, Edmund. The venture failed when the realm was claimed by Charles of Anjou, brother of the French King Louis IX, but it embroiled Henry in great expense at a time when he was also losing a fight at home against the independent Welsh prince, Llywelyn ap Gruffud.

Matters came to a head in 1258, when Henry tried to raise 135,000 marks – a third of the annual revenue of the realm – to pay the Pope the promised price of Edmund's Italian claim. Rebel barons, led by Simon de Montfort, Earl of Leicester and the King's own brother-in-law, presented demands for a programme of reform. Driven by financial necessity, the King unwillingly gave his assent to the Provisions of Oxford of 1258, which in effect turned England into a constitutional monarchy. Under the terms the King lost the right to choose his own advisers, agreeing instead to be bound by the guidance of a permanent council of 15 barons, chosen partly by the rebels. In addition, a Parliament made up of the 15 council members plus 12 elected representatives was to be summoned in an advisory capacity three times a year.

The Barons' Revolt

Henry soon reneged on his promises. In 1261 he got the Pope to declare the oath he had sworn to respect the Provisions of

Oxford null and void, just as his father had done before him with Magna Carta. Soon after, the dispute escalated into open war.

At first, fortune was with the rebels, who defeated the royalists at Lewes, in Sussex, in 1264, taking the King himself prisoner. Simon de Montfort then took over government in the name of the imprisoned king, calling two historic Parliaments that, for the first time in England's history, included representatives of the towns and knights of the shire.

De Montfort's revolt eventually collapsed, largely thanks to Henry's son Edward. The 26-year-old royal heir was very different to his father. Initially he had been sympathetic to the demands of the reformers, although he had sided with the King when open conflict broke out and had been taken prisoner with him at Lewes. In 1265 he escaped to rally the royalist forces. In the ensuing Battle of Evesham, the barons went down to defeat and de Montfort was killed.

On the surface, with de Montfort's death the Barons' Revolt had come to nothing. The ageing Henry III was restored to the throne and the leading rebels were disinherited of their lands. But the reformists' demands were never forgotten. The principle that the king of England could not rule solely at his own whim was not lost. Future monarchs would increasingly recognise the need to consult their subjects, particularly when extraordinary taxation was required, and advisory Parliaments would be a regular feature of future reigns.

A warrior king

Although Henry III remained king in name until his death in 1272, for all practical purposes, Edward took over the duties of kingship. He soon found opportunities to give proof of his abilities. Much of his reign would be taken up with the struggle to impose English rule on the nation's independently minded neighbours, Wales and Scotland. Wales was Edward's first target.

The nation of Wales had always been politically disunited, and the Norman kings had taken advantage of its divisions to colonise much of the country, particularly the border marches and the southwest (modern Pembrokeshire). The mountainous north and west, however, had remained in Welsh hands, ruled by their own princes in accordance with their own laws. Two strong Welsh leaders – Llywelyn the Great and his grandson Llywelyn ap Gruffudd – seized the opportunity offered by the baronial struggles in England to regain some ground. In 1267 Llywelyn ap Gruffudd won recognition of these gains from Henry III in the Treaty of Montgomery, which acknowledged Llywelyn's position as Prince of Wales, and recognised him as overlord of all the Welsh principalities.

A decade later Edward set out to take revenge. When Llywelyn ap Gruffudd refused to pay him homage, Edward led an invading army along the north coast and in a ruthlessly efficient campaign forced Llywelyn into submission. Llywelyn's brother Dafydd raised the flag of rebellion five years later, and Edward struck again, killing both brothers. Having subjugated the country, Edward then built a chain of strongholds, including Caernarfon and Conwy castles, to keep it permanently in check and formally annexed it in the Statute of Wales of 1284.

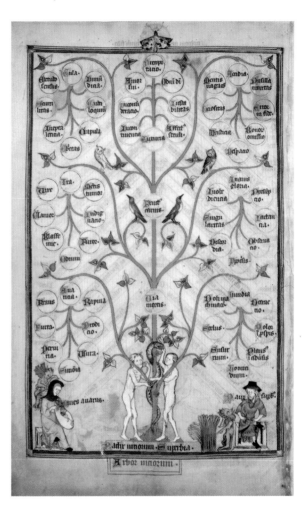

Book of devotions
Psalters were popular devotional works in medieval times, containing the text of the Biblical Book of Psalms to be recited by the faithful. This illustration depicting Adam and Eve and the Tree of the Knowledge of Good and Evil is from the Psalter of Robert de Lisle, dating from about 1310.

Fighting for independence
The death of the Scottish King Alexander III in 1286 opened an era of armed conflict between England and Scotland. The Scots won a decisive victory over the English and Edward II at Bannockburn in 1314, yet 13 more years would pass before his successor, Edward III, formally recognised Scotland's independence. This depiction of the battle is from the Holkham Bible.

A lethal new weapon

While campaigning in Wales, Edward was impressed by a weapon the Welsh used against his forces: the longbow. He rapidly equipped his own archers with the new weapon, and before long English bowmen were using longbows with astonishing skill. In the space of a minute, a practiced archer could let off six arrows or more at targets as far as 200m (650ft) away. At short range, an arrow from a longbow could penetrate an oak plank 9cm (3½in) thick; even from 200m it could punch through 2cm of wood. The crossbow, introduced a century earlier, had greater penetrating power at long distance, but the longbow had greater strategic value because of the speed with which the arrows could be loosed. The chainmail vests and leather jerkins that foot-soldiers wore in combat at the time could not offer effective protection against its power, and knights' horses were also vulnerable.

The struggle for Scotland

Having disposed of the challenge from Wales, Edward directed his attention to the Scots. The issue of Scottish sovereignty came to the fore after the death of King Alexander III in a riding accident one stormy night in 1286, a mishap that put a six-year-old girl on the throne. Following her death four years later, Edward intervened, first to assert his feudal right to choose between rival contenders to the throne, and then to assert royal rights that were resisted by John Baliol, the very candidate he had selected.

The result was war, first against Baliol, who was deposed and killed, and then William Wallace, who led the nationalist resistance to the tyrannical agents Edward appointed to rule in Baliol's place. In all, Edward sent eight expeditions to Scotland between 1296 and 1306, and although his forces had successes, eventually capturing and executing Wallace, they failed to strike the knock-out blow they had achieved against the Welsh.

The triumph of Robert Bruce

After Wallace's death, Robert Bruce was proclaimed King Robert I in 1306. Edward took personal command of a fresh campaign to unseat this new opponent. By that time, however, the monarch was 68 years old and a sick man. He died on the way to Scotland in 1307.

Edward's son and successor, Edward II, took up the struggle in the years that followed, but he made little headway and in 1314 led his army to a catastrophic defeat at Bannockburn. The battle effectively ensured Scotland's independence for the next three centuries and Robert's status as a Scottish national hero has endured to the present day.

The Knights of the Teutonic Order

In the course of the Crusades Christian knights founded military religious orders to fight in the Holy Land. The Knights of the Teutonic Order later settled on the Baltic coast, where they carved out a state that endured for over 300 years.

The knightly orders were a most distinctive feature of the age of the Crusades. Their members trained in the use of weapons like other knights, but they also took monastic vows of poverty, chastity and obedience. First to be formed, in the 11th century, were the Knights Hospitallers who originally ran a hospital for sick pilgrims in Jerusalem, but later turned their attention more to fighting. The Knights Templars followed in 1120, with the aim of protecting Christian pilgrims travelling in the Holy Land.

Winning papal backing

The Teutonic Knights were the last of the three great orders, formed in 1190 in the Christian enclave of Acre on the coast of Palestine. The Pope recognised them and gave them the same Benedictine-inspired monastic rule that the Templars lived by.

Soon, the new order received important privileges from Pope Honorius III, who issued more than 100 decrees in its favour, helping to establish it on a sound footing. Among other advantages, the knights were granted the income from indulgences sold to crusaders, who – in accordance with a provision dating back to the dawn of the crusading era – were promised a reduction in the time they could expect to spend paying for their sins in Purgatory in return for cash payments. The order was also permitted to practice the lucrative

business of moneylending. Private benefactors like St Elisabeth of Thuringia provided additional endowments. The money financed a hospital run by the monks in Acre, and also funded expansion elsewhere; before long the Teutonic Knights were running charitable institutions in parts of central Europe.

A presence in Europe

The order established a foothold in Europe soon after its founding. Early in the 13th century, it began setting up communities in Germany. These institutions are still reflected in street names – such as Teutonic Lords' Street or Teutonic Order Street – in German cities today, including Frankfurt and Nuremberg. The knights also had a military presence in Transylvania, where they were summoned by the King of Hungary to combat the Turkic Cumans threatening his eastern border. The King came to regret the

Symbol of power (background)
Comprising a church, chapter house and dormitory, the high castle at Marienburg, now Malbork, was completed sometime around 1280.

Licence to conquer
In the Golden Bull of Rimini (below) Emperor Frederick II charged the Teutonic Knights with the conquest of Prussia, granting them control of the territory.

The black cross
Once the property of a Grand Master of the Teutonic Knights, this shield displays the order's characteristic black cross on a white background.

invitation when the knights started importing German settlers to farm the lands they guarded, and in 1224 they were forcibly expelled.

The call to the Baltic

The order's involvement in the Baltic area began shortly after its expulsion from Hungary. In 1225, a Polish nobleman, Duke Conrad of Mazovia, sought help in fighting the pagan Prussians who were raiding his realm from the east and resisting all attempts to convert them to Christianity. The order's leader at the time, the charismatic Hermann von Salza, wanted above all to avoid another debacle like the Hungarian venture. He therefore took pains to establish a firm legal basis for the order's position in the region before accepting the request.

He approached his close friend, the Holy Roman Emperor Frederick II, who in 1226 issued the Golden Bull of Rimini, a sealed decree that spelled out the administrative structure of the order. It was influenced by that of Frederick's own efficiently run kingdom of Sicily.

At the head of the order stood the master, elected for life by a general chapter of all the knights. He was supported by five principal officials, the so-called 'Bidden Ones', who served for a fixed term – the marshal was responsible for military affairs, the grand commander for administration, the hospitaller for welfare, the quartermaster for clothing and the bursar for finances. Crucially, the bull also granted the order the right to undertake missionary activities in the pagan lands

Smiting the heathen
This illumination illustrating the Biblical battle fought in the last days against the forces of Gog and Magog depicts the leaders of the heavenly host bearing the insignia of the Teutonic Order.

east of Germany and to retain all conquered territory under its control. When this concession was subsequently confirmed by the Pope, von Salza had the formal authorisation that he needed to take up the challenge – and to lay the foundations of an independent state.

The knights still needed a base from which to launch their operations. By the Treaty of Kruschwitz of 1230, a local counterpart to the Golden Bull, Duke Conrad granted them the region around Chelmno on the River Vistula as their own sovereign territory. The knights then set up a military base on the eastern bank of the river. The city of Torun, which grew up on the site, is thought to take its name from Toron des Chevaliers, a crusader castle in Palestine.

Colonising Prussia

Over the ensuing decades the order founded many cities and fortresses as it set about the bloody business of suppressing the pagan Prussians and colonising the region with Christian settlers. The construction of the castle at Chelmno got under way in 1231, and work began on Marienwerder Castle (now in the Polish town of Kwidzyn) in the following year. The towns that grew up around the fortresses received their own charters, with the Chelmno Guarantee of 1233 serving as a model for those that followed.

The towns of Braniewo and Elblang in Poland and the port of Kaliningrad (now a Russian enclave on the Baltic coast) all developed from settlements founded by the Teutonic Knights. Many of the order's foundations advertised their origins with pious names, among them Christburg ('Christ's town', now Dzierzgon in Poland) and Bischofsburg ('Bishop's Town', today's Biskupiec). The commanders of the order took pains to site the new outposts no more than a day's ride from one another – a distance of about 40km (25 miles) – thereby creating a tight-knit network of neighbouring Christian communities.

Drive to the east

Besides founding towns, the order set out to expand the land area available for agriculture, recruiting peasants from northern Germany and the Low Countries to settle the newly cleared holdings. The farmers moved into what had previously been scantily populated regions of East Prussia and set about farming the land, felling forests and burning the stumps as they went.

Meanwhile, the knights drove ever farther north and east. The Prussians resisted doggedly, but they were vanquished in a series of pitched battles, until by 1283 all of the Prussian lands were in the hands of the order. Fresh waves of German settlers followed in the knights' wake, attracted by the prospect of large landholdings and low rents. The incomers were allotted plots by agents called locators, and were free of most feudal obligations other than the need to pay land rent to the order.

Union with the Sword Brothers

To oversee the spiritual life of the newly Christianised lands, four bishoprics were created at Kulmerland, Pomesania, Ermeland and Samland. Although the new sees were located on lands ruled by the order, they were subordinate in ecclesiastical terms to the newly created archiepiscopal see of Riga in present-day Latvia (previously a bishopric).

The Teutonic Order even inherited a presence of its own in Latvia and the eastern Baltic lands through its union in 1237 with the Sword Brothers, a fellow

FINLAND

SWEDEN

Tallinn

Lake Peipus

Gotland

B A L T I C   S E A

Riga

Daugava

Sovetsk

Neman

Gdansk

Kaliningrad

Malbork

POMERANIA

Chelmno

LITHUANIA

P O L A N D   Vistula

Warsaw

Teutonic Order states

14th century conquests

Important cities and places

EVERYDAY LIFE

EVERYDAY LIFE

The Teutonic life

Life within the order was austere in the extreme. The knights owned no personal property and were not allowed to consort with laymen. They kept silence at mealtimes, in dormitories, and on the march. Jousting was forbidden and they were only allowed to hunt animals that were considered harmful – mostly wolves, lynxes and bears.

Meat was off the menu not just at Lent but also for much of the year, and all sexual activity was strictly prohibited. Each man had to rise four times a night to attend holy offices, and on Fridays was expected to practice self-flagellation until blood was drawn.

Holy writ
An illuminated manuscript Bible, written on parchment with gold and coloured decoration. It was created in one of the Teutonic Knights' northern strongholds, c.1338-59.

monastic order founded in Riga in 1201. The Brothers had already forcibly converted much of what is now Estonia and Latvia to the Christian faith, but they had subsequently fallen out with the papacy. Following a crushing defeat at the hands of the pagan Lithuanians at the Battle of Saule in 1236, the remnants chose a path of confederation with the Teutonic Knights. Once the two orders' lands were joined, the combined statelet stretched from the River Vistula almost to the Gulf of Finland, leaving a gap for the pagan enclave of Samogitia (in present-day Lithuania north of the River Nemunas). This coastal arm of the inland Kingdom of Lithuania was to remain unconverted well into the 14th century.

Territorial expansion only increased the Teutonic Knights' hunger for fresh conquests. In extending their territory eastwards, however, they came up against the Orthodox Christian principality of Novgorod. In 1242 its ruler, Alexander Nevsky, checked the knights' ambitions when he inflicted a crushing defeat on them beside the icebound waters of Lake Peipus.

Knights, chaplains and lay brothers

One reason for the Teutonic Order's success was its total control over the lands it conquered. The order exercised all the sovereign rights of an independent state, even issuing its own coinage. It held a monopoly on amber found on the Baltic coastline, and appointed an 'amber master' to supervise collection of the precious resin, used for making rosary beads.

Membership of the order comprised three classes: knights, chaplains and lay brothers. The knights did the fighting, the chaplains looked after the spiritual welfare of settlers and converts within the order's lands, and the lay brothers, whose vows were less strict than those of the other two classes, worked the land. Each of the order's strongholds was manned by at least 12 knights – the number of Christ's apostles.

The heart of the state

In the early decades of Baltic expansion, the order was still officially based in the Holy Land. When Acre fell to Muslim forces in 1291, its headquarters briefly moved to Venice before transferring to Prussia in 1309. There the central seat of authority was the castle and town of Marienburg, now Malbork, near the Polish port of Gdansk. The castle stands on the east bank of the River Nogat. Construction began in the 13th century under Grand Master Konrad of Thierberg the Elder. Prior to that, a castle belonging to the Dukes of Pomerelia had stood on the site, but had been destroyed by local people in an uprising. As the knights expanded eastward through Prussia, Marienburg Castle assumed a decisive role at the heart of the state, serving as an almost impregnable stronghold, a residence for the Grand Master, and the hub of administration.

The castle was built in separate sections, surrounded by a huge moat. The high castle was the first to be built. It contained the church, assembly rooms, living quarters, refectory and dormitories – all the communal areas where knights came together. The mid castle, a Gothic red-brick jewel, contained the Grand Master's residence and accommodation for lay brothers and guests. A lower castle, comprising the armoury and a separate church, was also enclosed within the massive containing wall that stretched to the River Nogat. A second moat provided additional protection to the north and east.

Zenith and decline

The order reached the peak of its power in the mid 14th century under Winrich of Kniprode, a long-serving grand master who was responsible for building the mid castle at Marienburg. Each summer, knights from all over northern Europe would take part in raids into the Kingdom of Lithuania, a powerful realm that included present-day Lithuania and much of Belarus. It was the last remaining stronghold of paganism.

The order's success led to growing tension with the neighbouring Christian kingdom of Poland, a rising power to the south. At first Teutonic Knights and Poles had fought together, joining forces to campaign against the heathen Prussians. Relations soured after 1308, however, when the knights occupied the Polish coastal province of Pomerelia and the port city of Gdansk. In 1339 Poland's King Casimir III secured a papal ruling requiring the order to give back the province, but he could not enforce it. At the Peace of Kalisch, signed in 1343, he finally gave sovereignty over the province to the order in return for a promise of military aid against the Lithuanians. The treaty marked the zenith of the order's fortunes, which would start to decline after Lithuania's eventual conversion to Christianity some 40 years later – an act that removed the reason for the existence of a crusader Baltic state.

Power in brick and stone
From 1232 onwards, the Teutonic Knights built Marienwerder Castle in what is now Kwidzyn in the Masuria region of western Poland. The fortified stronghold was the residence of the bishops of Pomesania.

The struggle for power in Germany

For almost a century, the electors of the Holy Roman Empire effectively prevented a strong king from taking office in Germany – to the detriment of the people.

Unexpected emperor
In 1308, Henry VII became the first representative of the house of Luxembourg to be elected German king. During his five-year reign he married his son to the sister of King Wenceslas II of Bohemia, bringing that kingdom into the Luxembourg family. He also revived the imperial claims to Italy, and was crowned Holy Roman Emperor in Rome in 1311. These marble statues of Henry and his counsellors can be seen in Pisa.

The imperial election of 1257 was a cross between tragedy and farce. A new German king was needed to succeed William of Holland, who had been killed on campaign in Frisia the previous year. The electors were summoned to meet in Frankfurt to choose between two candidates, both foreign: Alfonso X, King of Castile, and Count Richard of Cornwall, brother of England's King Henry III. Two of the electors – Arnold II of Trier and Albert of Saxony – were in the pay of Alfonso. They took up quarters in the city in advance of the meeting, and on the appointed day proceeded to bar the other electors from entering the city.

The Great Interregnum

The excluded electors had no intention of being cheated of their voting rights. Setting up camp outside the city gates, they proceeded to elect their own preferred candidate, Richard of Cornwall, as king. Alfonso's supporters responded by holding a second election three months later at which King Ottokar II of Bohemia was persuaded to change his vote; having earlier supported Richard of Cornwall, he now came down in favour of Alfonso, who was duly elected.

So Germany had two separate elected kings, both hoping to win papal recognition as Holy Roman Emperor. The power vacuum that would go down in German history as the Great Interregnum had got under way.

As the electors had hoped, both claimants had other commitments that prevented them from taking much interest in Germany in any case. Richard made only four fleeting visits and Alfonso none at all. With no strong central authority, real power passed into the hands of the electors themselves.

Germany's leading noble families had concerns of their own to occupy their attention. In the Duchy of Swabia, Count Rudolf of Habsburg was waging a series of local wars to increase his possessions. In Bavaria the laws of succession were dividing up the estates of the Wittelsbachs, and shortly afterwards the Margravate of Brandenburg fragmented into five separate smaller principalities, each of whose rulers laid claim to the office of elector. Even the Sachsen-Wettin family, among the least powerful of the electoral council, was at loggerheads over which member should rightfully exercise the electoral vote. The situation was particularly bad in Thuringia, where the Margrave of Meissen was struggling – unsuccessfully – to assert his claims, the previous line of rulers having died out.

With no one in charge and the provincial noblemen distracted by their own troubles, lawlessness spread across the land. Peasants and city merchants suffered more than most from the prevailing chaos. In the countryside, farms were plundered and burned to the ground, while traders found themselves confronted with arbitrary tax demands. Even Church property was not safe from the robber barons.

The cities presented particularly tempting targets for plunder because they were thriving, with splendid buildings and busy markets – many were even minting their own coinage. Newly enacted laws stated that bondsmen who lived for a year and a day within their precincts were no longer obliged to return to service under their feudal lord. The new wealth offered opportunities for citizens to advance themselves and increase their earnings. But it also made the cities targets.

Rise of the Habsburgs

Of all the barons plundering southern Germany at this time, the most ruthlessly successful was Count Rudolf of Habsburg, who took advantage of the anarchy to lay

Wittelsbach versus Habsburg
On the death of Henry VII two rival claimants asserted their right to the title of German king. The dispute was settled in 1322 outside the town of Mühldorf on the River Inn. Frederick the Fair, the Habsburg candidate, assembled an army of 2200 knights, 6600 foot soldiers, and 4000 mounted Hungarians and Mongols to face an army of similar size fighting for Ludwig IV of the Bavarian Wittelsbach family. In what turned out to be the last great battle of the pre-gunpowder era, Ludwig's forces won the day, and he ruled as undisputed king for the next 25 years.

the foundations for the future Habsburg dynasty. When the Pope threatened to choose a new Holy Roman Emperor himself in order to end the chaos of the Interregnum, the electors were sufficiently alarmed to take action. In 1273 they met to elect their new king, and Rudolf's ambition and belligerence made him the obvious choice.

Yet this was too little and too late to restore imperial prestige. What followed was a lengthy struggle for power between the rival houses of Habsburg, Luxembourg and Wittelsbach that so dissipated the authority of the imperial office, it never again attained its previous status of power. Richard of Cornwall had died the year before, so was no longer a contender, but Alfonso X of Castile was still alive and

The Lion of Bavaria
Eight years after first laying claim to the title of German king in 1314, Ludwig IV of Bavaria confirmed his position by victory in battle. The six sons who succeeded him as rulers of Bavaria were paper tigers by comparison, and during their reigns the area under Bavaria's rule fragmented and collapsed.

maintained his claim to the crown. He disputed Rudolf's election, counting on Ottokar of Bohemia's support.

Ottokar had reasons of his own for not wanting to see a new, more assertive ruler on the throne. Like Rudolf, he had taken advantage of the period of anarchy to expand his realm and had no wish to abandon the gains he had made. Rudolf, however, wanted to get his own hands on Austria, Styria, Carinthia and other provinces that Ottokar had annexed. The scene was set for conflict.

The dispute was finally settled on the battlefield. Ottokar lost, and in 1276 was forced to cede the territories. Two years later he regrouped his forces, but was defeated at the Battle of the Marchfeld.

A succession of short-lived rulers then followed one another onto the German throne. Rudolf was succeeded by Adolf of Nassau, who was known to be deeply in debt and chosen by the electors as a puppet king. When he proved less than compliant, however, he was deposed and replaced by Rudolf's son Albert. Ten years later Albert was assassinated, making way for Henry VII, Count of Luxembourg, who held the throne for just five years.

The last knightly battle

When Henry died in 1313, an election took place in which Frederick of Habsburg received exactly the same number of votes as the Wittelsbach Ludwig of Bavaria. An eight-year civil war ensued, ultimately settled in Ludwig's favour at the Battle of Mühldorf on the River Inn. Some 1400 Habsburg knights fell during this eight-hour, hand-to-hand struggle, not counting the losses among the foot-soldiers; around 1000 knights perished on the Bavarian side.

Ludwig's subsequent attempts to revive the old imperial claims to Italian territory roused the ire of Pope John XXII, who disputed his title on the grounds that his election had not been sanctioned by the papacy. When Ludwig ignored his complaints, the Pope excommunicated

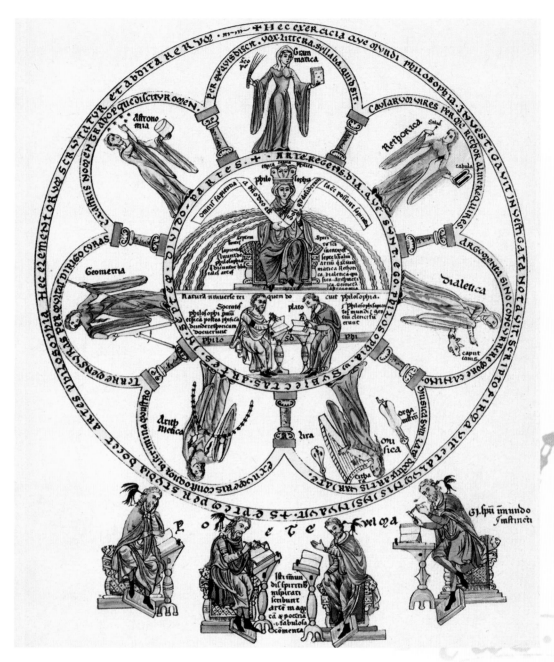

Advanced education
The first universities of Christian Europe grew up between the 12th and 14th centuries in Italy, France, England and Germany, developing mostly out of earlier ecclesiastical institutions. This illustration from a 12th-century work by Herrad von Landsperg, Abbess of Hohenburg Convent, represents the seven liberal arts – grammar, rhetoric, dialectics, music, arithmetic, geometry and astronomy.

him. Ludwig responded by marching on Rome, where he was crowned Holy Roman Emperor in 1328 by one of his own placemen. Enraged, the Pope declared him deposed and called for a crusade against him. Ludwig retaliated by having Nicholas V elected as anti-pope.

The Pope's intervention angered the German electors, who claimed sole right to decide who should be chosen as their king. In July 1338 they met at Rense, near Koblenz, and with the support of the Archbishop of the Rhineland agreed

to oppose anyone who threatened to infringe their rights. They thereby formally rejected the influence of the Pope in imperial affairs, bringing to an abrupt end the centuries-long link between Pope and Holy Roman Emperor.

After yet another contested election had produced two rival claimants for the imperial throne, the accession, in 1347, of Charles IV from the house of Luxembourg finally brought Germany a semblance of peace. He was to rule for the next 31 years.

The birth of Switzerland

The Swiss struggle for freedom from Habsburg overlordship gave rise to many legends surrounding the nation's origins.

Habsburg ruler
A stained-glass window in St Stephen's Cathedral, Vienna, shows Albert I, who reigned as German king from 1298 until 1308, when he fell victim to a family feud. Under his rule, Habsburg power in Switzerland reached its peak.

When the Holy Roman Emperor Rudolf I died on July 15, 1291, it took the imperial electors almost 10 months to settle on Adolf of Nassau as his successor, preferring him to Rudolf's sole surviving son, Duke Albert of Austria. During this period of uncertainty the Swiss feared for their freedom, especially those living in the forest cantons of Uri, Schwyz, Nidwalden, and Obwalden around Lake Lucerne.

Uri and Schwyz had been granted direct rule in charters issued by the Hohenstaufen emperor Frederick II, in 1231 and 1240 respectively. These made them directly answerable to the King rather than to the Habsburg counts. Even so, Habsburg influence was spreading through the Swiss lands, for the counts had taken charge of as many Alpine passes as they could in order to control the trade routes to Italy. For this reason Rudolf I – himself a Habsburg – had refused to confirm the Swiss freedom charters.

An alliance of cantons

Early in 1291, a meeting was convened at which representatives of the three cantons of Uri, Schwyz and Nidwalden put their signatures to a Latin document swearing 'in God's name' to form an 'everlasting league'. The canton of Obwalden signed in December.

This vow of mutual support and defence, which has gone down in history as Switzerland's original Charter of Alliance, was not intended as a declaration of independence from the Holy Roman Empire, but rather to protect the cantons' existing rights to a degree of autonomy within the empire. In the late Middle Ages, many communities exercised the right to form alliances. Their principal intention was usually to secure existing rights and possessions as well as to ensure that peace was preserved in the land. Long-term covenants aimed at the foundation of independent states were unknown, since sovereignty resided in dynastic ownership, feudal ties and royal privileges.

In Swiss eyes, the Charter of Alliance is often seen as the document that gave birth to a nation. In fact, there was nothing in the charter to prefigure the future Swiss Confederation. The agreement was not even particularly democratic. It was drawn up at the instigation of the leading figures in the cantons concerned and was intended to confirm and underpin their interests. But it did set in motion the lengthy process that would one day result in the creation of Switzerland.

William Tell and legends of nationhood

The early days of Swiss independence have long been shrouded in legend. Two hundred years after the event, the story of the freedom fighter William Tell became popular in Switzerland, later providing the German poet Friedrich von Schiller with the subject matter for a famous play.

The tale recounts how Tell, a hunter from the village of Bürglen in the canton of Uri, was forced by the evil Habsburg governor Gessler to shoot an apple off the head of his son. A renowned bowman, Tell accomplished the feat, but later took revenge for the ordeal by luring Gessler to the Hohle Gasse ('Sunken Alley') in the village of Küssnacht, east of Lucerne, where he killed him.

Historical sources provide no clear evidence that either William Tell or his enemy Gessler ever existed, but it became one of Switzerland's great founding myths, justifying the Confederation's subsequent struggle for independence from Habsburg tyranny. Late in the 19th century a huge memorial to Tell was erected in the village of Altdorf, where the celebrated shooting was said to have taken place. The monument even puts a date for the incident in stone: 1307.

Schiller's play *William Tell* incorporated another incident with a hallowed place in the Swiss national conciousness: the Rütli Oath, sworn by representatives of the three forest cantons in a meadow on the bank of Lake Lucerne in 1307. The oldest

Mountain fastness
The fortress of Sargans, near Switzerland's modern border with Lichtenstein, was built between the 12th and 15th centuries for the counts of Sargans, who were in the service of the Habsburgs. Habsburg itself – the seat from which the dynasty took its name – was in the northern canton of Aargau.

An explosive inheritance
Before his death, in 1291, the Holy Roman Emperor Rudolf I of Habsburg (right) succeeded in bringing much of Switzerland under his rule. When he also secured for himself the role of patron and governor of the monastery at Einsiedeln, the scene was set for future conflict.

written source for the incident, the *White Book of Sarnen*, postdates the event by more than 150 years. It was written by a local chronicler, Hans Schriber of Obwalden, who gathered together documents and legends concerning the origins of the Confederation in about the year 1470.

It seems likely that the Rütli Oath may have more historical validity than the William Tell story. The *White Book of Sarnen* mentioned only the surnames of the three representatives who swore the oath, but historians have since tracked down possible candidates from other contemporary sources and provided them with Christian names: Werner Stauffacher from Schwyz, Walter Fürst from Uri, and Arnold of Melchtal from Unterwalden.

Jostling for position

When Adolf of Nassau was finally confirmed as German king, his position was weakened by the many concessions he had been forced to make to the electors to secure his accession. Yet he proved to be a subtle tactician. Thanks to skilful diplomacy, he managed to persuade his Habsburg rival, Duke Albert, to hand over all the imperial insignia. Adolf subsequently took advantage of his position to assert his overlordship of the Habsburg lands in southwest Germany, Alsace and the Swiss cantons. The move turned out to benefit the latter, for he proved willing to confirm their privileges. In 1293 he gave his official approval to the privileges accorded to the cantons of Zurich, Berne and Constance; four years later he reaffirmed the rights of Schwyz and Uri.

Shortly after, however, Adolf over-reached himself by attempting to expand his power base into the Palatinate. Fearful for their own positions, the imperial electors declared him deposed in 1298 and chose Duke Albert of Habsburg to replace him. Adolf took to arms to defend his title, but his forces were no match for Albert's, and he died in battle at Göllheim in the Palatinate just nine days after his deposition.

Albert held the throne for the next 10 years. In that time he managed to restore the Habsburg position in southern Germany and Switzerland and did all in his power to bring the Swiss cantons under the family's sway once more. But he, too, fell victim to family rivalry. His nephew and ward Johann demanded the possessions that were his entitlement in Swabia, the German region to which the Swiss cantons officially belonged. When Albert refused to hand them over,

---

TIME WITNESS

The Rütli Oath

Generations of Swiss schoolchildren have grown up believing that the founding of the Swiss nation could be traced back to an oath sworn in Rütli meadow beside Lake Lucerne on November 7, 1307. Legend has it that delegates from the forest cantons of Uri, Schwyz and Unterwalden (Nitwalden and Obwalden) met there to pledge resistance to Habsburg tyranny. Historians have since cast doubt on the story, particularly following the discovery in the 19th century of a Charter of Alliance between the three cantons dating back to 1291. Even so, the oath holds a cherished place in Swiss tradition. One early source catches the patriotic fervour that underlies the story:

'On the Rütli meadow, surrounded by woods, a small fire was burning. Three men kept watch by its flickering light. Suddenly, Werner Stauffacher spoke up: "Brothers, as we stand here, let us join hands in God's name. A single will and a single goal unites us: we wish to be free. We hereby promise to help one another in times of desperate need, and to stand together in the fight against the [Habsburg] governors and not yield to any force. If there is any one among you who is not prepared to sacrifice his life, his land and his blood, let him leave this circle now!" There was silence, and no-one stirred.'

The Rütli confederates
After they had sworn the oath, Stauffacher, Melchtal and Fürst said a prayer, then they set off back to their farmsteads under cover of darkness.

Johann took his revenge. On May 1, 1308, he stabbed the monarch to death on a Swiss riverbank.

The first great Swiss victory

Henry VII of Luxembourg succeeded Albert as king of Germany and Holy Roman Emperor, and in 1309 he confirmed the confederated cantons in their privileged positions as directly answerable to the Emperor and not to any feudal intermediaries. The situation deteriorated again, however, on Henry's death in 1313, when the election to choose his successor produced a tied vote. Civil war broke out between the rival candidates – Frederick III of Habsburg and Ludwig of the Bavarian Wittelsbach family. When the Swiss took Ludwig's side against the old Habsburg enemy, Frederick plotted revenge.

He found the pretext he needed when a long-simmering dispute between the canton of Schwyz and the monastery at Einsiedeln suddenly erupted into violence. On January 6, 1314, a Swiss force attacked the monastery, which was under Frederick's protection. According to Habsburg sympathisers, the monks were imprisoned and everything moveable, including religious artefacts and reliquaries, was looted. The Swiss were also accused of drinking the wine cellars dry, of relieving themselves on the church altar, and of driving the monks' cattle from their stalls.

The raid provided an excuse for Frederick to send his brother, Duke Leopold I of Austria, to bring the rebel Swiss to heel. Faced by the onslaught of a well-equipped army of knights, the numerically inferior Swiss forces resorted to guerrilla tactics.

On November 15, 1315, on the northern border of the Schwyz canton, they blocked the Morgarten Pass at its narrowest point with tree trunks, and ambushed the Austrian army. Trapped, the knights could neither fight nor flee as arrows and heavy boulders poured down upon them from the slopes above. Duke Leopold survived the bloodbath, but few of his knights did. Morgarten was the Swiss Confederation's first great victory. Many more battles lay ahead, but full independence was finally achieved more than a century later.

Celebrated victory
Foot-soldiers from the Swiss cantons defeated Duke Leopold I of Austria and his army of mounted knights at Morgarten in 1315. The victory, shown here in an illustration from c.1450, was an important step on the road to Switzerland's independence.

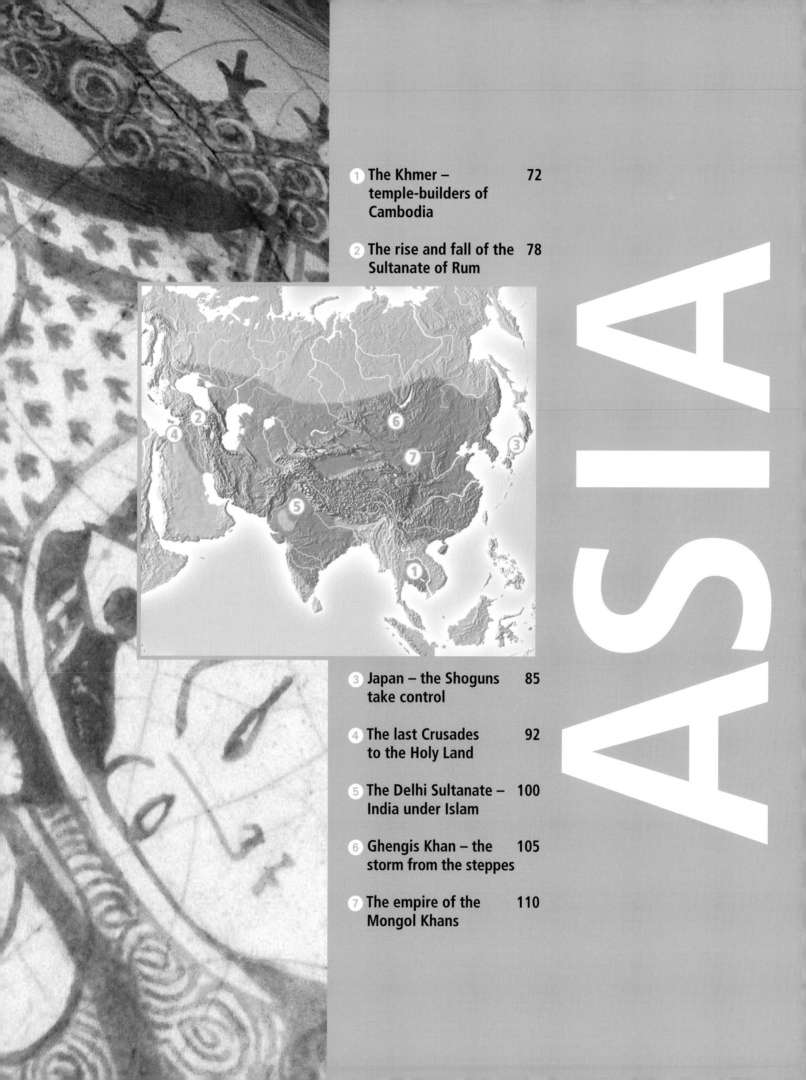

ASIA

The Khmer – temple-builders of Cambodia

The Khmer people built an empire centred on the Mekong Valley in Cambodia, and left a legacy of vast ceremonial complexes, constructed in stone.

Few sights can match the five towers of Angkor Wat at sunset, outlined against the dark backcloth of the Cambodian jungle. Almost 900 years after it was built, the huge temple – along with the adjoining palace complex of Angkor Thom, built half a century later – bears enduring witness to the might of the medieval Khmer Empire. Only the stone buildings now remain. The wooden structures – including royal palaces and libraries housing thousands of manuscript rolls made of palm leaves and animal hides – have not survived the centuries, rotting away in the hot, damp climate.

Building work on Angkor Wat was almost complete in 1150 when its creator, Suryavarman II, died on campaign against the neighbouring Cham people. Under his rule, the Khmer empire had reached its

Temple city
The moat that surrounds the temple complex of Angkor Wat is 190m (620ft) wide and believed to be the largest in the world. Scholars have estimated that 800,000 people may have worked on the temple-city's construction. Bas-reliefs stretch for several kilometres along its walls, depicting scenes from Khmer history and Hindu legend.

Great leader
Standing almost 1.5m (5ft) high and weighing 100kg (225lb), this sandstone statue of the last great Khmer king, Jayavarman VII, is one of very few representations of rulers from Cambodia's imperial period to have survived to modern times. Jayavarman's image still finds a place today in Cambodian hospitals and hotels.

subjects viewed him with awe as a god-king, the earthly incarnation of the god Vishnu. To create a residence fit for his semi-divine status, he gave orders for major construction works at Angkor. He dedicated the great temple of Angkor Wat to Vishnu himself, hoping to be united with his patron deity after death. Suryavarman wanted the temple complex – which would become the largest in the entire Hindu-Buddhist world – to be the crowning glory of his reign.

Homes for the gods

The Khmer temples were not intended as places of communal worship. Rather, like the Hindu shrines of India, they were regarded as homes for the gods, who were thought to take up residence within them, their holy presence symbolised by statues that graced the interiors.

greatest extent. Khmer forces had conquered the Thai peoples to the north and the Cham of Vietnam to the east, and had brought under their control an area stretching from the Malay peninsula to the China Sea. Suryavarman had chosen Angkor – founded as a settlement long before his time – as his capital and seat of government.

Suryavarman was a follower of the Hindu faith, imported by his predecessors many centuries before from India. His

The temples were designed as a tangible portrayal of the Hindu world order. Most were rectangular in shape. In the centre stood the *prasat* – the highest tower, sheltering the principal shrine – which symbolically represented Mount Meru, the mythical home of the gods. Smaller towers surrounded this central pinnacle, many of them phallus-shaped, for the Khmers revered the lingam, a stone pillar symbolising the virile power of the god Shiva. Around each sanctuary ran a wide moat, which represented the ocean thought to encircle the world.

Each of the towers was home to a different deity. At Angkor Wat one was dedicated to a *naga* or snake goddess, thought to have been the mythical progenitor of the Khmer royal line. Legend had it that every night she would renew her congress with the King; if she failed to put in an appearance, it was a sign that the King was in danger and that a new ruler might soon be on the throne. In addition to the five main temples, there were many other lesser shrines, and the precincts also contained accommodation for priests, musicians and dancers.

An empire built on irrigation

Suryavarman introduced many reforms, encouraging the Khmer society of rice farmers, priests, monks, soldiers and merchants to develop along hierarchical lines. His most important contribution, though, was to put water at the very top of the royal agenda, for the secret of the empire's prosperity lay in the careful management of water.

The King chose Angkor as the royal capital partly because of its proximity to Tonle Sap, a great lake teeming with fish that lies at the centre of Cambodia, trapping the floodwaters of the Mekong River. To get the maximum advantage from its waters, successive Khmer kings built an extensive network of canals feeding a system of reservoirs, irrigation ditches and drainage channels.

Water management allowed the Khmers to harvest two or more rice crops a year. They worked out how to store the monsoon rains in massive basins and then put them to use to produce food surplusses for export. The reservoirs also helped to prevent flooding by soaking up excess water, and the canals doubled as a transport network, greatly improving communications in the heavily forested landscape.

With such efficient irrigation, the Khmer Empire prospered and was second only to China among Asian nations. In the mid-12th century there were 1.5 million people living in the Angkor region – at a time when Paris, in comparison, had just 30,000 inhabitants. Angkor, in its heyday, was probably the largest city on Earth.

The Cham sack Angkor

Suryavarman's death triggered trouble in the Khmer lands. The King's huge building programme had exhausted the state treasury, and rival contenders vied for the throne. The neighbouring Cham people took advantage of the situation to launch an invasion. In 1177 they defeated the severely weakened Khmer in a naval battle on Tonle Sap, and went on to sack the city of Angkor itself. It was at this low point in the empire's fortunes that

Angkor from the air (background)
An aerial view of the Angkor Wat temple complex gives some idea of its vast size. The temple alone covers more than 1km² (0.4sq miles).

Seven-headed serpent
The *naga* or cobra was a frequent symbol in Khmer art, reflecting a tradition that the Khmer people traced their origin to the union between one of their early kings and a snake queen. The seven-headed *naga* is thought to represent the seven different classes of the naga race.

Religious revolutionary
Huge images of the Buddha, perhaps sculpted in the likeness of the city's royal founder, are omnipresent at Angkor Thom, the new capital Jayavarman VII had built at the close of the 12th century on a site adjoining the Angkor Wat complex. Jayavarman favoured Buddhism over the Hindu faith which is celebrated in the earlier temple.

another charismatic leader emerged to turn the situation round. Just a year later, Jayavarman VII, a cousin of Suryavarman II, routed the invaders in another naval encounter on the lake. The victory was decisive, although commemorative inscriptions no doubt exaggerated when they recorded Jayavarman smiting the enemy with 100 million arrows and drowning them in a sea of blood. The victorious admiral was crowned king three years later, in 1181.

Jayavarman's 40-year reign was a golden age for the Khmer, during which external trade doubled thanks to closer ties with China to the north and the opening of a sea route through the Gulf of Thailand in the south.

A change of religion

The new king broke with the nation's long-established Hindu traditions to embrace Buddhism. He restored or rebuilt most of Cambodia's existing temples and had many new buildings erected in honour of the Buddha, who became the focus of the new state religion.

The change of faith had implications for the monarchy itself, for Jayavarman lost his royal status as a god-king. Socially, the switch loosened the bonds of caste that had made Khmer society so rigid, forcing it to develop a new, populist edge.

To proclaim the change, Jayavarman established a new capital, Angkor Thom, at a site adjoining the existing city of Angkor. He inaugurated his foundation in the year 1200. At the centre of the city stood a huge new temple, the Bayon, raised on an artificial earthen mound and graced by 49 towers. Each one was adorned with massive stone portraits of the Buddha, smiling impassively to all points of the compass and broadcasting for miles around the sense of inner well-being that the faithful hoped to find one day.

The splendours of Angkor Thom

To build his new capital, Jayavarman called on the labours of thousands of workers, many of them slaves, as well as 50,000 elephants that provided muscle power for shifting and carrying. The complex was designed on a grand scale. An artificial lake 700m long by 300m wide (2300 by 1000ft), known as Sra Srang, surrounded the two main temples of Bayon and Ta Prohm; the King himself would discuss policy with his advisors while bathing in its waters. Close by was a ceremonial platform, known as the Elephant Terrace from the sculptures that adorned it; bas–reliefs found there suggest that the open space it overlooked was a venue for polo matches, wrestling bouts and military parades.

Surviving records show that Jayavarman provided lavishly for his people. He had schools and hospitals built throughout the country. Hostels for pilgrims, merchants and other travellers lined the main roads in and out of the kingdom.

An envoy from China named Zhou Daguan arrived in the kingdom in 1296. Although the Chinese had traditionally regarded the peoples beyond their borders as barbarians, he was impressed by what he saw. He noted with astonishment that some of the towers, bridges and statues of lions and Buddhas that adorned Angkor Thom were made of pure gold, as were the parasols that protected the king himself from the rays of the sun.

End of a golden age

Such magnificence was costly, and Jayavarman's extravagant building exhausted the empire's resources. The King himself died mysteriously in about 1220; according to one legend he had leprosy, which might explain his passion for building hospitals. With his demise the great age of the Khmer drew to a close.

Jayavarman VIII, who reigned from 1243 to 1295, reversed the Buddhist experiment and restored Hinduism as the state religion. Although he enjoyed a long reign, Jayavarman VIII left no monuments to rival those of his predecessors and no new temple complexes were constructed in his day. Instead, he contented himself with converting the empire's many Buddhist sanctuaries back to Hindu worship. He is also said to have had 10,000 statues of the Buddha from all parts of the country destroyed.

The Khmer Empire never recovered its former greatness. The irrigation system gradually fell into decay, as the power of the state was sapped by a combination of economic decline and religious strife. Outlying provinces of the empire fell one by one to the assaults of the Thai and the Cham. The end finally came in 1431, when Thai forces overran the Cambodian heartland, seizing Angkor itself the following year. The Khmer Empire became a memory, and its great capital was swallowed by the jungle, where it lay forgotten for centuries.

Royal beasts
A section of Angkor Thom's 300m-long Elephant Terrace, from which Khmer kings watched parades and sporting events.

Ceremonial dagger
By the 12th century the Khmer had an iron industry capable of producing sophisticated objects like this dagger. Elsewhere in Southeast Asia, the metal had to be imported from China. Bronze bells (background) were fixed to the saddles of elephants to warn bystanders of their approach.

The rise and fall of the Sultanate of Rum

Asia Minor thrived under the Seljuk Sultanate of Rum. But their state collapsed in the wake of a Mongol invasion, allowing the Ottomans to rise to prominence in the region.

Whirling dervishes
The poet and scholar Jalal ad-Din Rumi, founder of the Mevlevi Order of whirling dervishes, sits amid companions seeking mystic rapture through dance. Performed until the dancer reaches an ecstatic trance, the spinning gyrations aimed to bring the soul closer to God.

They called the land Rum after imperial Rome, for when the Seljuk Turks first arrived in Anatolia the region was still a heartland of the Eastern, or Byzantine, Empire. All that changed with a decisive battle, fought at Manzikert in eastern Anatolia in 1071. The Byzantine forces were routed, and at a stroke, the land known in classical times as Asia Minor lay open to the Seljuk Turks.

The Seljuk leader Alp Arslan – literally, 'Heroic Lion' – was assassinated the following year while putting down an uprising on the other side of the empire. But his victory had opened the gate for other Turkomans – Turkic peoples who converted to Islam – to flow into eastern Anatolia and carve out kingdoms of their own. The Sultanate of Rum was the greatest of these. It was proclaimed by Sulayman, a distant cousin of Alp Arslan, in 1078. Sulayman rivalled Alp Arslan's successor, Malik Shah, who reigned over the main Seljuk Empire from Baghdad. Even though Sulayman himself died in battle in 1086, his successors held onto power. While the Seljuk Empire fragmented following Malik Shah's death in 1092, the Rum

sultanate continued to flourish. It also bore the brunt of the Christian crusader armies that invaded the Holy Land from 1096 onwards.

Sulayman's successors built a prosperous and cultured realm in a kingdom that stretched across the central Anatolian plateau from the Black Sea to the Mediterranean. The Moroccan traveller Ibn Battuta was full of praise. 'The land of Rum is one of the finest in the world,' he wrote. 'Here, God has brought together in one place all the qualities that are elsewhere spread over many countries. Of all peoples, its inhabitants are the handsomest in appearance and the neatest in their apparel, and they have the best food and are the friendliest of all God's creatures.' Another chronicler remarked of Konya, the sultans' capital, that 'an hour spent there is better than a thousand months in other lands'.

Coming to power in 1156, Sultan Kilic Arslan II was a gifted and clever ruler who built on the achievements of his forebears. At home he overcame political rivals and broke the power of the emirs who had established independent power bases in outlying parts of his realm. Abroad, he held his own against the other rival states formed from the fragments of Malik Shah's empire, and also won an important victory against the Byzantine Emperor Manuel I at Myriocephalum in 1176. By the end of the 12th century,

The most famous landmark of Konya is the tower of the Mausoleum of Rumi, the founder of the Mevlevi Order, which is decorated with green ceramic tiles.

Kilic felt secure enough financially and politically to embellish Konya, the former Byzantine city of Iconium, which had been established as the capital of the sultanate earlier in the century.

A time of greatness

The latter part of Kilic Arslan's reign was embittered by infighting between his many sons. The youngest of them, Kay-Khusraw, eventually put the empire back on an even keel. During the preceding time of troubles, he had been in exile in Constantinople, where he married a Byzantine noblewoman. Coming to power in Rum in 1204, shortly after the forces of the Fourth Crusade had taken the Byzantine capital, he allied with the exiled Greek rulers against the Latin crusaders. He took the port of Antalya from the Latins in 1207, giving Rum an outlet on the Mediterranean that opened up great prospects for foreign trade.

The sultanate was at its height under Kay-Khusraw's two sons, Kay-Kavus I and Kaykubad I, who ruled respectively from 1211 to 1219 and from 1219 to 1237. Between them, the two sultans revitalised agriculture and promoted trade. They launched irrigation projects that enabled farmers to grow fruit and vegetables in the barren interior of their domain, even in the infertile land around Konya itself. Trade benefited from the capture of additional ports, notably Sinope on the Black Sea in 1214, and Alanya on the Mediterranean. In Sinope, the riches of Russia were unloaded: slaves from the Caucasus, thoroughbred horses from Georgia, cobalt, furs, cotton fabrics, silks. Alanya opened the door to Western trade.

Spreading prosperity

Kaykubad struck an advantageous trade deal with the Venetians, who could import and export precious stones, pearls and gold and silver ingots duty-free in return for paying a 2.5 per cent tariff on all other goods. Kaykubad invested the money in developing the infrastructure of the state.

In particular, he commissioned Abu Ali, a Syrian from Aleppo, to extend the port facilities at Alanya, which when completed were unequalled in all the Mediterranean region. Abu Ali built a new harbour wall whose centrepiece was the octagonal Red Tower. These fortifications protected a unique shipyard that extended 80m (260ft) back into the cliff-face. Within its depths, ships could be built and stored in five vaulted galleries, shielded from the prying eyes of inquisitive foreigners. Over time, the harbour at Alanya became the Seljuks' most important naval base.

Hostels for travellers

The cities of Konya, Sivas and Kayseri all stood at the intersections of major trade routes and flourished with commercial activity. The sultans encouraged the trend by developing the transport network, improving existing caravan routes, renovating old bridges and building strong new ones of stone. For the comfort of travellers, they ordered the construction of a chain of caravanserais, each built a day's

journey apart – about 30km (20 miles). Most of these hostels were spacious and well appointed, with everything a traveller could need. There were store rooms for goods, stalls for camels and horses, even a workshop where repairs to axles, wheels or harnesses could be made. Each had a mosque with a fountain where visitors could pray and ritually cleanse themselves, and there were coffee rooms and a *hamam* or bathhouse as well as sleeping quarters.

Trade filled the sultans' coffers, enabling them to enjoy a luxurious lifestyle. Kilic Arslan II had reigned in the manner of an old-style tribal chief, but his successors had a far more lavish court resembling that of the Persian kings. They imported spices and sugar from Egypt and musk and essence of aloes from Mesopotamia. They demanded the finest, most delicate woollen cloth from Baghdad for their turbans and Chinese silk for their robes. Their jewels were brought all the way from Central Asia.

Coronations, military parades and other ceremonies were celebrated with great pomp. The sultans hosted spectacular banquets at which the diners ate from jewel-encrusted plates.

The palaces where the sultans lived have long since disappeared, but they are known to have covered a wide area. The palace complex that Kaykubad laid out beside Lake Beysehir, 55km (35 miles) west of Konya, even had a game park.

Mosques and madrassas
The main focus of the sultans' building programmes, however, was mosques. The architects of Rum developed a distinctively Anatolian style of mosque design that featured a nave and side aisles,

Paddle power
A manuscript illumination shows an experimental boat driven by a paddle wheel. The Seljuk sultans encouraged scientific speculation and were especially interested in technical matters such as problems of mechanics.

Safe crossing
Among the Seljuk sultans' enduring legacies was an advanced road network that benefited from solidly built stone bridges, such as this one at Erzurum in eastern Turkey.

Place of learning
In madrassas like this, shown in a 16th-century illustration, Islamic scholars taught not just theology and shar'ia law but also medicine and the natural sciences.

rather in the manner of Christian basilicas. The inner courtyard, which was usually left open to the elements, was covered with a flat roof to protect worshippers from the raw climate of the high plateau; in later years, the roof was replaced by a dome. Tiles, glazed or plain, covered the inside walls, while a small forest of columns supported the vaulted ceilings. Forty-two ancient pillars were reused in the Ala ad-Din Mosque in Konya, and the mosque in Sivas had 90. Minarets were added from the 13th century onwards.

Apart from the mosque, the madrassa, or Islamic seminary, formed the core of the spiritual life in every city. By the year 1300 there were about 70 such schools in Anatolia. Classrooms and living space for teachers and pupils were grouped around a rectangular courtyard, often roofed against the elements. Hospitals and orphanages formed part of many of the complexes, whose domed gateways were decorated with bas-reliefs and faïence mosaics, making them feasts for the eye. The decorative elements incorporated motifs reflecting a wide range of artistic influences, from Persia and Syria to Armenia and Georgia.

Dating from Kaykubad's reign, the city walls of Konya reflected Anatolia's role as a cultural melting-pot. They were adorned with 108 towers and decorated with old statues from Graeco-Roman times.

Another distinctive feature of Seljuk architecture were the tower-like tombs known as *kümbets*. Surmounted by a cupola, these two-storey mausoleums were richly decorated inside with inscriptions and with plant and animal motifs, forbidden in some Islamic traditions. The Great Kümbet in the Ala ad-Din Mosque in Konya contained the tiled sarcophagi of eight sultans.

Stirrings of unrest

Luxury separated the Seljuk sultans not only from their nomadic tribal roots, but also from many of their subjects. The new wealth created by the upsurge in trade was very unevenly distributed, which helped itinerant preachers from Iran to foment unrest in Seljuk lands. Increasingly, wandering pilgrims and holy men called for the people to resist the Sultan's rule.

In about 1200, a charismatic preacher called Ilya came to Rum from Khorasan, the Seljuks' former homeland in north-eastern Iran. His teaching won him many followers who came to regard him as a messiah sent by Allah. Although Ilya himself avoided politics, his disciple Baba Ishak whipped the faithful up to revolt. The rebellion he inspired spread to the important trading city of Sivas in 1240. Sultan Kay-Khusraw II responded by sending troops, who suppressed the uprising with extreme brutality. Baba Ishak and many of his followers were hanged, and their possessions distributed among the soldiers.

Home of the dervishes

Asia Minor was a meeting-place of religions, a point well illustrated by the career of the dervish mystic Haji Bektash. Bektash's teachings combined elements of Buddhism and ancient Turkic animism as well as Islam, and borrowed the concepts of confession, absolution and celibacy from the Christian tradition.

Another group that helped to bring a fresh mystical vision to Islam was the Mevlevi Order of whirling dervishes, founded by the poet and mystic Jalal al-Din Rumi. Although his name means 'of the Sultanate of Rum', Rumi originally came from Balkh in Afghanistan. He studied at madrassas in Aleppo and Damascus as well as in Konya. Rumi was an adept of Sufism, a mystical strain of Islam that strives to approach God through ecstatic experience. Rumi established his order, which incorporated some Christian and Buddhist elements in its beliefs, in Konya in the mid-13th century. Its influence spread quickly through Anatolia, attracting many people of substance to its ranks.

The Mongol invasion

By the time that Haji Bektash and Rumi were elaborating their philosophies, the Seljuk world was already in danger. In the steppe lands far to the east, Genghis Khan had united the Mongol tribes. Rumours of Mongol atrocities had been heard in Anatolia decades before the Seljuks had their first direct contact with the mounted warriors. This occurred in 1241, when a horde sacked the city of Erzurum in the far east of their realm.

Two years later, the Mongols were back in greater force. Sultan Kay-Khusraw II raised an army of 80,000 men to confront them, but even so the Seljuks went down to a decisive defeat at the Battle of Kose Dagh. The victors followed up their triumph by sacking the cities of Sivas and Kayseri and plundering everything in their path. Panic gripped the country, and the Sultan himself was killed.

The Mongols had other targets in their sights and were happy to let the Seljuks remain in control, but only in return for accepting vassal status and agreeing to pay a large annual tribute. So it came about that the once mighty sultans were reduced to puppets of the Mongol Il-Khans, whose power base lay in Iran.

In the years that followed defeat at Kose Dagh, the sultanate briefly split into three, ruled by the three sons of Kay-Khusraw. It was reunited under one of the trio, Kilic Arslan IV, but his power was undermined by his principal minister, Muinaddin Sulayman, known by his nickname of Pervane ('Butterfly'). The Sultan died in 1265, probably killed on Pervane's orders. For the next 12 years Pervane was the real ruler of the country, until he rashly conspired with the Egyptian Mamlukes against the Il-Khans, and was put to death.

By that time the empire was in unstoppable decline. The sultanate had fragmented into a multitude of smaller

Ceramic talent
Seljuk potters were masters of decoration. The spout of this 13th-century water jug is in the shape of a hen's head, while the body is covered with an intricate basketwork design. Although Islamic tradition generally frowns on representations of the human figure, Seljuk art frequently portrayed people (background), reflecting Anatolia's time-honoured openness to the influence of foreign cultures.

states ruled by emirs from rival Turkoman groups that had been happy to accept its overlordship in more fortunate times. One such, the Karamanids, seized Konya in 1308, finally putting an end to Seljuk rule.

Rise of the Ottomans

Yet new life soon stirred among the ruins. Of the dozen or so petty states that filled the power vacuum left by the Seljuk decline, one soon rose to prominence. A tribe of ghazis or 'holy warriors', led by a warlord named Ertugrul, had settled, with Seljuk permission, in the far west of Anatolia in a frontier province confronting the Christian Byzantine lands. This was to be the base from which the mighty Ottoman dynasty eventually rose to power. Ertugrul's son, Osman, set the Ottomans on the road to empire. He won a first victory against his Christian neighbours outside the Byzantine stronghold of Nicomedia (modern Izmit) in 1301. In 1326, he made another major advance, capturing Byzantine Bursa. He died shortly after and was buried in the city he had conquered, fulfilling a lifelong wish.

Osman's son and successor, Orhan, was the real founder of the Ottoman Empire, driving its territorial expansion and shaping its structure. Under Orhan's direction, Islam became the guiding force of the new state. He founded institutions aimed not just at providing for his people's spiritual needs but also

The first Ottoman
Osman I came to power in 1280 as the ruler of one of the smaller principalities into which the Seljuk lands had fragmented. He started the process of empire-building that was to mark the history of the Ottoman dynasty, which took its name from him. Here he is seen in an 18th-century water colour painting.

their material welfare – soup kitchens for the poor, for example, and hospitals for the sick. In Bursa he built a great mosque, showing himself a worthy successor to the Seljuks in his architectural ambitions.

'The Sultan Orhan Beg is the mightiest of the Turkoman kings,' a contemporary observer reported. 'He has the richest treasures, and the greatest number of cities and soldiers. He has almost 100 fortresses.' Orhan encouraged a revival of silkworm cultivation, bringing Bursa new prosperity. Under his watchful eye, the city became a commercial centre of the first rank.

A first foothold in Europe

One of Orhan's chief priorities was to reorganise the army. An ancient tradition maintains that it was he who established the first janissary unit, made up of Christian prisoners of war. Certainly he created a professional standing army, with an elite corps of *sipahis*, or regular cavalry, that won him victory after victory. He was helped by the internal problems of the Byzantine Empire, which was riven by strife over the succession to the throne, preventing the Emperor in Constantinople from mounting an effective resistance. In 1331, the Sultan captured Nicaea (Iznik), a city whose name resounded in Christian ears as the site of a crucial council of the early Church. Shortly afterwards Nicomedia also fell.

Further weakened in 1347 by the ravages of the Black Death, the Byzantine Empire proved unable to resist the Ottoman advance. Instead, it actively encouraged Orhan by employing his forces as mercenaries in its own wars. The Sultan took the hint and, in 1354, took advantage of an earthquake that struck the Gallipoli peninsula on the European side of the Dardanelles to sieze Gallipoli itself, establishing the first Ottoman presence in Europe. It would not be the last. The Christian West now faced a rising new power on its eastern borders that over the ensuing centuries would make deep inroads into its heart.

Japan – the shoguns take control

Minamoto Yoritomo, Japan's first shogun, changed the country from a land ruled by emperors into a feudal warrior state, creating a new form of government that would steer the policies of the island nation for centuries to come.

O n April 25, 1185, a naval battle was fought at Dannoura off the coast of Kyushu, Japan's southernmost island, that was to determine the future course of the nation. The victorious commander, Yoritomo, was of the Minamoto family, which represented a rising force in 12th-century Japan: the provincial warrior caste, which had mobilised against the decadent imperial court in Kyoto. With the help of a few noblemen who had been expelled from the imperial court, this military class – also known as *bushi* – went on to forge a new system of government and put an end to the extravagance of the preceding age.

Defeating the Taira

The Minamoto clan were fortunate that Yoritomo's young half-brother, Yoshitsune, turned out to be a military genius whose tactics were subtle, occasionally underhand, but ultimately successful in ensuring Yoritomo's victory. Yoshitsune joined the fight at just 15 and won almost every battle he fought. In later years his military prowess as a daring commander would be celebrated in legends.

A new kind of ruler
The Kamakura shogun shunned imperial display and luxury. He chose instead to wear severe black robes, emphasising the ascetic lifestyle of the warrior caste.

Dressed to kill
Samurai warriors underwent intensive weapon training and were skilled in the martial art of ju-jitsu, a form of unarmed combat. The elaborate armour they wore indicated their rank. One feature was a fearsome mask intended to intimidate opponents even before fighting began. This suit of armour belonged to a 12th-century samurai.

Fighting against the Minamoto were the Fujiwara – a rival family who had effectively ruled Japan for most of the Heian era, which had begun in 794 – and the Taira who had ousted the Fujiwara in 1156. Ambiguity over who actually ruled Japan had limited the power of the court nobility for almost four centuries. While in theory the emperor was absolute ruler, in reality his role had become increasingly ceremonial and real power was exercised by co-regents from the Fujiwara or, more recently, the Taira clan. By 1185, however, the governing regime was losing control and the bureaucratic apparatus was stagnating. It was simply a matter of time before a new power arose that was sufficiently organised to bring the old order down.

The first shogun

Minamoto Yoritomo, who lived from 1147 to 1199, was the man who finally put an end to court rule. He replaced imperial absolutism with a feudal military state, and became Japan's first military ruler, or *shogun*. He let nothing, including family ties, get in the way of attaining his goals: he cold-bloodedly dispatched every relative who opposed him. He even hounded Yoshitsune to his death, in 1189, fearing that the talented warrior's popularity might give him the power to threaten his own position. Once in power, Yoritomo surrounded himself with the finest warriors and appointed military governors who could help him to reform the system of property tenure. The Taira and Fujiwara lost their lands and took flight; many were killed in brutal skirmishes. Their fate was described in *The Tale of Heike*, a 13th-century epic popularised by blind monks who wandered the land singing it to the accompaniment of the *biwa* or short-necked lute.

Yoritomo based himself in the small coastal town of Kamakura, 480km (300 miles) east of Kyoto. It was there, far from the imperial capital, that he built up his strength for the assault on the Taira, and consolidated his administrative power base, vesting authority in provincial military officials known as *shugo* (constables) and in tax gatherers called *jito* (district stewards).

In 1192, at the peak of his power, Yoritomo took the title of *seitaishogun*, literally 'barbarian-subduing general'. It was an historic move: for the next 700 years the shoguns, as they became known, would be the real power in the land, and the emperors they served would be little more than ceremonial figureheads.

Feudal rule

The Kamakura shogunate that Yoritomo established was centred in the lawless east of the country. It survived until 1333. The Japanese called the system of government that he set up the *bakufu* or 'tent government' – a term, derived from the shogun's huge field headquarters, that emphasised the regime's military origins.

On taking power, Yoritomo divided the country into *shôen* or great estates, roughly corresponding to the fiefdoms of medieval Europe. As in European feudalism, a system of rights and responsibilities regulated the relationship between landowners and the peasants who worked the land. Feudalism guaranteed the rule of law as well as providing a ready-made military hierarchy in wartime.

Yoritomo needed a bureaucracy to complement the naked military force on which his rule rested. With that goal in mind, he established the Mandokoro or 'Bureau of Administration', to supervise the implementation of government policies and revenue collection. The Monchujo ('Bureau of Questioning') was the

highest legal authority, responsible for the administration of justice and the framing of laws. Most important of all was the military Samurai-Dokoro (the 'Board of Retainers'), which oversaw the privileges and duties of the army.

Birth of the samurai

Under Yoritomo's shogunate, the warriors who had previously served the emperor developed into the legendary samurai caste. These aristocratic fighting men were skilled in the used of every form of weaponry then known. Courage, bravery, loyalty to one's feudal lord and adherence to Buddhist teachings were all integral parts of their code of honour.

Before he could call himself a samurai, a young warrior had not only to learn martial skills but also to accept a knightly code that included the duty to take blood vengeance and, if required, to commit suicide rather than accept dishonour. A samurai warrior was expected to be as quiet as the forest, as firm as the mountain and as cold as fog. In his resolve he had to be as swift as the wind, in battle as violent as fire. The traditional samurai code of self-discipline, bravery and simple living came to be known as *bushido*.

Warrior wear

The samurai rarely faced foreign enemies, since the sea protected the islands from invasion. Feuds between clans were normally settled by bloody duels. The warriors would face one another calmly, protected by sophisticated fighting gear unequalled anywhere else in the world. The inflexible armour worn by European knights at the time usually weighed about 35kg (75lb). In contrast, samurai armour was made up of individual metal plates laced together with cords – and it weighed just 12kg (25lb). Japanese warriors could mount their horses unaided,

Temple view (background)
Parts of the Engakuji Temple near Kamakura date from the time of the first shoguns.

Warrior's weapon
The typical samurai sword – called a *tachi* – had a curved blade up to 1.2m (4ft) long. The elongated grip meant it could be wielded with two hands. When sheathed, the sword was worn on the left side of the body, hanging on straps attached to a belt.

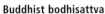

Buddhist bodhisattva
Kannon, an embodiment of compassion and a principal figure of Mahayana Buddhism, is usually portrayed as female, but this sculpture from Japan's Kamakura period shows Kannon as male.

and could run, jump, climb and even swim dressed for battle. One piece of equipment no warrior every forgot was his iron neck-guard, worn beneath a magnificent fighting helmet. It was needed because, following the rules of engagement, opponents' heads were severed and exhibited after each battle for the macabre custom known as *kubi-jikken* – inspection of decapitated heads. On the battlefield severed heads were collected in *kubi bukuro*, net-like bags attached to a warrior's armour or saddle. A warrior could expect reward commensurate with the status of the man he had killed. Occasionally, *kubi-jikken* would reveal that a samurai had mistakenly beheaded an ally rather than an enemy, in which case he could expect to pay for the error by having a finger cut off his right hand.

Ritual suicide

For a samurai, the sword was his most important weapon: a warrior who lost his sword was considered dishonoured and risked severe punishment, for his sword was his soul. In the Kamakura period the preferred weapon was a *tachi*, or 'long one'. In addition, each warrior always carried a small dagger known as *wakizashi*. Rather than be captured or killed by an enemy, he was expected to use it on himself in the last resort to commit the ritual suicide known as *seppuku*. To perform *seppuku* – also known as harakiri in some regions – the warrior

Kamikaze – the divine winds

In the Kamakura period, the Mongols under Kublai Khan sought to invade Japan from China. Huge invasion fleets appeared off the southern island of Kyushu. But on both occasions nature came to Japan's rescue in the form of typhoon winds that destroyed much of the enemy shipping, forcing the survivors to abandon the attack and return to China. The Japanese called the storms *kamikaze*, 'divine winds', a word borrowed in World War II to describe Japanese pilots on suicide missions. Even today there are people in Japan who believe that the original kamikaze were divinely ordained, showing their islands are protected by a higher power.

sat down cross-legged on the floor with his stomach bared, then thrust the *wakizashi* dagger into his intestines, causing him to quickly bleed to death.

Shogun succession

Yoritomo made provision for the title of shogun to be hereditary, but he failed to provide a suitable heir. His sons lacked not only their father's martial spirit but also the tactical subtlety of their mother, Masako, who became the real power in the land on her husband's death in 1199. Nicknamed the 'nun-general' because she followed custom by taking religious vows on being widowed, she remained politically active until her death in 1225. Masako was instrumental in setting up a curious system of government by which the title of shogun passed to the Fujiwara family, their old enemy, but became largely ceremonial. Real power was exercised by regents appointed from her own Hojo clan. For the next 100 years Hojo regents, or *shikken*, were at the head of the *bakufu*, steadily reducing the authority of the shoguns, who were very often still minors.

The Hojo secured their grip in the provinces with the assistance of feudal lords known as *daimyo*, a rising force in the land. With the *daimyo* to execute their orders, the Hojo established themselves as worthy rulers, not just for their military skills but also for their openness to the new religious movements that did much to shape Japanese culture at the time.

Paradise of the Pure Land

Japan's sects all derived from Buddhism, which had reached Japan from China and Korea in the 6th century AD. The first was the Pure Land cult, founded by the monk

Honen, who lived from 1133 to 1212. Having tried for much of his life to attain salvation through his own efforts, he concluded that mankind was so corrupt it could only be saved by the divine grace of the Buddha and his bodhisattvas, who delayed their own attainment of nirvana to help their fellow creatures. At Honen's suggestion, his followers prayed to the Amida Buddha, a compassionate incarnation of the great teacher, dwelling in the Western Paradise. Devotees of Pure Land believed that they could attain salvation by reciting, regularly and with intense concentration, the nembutsu prayer: 'Homage to Amida Buddha'. For some, 'regularly' meant 'incessantly': Honen himself is said to have repeated the phrase 70,000 times a day.

Salvation through divine grace

Honen's pupil Shinran took a more radical view of the path to salvation. Having spent 20 years living among peasants in the Ibaraki region of eastern Japan, he knew the poverty in which most people lived and realised that they had to hunt and fish to survive, even though this meant breaking the Buddhist prohibition on killing living creatures. Shinran concluded, as Honen had done, that only the Buddha's divine grace could guarantee salvation, but in his view it was only necessary to say the nembutsu prayer once in one's life, so long as the sentiment was heartfelt, in order to attain rebirth in the Pure Land. The True Pure Land school that Shinran founded maintained that it was actually easier for wicked people to attain paradise than for the good, since they were more in need of the Buddha's compassion. The True Pure Land doctrines had a special appeal for samurai, since they offered the prospect of salvation even for those who regularly took lives.

Zen Buddhism, which reached Japan from China during the Kamakura period, was also popular with the samurai. Zen rejected ritual and scholarship as aids to enlightenment in favour of meditation and physical labour. The warriors liked the stress that Zen laid on self-discipline, concentration and composure, all qualities that they cherished. Several Hojo regents became Zen devotees, and one, Hori Toji, renounced the regency in 1256 to enter a Buddhist monastery.

The Great Buddha
Most seated statues of the Buddha actually depict the Amida Buddha worshipped by followers of Japan's Pure Land sect. This bronze statue, known as Daibutsu, is the second largest such image in Japan, rising almost 12m (37ft) high. It was erected in 1252 in Kamakura in eastern Japan, where it can be seen to this day.

Spreading the word
A manuscript scroll shows disciples of the Pure Land sect carrying their message to the countryside. The sect's followers did not shut themselves away in monasteries like the devotees of Zen Buddhism. Instead, they travelled the length and breadth of the land, taking the sect's teachings to the peasantry.

Writing box
This elegant lacquered wooden box, decorated with gold inlay, would have held the four traditional writing implements – paper, brush, ink and erasing stone – used by literate Japanese, primarily priests or nobles.

Cycle of calamities
A series of natural disasters rocked Japan in the mid 13th century and threw the Hojo administration into crisis. A great famine in 1231 was followed by an earthquake in 1257 and a deadly epidemic in 1259–60. These catastrophes spread hunger and misery in their wake, and the regents had difficulty containing the ensuing crime wave.

A monk named Nichiren, born in 1222 in a fishing village on Japan's Pacific coast, began to proclaim publicly that the disasters stemmed from people's failure to follow the true Buddhist path. Like Honen, he preached that the way to salvation lay through a single sacred text, but in his case the holy writ was an ancient Buddhist scripture known as the Lotus Sutra. But his was an exclusive sect. He called on Japan's people to abandon all other cults and unite behind his banner. Otherwise, he insisted, national disaster was imminent.

The Mongol invasions
Nichiren's claims seemed more plausible when Japan found itself threatened by an aggressor. Having conquered China and Korea, the Mongol leader Kublai Khan turned his gaze on Japan. From 1268 onwards he sent repeated envoys to Kamakura bearing demands for tribute, which the Hojo regents simply ignored. Losing patience, Kublai resorted to force. In early October 1274 he sent an army of 25,000 men on 900 ships that landed on the northwestern coast of Kyushu.

Mounted samurai, skilled in one-to-one combat, stood little chance against the massed ranks of the Mongolian infantry, with their terrifying gunpowder-packed rockets, courtesy of Chinese technology. In two days of fighting, the Japanese suffered heavy losses. But when the Mongolian warriors returned to their galleys for the second night, a violent storm blew up. More than 200 ships were sunk and the rest were forced to sea, where they beat a retreat back across the Korea Strait to the mainland.

Kublai Khan did not accept defeat gracefully. Seven years later he sent another invasion force, several times larger than the first, but was thwarted once more when a typhoon destroyed much of his armada. The Japanese subsequently gave thanks to the gods for the kamikaze ('divine winds') that had delivered them from their attackers.

The trauma of the assaults was profound, and the military costs to the Hojo regents plunged the government into financial ruin. The samurai also suffered financial losses, both from the time spent away from their estates and from the costs of building up coastal defences. They demanded compensation, which the regents could not pay. Discontent spread, quickly turning to active resistance against the Kamakura government. Infighting within the Hojo clan itself further weakened the regents.

The end of the Kamakura era

At the imperial court in Kyoto, Emperor Go-Daigo and his allies realised that their hour had come, especially since the incumbent Hojo regent Takatori devoted his time to pleasure rather than politics. Go-Daigo returned from exile in 1331 and quickly gathered support among provincial warlords eager to end the Hojo administration. He appointed his own son Prince Morinaga as shogun.

In 1333 the rebels captured Kamakura and set the city on fire. Rather than be taken prisoner, the leaders of the Hojo clan retreated to the cemetery of the Tosho-ji Temple, where they drew their daggers and committed *sepukku* one after another. Their mass suicide spelled the end of both the Kamakura shogunate and of the Hojo clan as a political force.

Go-Daigo took on the mantle of government himself, but this action unleashed a fresh power struggle with the provincial warlords. One of the warlords, Ashikaga Takauji from the province of Shimotsuke, seized the opportunity to switch his allegiance to the opponents of the emperor. Building up a rebel army, he took the city of Kamakura in 1335, then marched on Kyoto and set up his head-quarters in the suburb of Muromachi. He had Prince Morinaga murdered and in 1338 he took the position of shogun for himself, inaugurating the Ashikaga (or Muromachi) shogunate, which was to hold power for the next 150 years.

Warrior patron
The samurai Takezaki Suenaga, shown here on horseback, was one of the victorious warriors who saw the Mongol forces destroyed by typhoons in 1274 and 1281. To commemorate the victory, Takezaki commissioned two painting scrolls, the *Moko Shurai ekotoba*, from one of which this detail is taken.

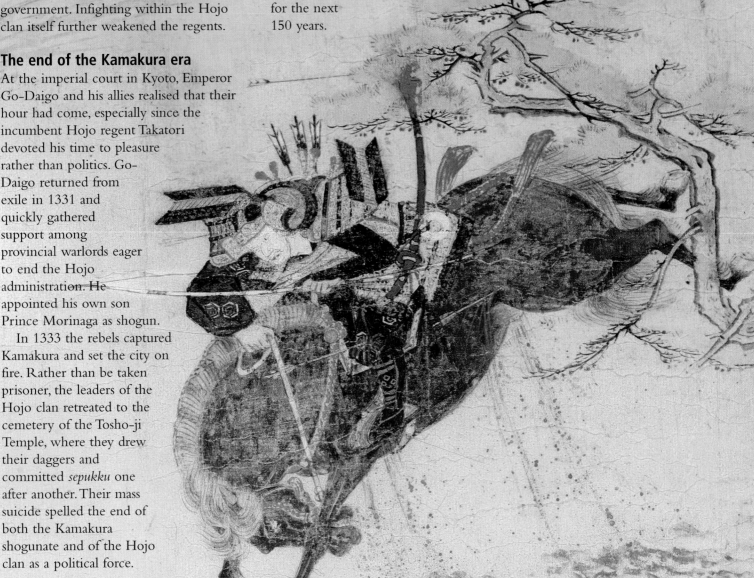

The last Crusades to the Holy Land

During the 13th century, the crusaders who had established the Latin Kingdom of Jerusalem were forced, one by one, to abandon their strongholds in the Holy Land. The last, Acre, fell to Muslim forces in 1291.

The Lionheart and Saladin
The two great adversaries of the Third Crusade were the Muslim leader Saladin and King Richard the Lionheart, shown here engaged in an imaginary joust in a miniature from the Luttrell Psalter. Richard got the better of Saladin's forces in a series of skirmishes, but eventually negotiated a compromise peace settlement that left Jerusalem in Muslim hands. The two never met in personal combat.

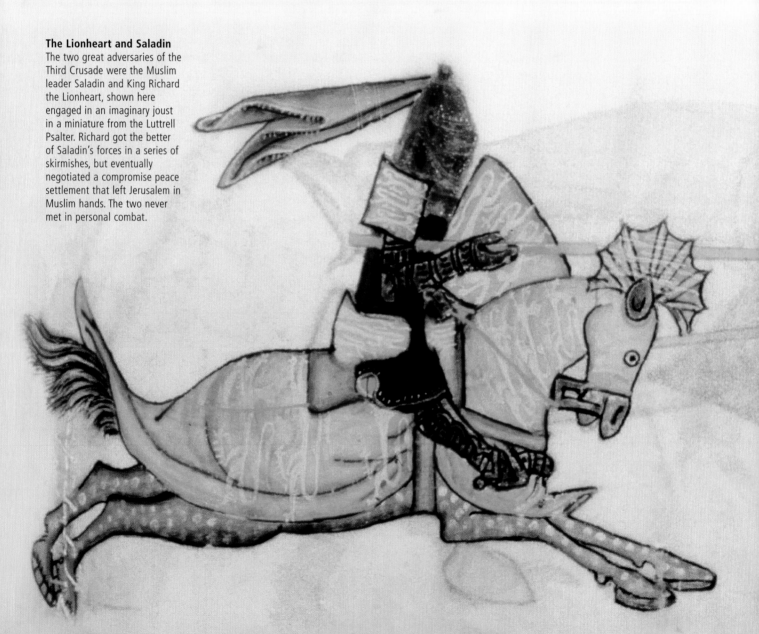

In 1187 the charismatic Muslim leader Saladin conquered Jerusalem from the Christian crusaders who had held it for the previous 88 years. The victors knocked down the cross the Christians had raised over the Dome of the Rock – one of Islam's holiest mosques, built on the site from which the Prophet Muhammad was said to have ascended to Heaven. According to a contemporary chronicler, 'a great cry rose all around, in which the shouts of joy of the Muslims were mingled with cries of anguish and rage from the Christians'.

The cry echoed loud across Christian Europe, rousing the Continent from its lethargy. Pope Clement III called for a Third Crusade to recover lost territories, and the three most powerful rulers of Western Europe – the Holy Roman Emperor Frederick Barbarossa, King Philip II Augustus of France and King Richard 'the Lionheart', ruler of the Angevin Empire of England and western France – heeded his call. Thousands rallied to their banners, and in 1189 the largest crusader force ever assembled embarked for Palestine. Knights from all over western Europe came together to win back the holy sites of Christendom.

The Third Crusade

The German contingent took the overland route to the Holy Land, but the expedition quickly fell apart when the 67-year-old Barbarossa died, possibly of a heart attack, while swimming a river in eastern Anatolia. The English and French forces went by sea, and in 1191 had a stunning initial success in helping beleaguered crusader forces to capture the key port of Acre. Soon, though, discord reared its head. Rivalry between the

Bronze crusader
A bronze sculpture of a crusader wearing chainmail, sleeveless tunic and the typical pot-shaped helmet of the 13th century.

The Emperor's end
Emperor Frederick I Barbarossa drowned on June 10, 1190, while trying to swim the River Saleph in Asia Minor – now the Göksu in Turkey. After his death only a small contingent of his army, led by his son Frederick of Swabia, carried on to join the English and French troops in the Holy Land on the Third Crusade. The 13th-century illustration and text above are from the Saxon Chronicle of the World.

French and English kings led Philip to abandon the Crusade and return to France. Another dispute, between Richard and Duke Leopold of Austria, brought about the Duke's sudden departure.

Richard's forces clashed with Saladin's archers at Arsuf. The battle was indecisive and the two subsequently concluded a three-year truce that left the crusading forces in control of a coastal strip stretching from Tyre (in modern-day Lebanon) to Jaffa (today part of Tel Aviv in Israel). In addition, the truce guaranteed Christian pilgrims safe conduct to visit the holy places of Jerusalem. Richard set off for home in October 1192, with Saladin's victorious progress checked, but Jerusalem still in Muslim hands.

A great Muslim leader

The Third Crusade's achievments were hardly commensurate with the enormous effort that had gone into its preparation.

The Christian camp was riven with discord at a time when the Muslims were newly united. And in Saladin, the crusaders faced a worthy opponent.

Born a Kurd, Saladin began his career in the service of the Seljuk Sultan Nur ad-Din in Damascus. Nur ad-Din, himself a Sunni, dispatched him to Shi'ite Egypt, which was falling into chaos and was under threat from the Franks. There, Saladin first rose to become the country's vizier or chief minister, then on the death of the last of the Fatimid caliphs in 1171, he took power. When his former mentor Nur ad-Din died, Saladin inherited his lands in Syria. By linking Egypt and Syria he founded the Ayyubid Empire (named for his father, Ayyub), creating a single, united power bloc across the Near East.

Saladin was able to use religion to bolster his claim on power. Having deposed the Shi'ite Fatimids in Cairo, he could legitimately claim to be the rightful defender of mainstream Sunni Islam and so could rely on the support of the caliphs in Baghdad. In the jihad or holy war that he launched, he succeeded in uniting his co-religionists against Muslim opponents of Sunni orthodoxy as well as against the Christians. The conquest of Jerusalem boosted his reputation immeasurably, because the city was just as sacred in Islamic eyes as it was to Christians and Jews.

While the forces of Islam were coming together, Christendom was divided by bitter quarrels. When Pope Innocent III called for a Fourth Crusade in 1201, the assembled forces were diverted by Venetian chicanery and other circumstances against Christian Constantinople rather than any Muslim target. Instead of landing in Egypt in preparation for an assault on Jerusalem, the crusaders sacked the capital of the Byzantine Empire, setting up a short-lived Latin Kingdom there, instead.

After the fiasco of the Fourth Crusade, the crusading movement lost much of its idealistic momentum. Successive popes continued to issue appeals for fresh campaigns, but the response was

BACKGROUND

Children's Crusade

The Children's Crusade of 1212 was a tragic example of the enthusiasm that the common people had for Crusades. A 12 year old shepherd boy called Stephen, from the Orléans region of France, had a vision that led him to preach to other children to go on Crusade. By strange coincidence, a farmer's boy named Nicholas of Cologne was doing the same in the Rhineland. Both built up huge followings, and they set off to rescue the Holy Land from the infidel.

The French children reached Marseilles, where traders shipped many into slavery in North Africa. The Germans got only as far as Italy. Few found their way home. The legend of the Pied Piper of Hamelin may have had its origins in this tragedy of lost crusading children.

generally disappointing. A Fifth Crusade, launched in 1216, succeeded in capturing the Egyptian port of Damietta and holding it for two years.

The accession of Frederick II, first as German king in 1215 and then as Holy Roman Emperor in 1220, raised hopes. The charismatic young ruler spoke enthusiastically of a fresh assault on the Holy Land, but he kept postponing his departure and failed to turn up for the Fifth Crusade, even though he was constantly expected. Eventually, Pope Gregory IX lost patience and excommunicated him.

The Sixth Crusade

Frederick finally set off for the Holy Land in 1228. By then he had married Princess Isabella, heiress to the crusader throne of Jerusalem, and the timing of the venture looked favourable. Saladin had died in 1193, and his heirs had been squabbling over his inheritance ever since. On his arrival in Outremer, Frederick found the Muslims there were more willing to negotiate with him than the Franks were to accept his leadership as an excommunicate.

Crusader's tomb
Many crusaders, like this English knight from Dorchester, never saw their homeland again. They either died in combat or from the wounds and diseases that they picked up.

Cultural exchange
The game of chess, which originated in India, is thought to have reached Europe via the Holy Land at the time of the Crusades. It was known as the game of kings since it taught players the art of strategic thinking. This depiction is in a 14th-century altarpiece.

Frederick took to the task of diplomacy with a will. An Arabic speaker well versed in Islamic culture, he was able to negotiate a 10-year truce with the Ayubbid ruler of Egypt that achieved more for the Christian cause than any military force had managed in well over a century. The Sultan agreed to hand over Jerusalem, together with Bethlehem and a corridor running to the sea, saving only that Jerusalem's Dome of the Rock and Al-Aqsa Mosque were to remain in Muslim hands. On March 17, 1229, Frederick was able to ride in pomp to the Church of the Holy Sepulchre and set the crown of the Kingdom of Jerusalem on his own head. Claiming the Holy Land as an imperial fief, he then returned to Europe.

Learning to live together

Religious zealots on both sides were incensed by so amicable an agreement. The Pope at first wanted nothing to do with a compromise of this kind, especially not one concluded by a man he had excommunicated. Jerusalem was placed under a temporary interdict, only lifted after Frederick eventually made his peace with the papacy in 1230.

In the Holy Land itself, Christians and Muslims were learning to live side by side. Neither group showed any great tolerance or understanding of the other's religion, but they accepted the principle of peaceful coexistence. Relations were most relaxed among the nobility, who organised joint hunting parties, played chess together, and forged politically convenient alliances whenever the need arose. Christian and Muslim leaders made numerous

agreements safeguarding each other's rights in regions where their spheres of interest overlapped.

Above all, trade flourished. Even in Saladin's day Venice and Egypt had been active trading partners, exchanging raw materials from the northern lands – notably iron and wood for shipbuilding – for oriental spices, sugar, jewels and perfumes. By the mid-13th century Pisa too supported a merchant community in the Egyptian port of Alexandria. The Venetians were given leave to build a church and bath-house there, and even maintained a wine cellar in spite of the Islamic ban on alcohol. The ports of the Levant also flourished, and Acre became an important commercial centre.

Over time, Frankish lords began to adopt oriental lifestyles. Their palace floors were decorated with priceless rugs, their windows plated with glass (a novelty in the West at the time) and screened with curtains in the best eastern manner. Second-generation knights developed a taste for damasks and muslins, cosmetics and exotic fruits, while also learning to appreciate the fine-grade steel produced by Levantine metalsmiths. In art, a unique crusader style developed, blending Islamic, Byzantine and Western elements.

The Christian presence

The crusader castles built to protect the Christian enclave stand to this day as an enduring legacy of the period. With their massive walls and battlements, the strongholds of Montreal (in what is now Jordan), Krak des Chevaliers in Syria and Montfort near the port of Haifa in Israel set a trend for subsequent developments in European military architecture. Among the innovations that first made their appearance in Outremer were massive defensive outworks, and gatehouses with oblique approaches and ingenious defensive arrangements of portcullises, loopholes and machicolations.

For despite the blossoming of trading contacts and artistic cooperation, it was still naked force that preserved the

Poet as peacemaker
This miniature shows the German poet Wolfram von Eschenbach seeking to reconcile a Muslim, a Jew and a Christian crusader. The age of the Crusades saw a disturbing upsurge in religious intolerance, with Jews as well as Muslims picked out as targets for Christian wrath.

Imposing walls
The fortress of Margat (now known as Marqab) in Syria was originally built by Muslim architects but captured by crusaders in the 12th century and subsequently extended by the Knights Hospitallers. It finally fell to the Mamelukes in about 1285, shortly before the final collapse of the crusader kingdom.

Islamic coin
A coin from the time of the Crusades proclaims the Ayubbid ruler for whom it was minted to be the 'Ruler of Islam and all Muslims'.

Christian enclaves in what were predominantly Muslim lands. The military presence was necessary because Muslims living in the Christian principalities were generally oppressed, treated as second-class citizens and forced to put up with high taxation and legal discrimination.

A key part in the defence of the Holy Land was played by military religious orders. The Order of the Knights of St John and the Knights Templars had been in existence since the beginning of the 12th century, and they were joined in 1190 by the Teutonic Knights. In that year, merchants from Bremen and Lübeck established a field hospital outside Acre and set up the Teutonic Order in order to care for the sick. The knights soon found a military vocation and this was officially confirmed in 1199 when Pope Innocent III instructed the order to fight against all enemies of the faith.

EVERYDAY LIFE

The Nureddin Hospital in Damascus

The standard of medical expertise in the Islamic world was far superior to that in contemporary Europe. Using new, improved instruments such as scalpels, forceps, scissors and clamps, Muslim doctors knew how to open up the abdominal cavity, operate on tumours and ruptures, remove tonsils, and undertake a whole range of complicated amputation procedures.

Sultan Nur ad-Din founded a hospital in Damascus in 1154 that was a model of good organisation. It employed a permanent staff of doctors, and was equipped with an excellent medical library. Separate wards specialised in surgery, orthopaedics, fevers and mental illnesses.

On their morning rounds, the doctors would diagnose the patients' conditions and prescribe treatment that combined therapeutic and dietary measures. To lift the patients' spirits and speed their recovery, there were musical performances each afternoon in the hospital courtyard.

Medical encyclopedia
A medieval Islamic medical manuscript illustrating surgical implements.

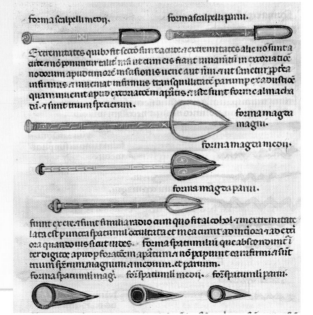

The last crusader king

After the truce that the Emperor Frederick II had negotiated came to an end, the papacy once again called for crusaders to take up arms against the Muslims, but the only response was a campaign conducted between 1239 and 1241 by Count Theobald of Champagne and Richard of Cornwall, who achieved little. In contrast, the Muslim forces were growing stronger, reinforced by a flood of Turkish warriors displaced westward by invading Mongol hordes. In 1244 Jerusalem once more fell to the Muslims.

In response, France's devout King Louis IX – later known as St Louis – announced his intention, with papal approval, to launch a Seventh Crusade. He spent three years preparing, then in 1248 set off by ship from the port of Aigues-Mortes in Provence, specially built as an embarkation point for the enterprise. He took his army by way of Cyprus to the Egyptian port of Damietta, previously captured in the course of the Fifth Crusade.

Although he took Damietta, Louis then squandered his chance of victory by allowing his opponents to regroup and rally their forces. An ill-judged march on Cairo ended in a reverse at the Battle of al-Mansura, then a disastrous retreat as the Muslim forces moved in. Louis himself was captured along with many of his knights, and was only released on payment of a large ransom.

The Mamelukes

After Damietta fell to the crusaders, Turkish slave soldiers in the service of the Ayyubids, known as Mamelukes, deposed their masters, seizing power in their own name in 1250. These elite troops, who originated from the steppes of southern Russia, were passionately committed to the Islamic cause and to

Abortive assault
King Louis IX of France invested six times his annual income in the Seventh Crusade. Although his forces initially succeeded in capturing the Egyptian town of Damietta (shown here in a manuscript miniature), Louis was subsequently captured and only released in exchange for the return of the port and the payment of a huge ransom.

jihad or holy war. They established a tightly controlled, centralised state system in Egypt that withstood even the onslaught of the Mongols. In 1260, Mameluke forces defeated the horde led by Hulagu that had recently sacked Baghdad and executed the caliph. This Battle of Ain Jalut, fought near Nazareth in Palestine, halted the Mongol advance in the Near East and made the Mamelukes the leading power in Egypt and Syria.

The crusader states soon felt the effects of the victory. Baybars I, the first Mameluke sultan, quickly overran most of the remaining Christian enclaves in Palestine, massacring the inhabitants. The cities of Caesarea, Haifa and Arsuf all fell in 1265, Antioch followed in 1268.

Shocked, King Louis IX launched an Eighth Crusade in 1270. He landed in Tunis on the North African coast, in order to attack the Mamluke homeland of Egypt, but died of the plague.

Baybars was able to resume his triumphal progress unhindered. Even the strongholds of Krak des Chevaliers and Montfort succumbed to his onslaught. Baybars himself died in 1277, but his successors continued to whittle away the final bastions of Christian power. The last to fall was Acre, which capitulated after a desperate defence in 1291. The age of the crusades was finally over.

The surviving crusader forces, deeply humiliated by their defeat, withdrew to Cyprus, never to see the Holy Land again.

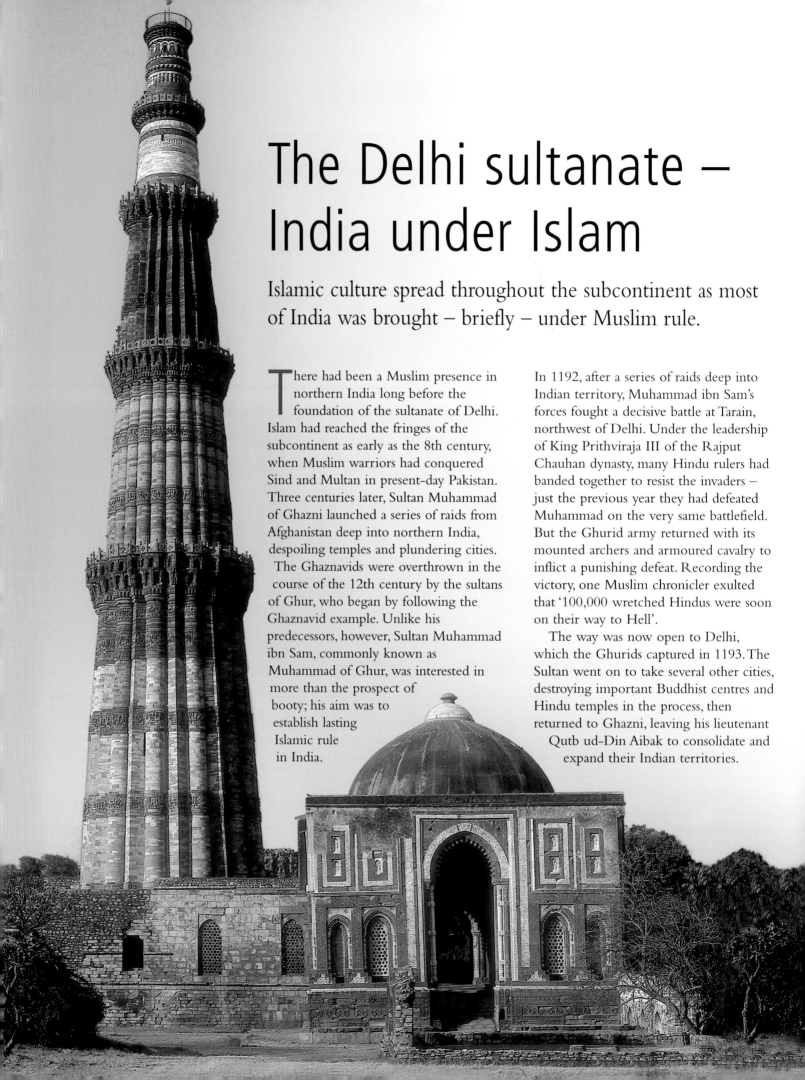

The Delhi sultanate – India under Islam

Islamic culture spread throughout the subcontinent as most of India was brought – briefly – under Muslim rule.

There had been a Muslim presence in northern India long before the foundation of the sultanate of Delhi. Islam had reached the fringes of the subcontinent as early as the 8th century, when Muslim warriors had conquered Sind and Multan in present-day Pakistan. Three centuries later, Sultan Muhammad of Ghazni launched a series of raids from Afghanistan deep into northern India, despoiling temples and plundering cities.

The Ghaznavids were overthrown in the course of the 12th century by the sultans of Ghur, who began by following the Ghaznavid example. Unlike his predecessors, however, Sultan Muhammad ibn Sam, commonly known as Muhammad of Ghur, was interested in more than the prospect of booty; his aim was to establish lasting Islamic rule in India.

In 1192, after a series of raids deep into Indian territory, Muhammad ibn Sam's forces fought a decisive battle at Tarain, northwest of Delhi. Under the leadership of King Prithviraja III of the Rajput Chauhan dynasty, many Hindu rulers had banded together to resist the invaders – just the previous year they had defeated Muhammad on the very same battlefield. But the Ghurid army returned with its mounted archers and armoured cavalry to inflict a punishing defeat. Recording the victory, one Muslim chronicler exulted that '100,000 wretched Hindus were soon on their way to Hell'.

The way was now open to Delhi, which the Ghurids captured in 1193. The Sultan went on to take several other cities, destroying important Buddhist centres and Hindu temples in the process, then returned to Ghazni, leaving his lieutenant Qutb ud-Din Aibak to consolidate and expand their Indian territories.

From slave to ruler

Aibak was a *ghulam* – one of the slave soldiers of Turkic extraction who made up the bulk of the Ghurid army. These men were bought into military service in childhood; they were not necessarily from humble backgrounds and did not lack rights, but they were completely dependent for favour and promotion on the master they served. A *ghulam* who won the trust of the Sultan could attain high rank, and none had given better service than Aibak, who by now had conquered a realm stretching 1200km (750 miles) east and west of the new Muslim capital of Delhi. His reward was control of all territories 'from the gates of Peshawar to the remotest parts of India'.

Shortly after Aibak's appointment, Muhammad of Ghur was murdered in Lahore. His death unleashed a power struggle that left Aibak *de facto* ruler of the lands he had conquered. This position was confirmed when Muhammad's successor sent him the gift of a ceremonial *baldachin* (a richly decorated fabric canopy) effectively recognising him as ruler of an independent empire incorporating all the Muslim lands in India – the first Sultan of Delhi.

The sultanate takes root

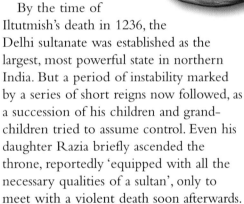

On assuming control of Ghurid lands in India, Aibak moved his headquarters to Lahore. His reign was short-lived, however, as he was killed in a polo accident just four years after the death of Muhammad of Ghur. Aibak's son-in-law and successor, Iltutmish, chose Delhi as his capital; it occupied a good strategic position with ready access to the Ganges Valley to the east. In the course of a 26-year reign, Iltutmish skilfully avoided the threat of Genghis Khan's forces, who encroached on his lands from the northwest. By deploying his troops in a chain of newly built fortresses – and by not supporting his hard-pressed neighbours – the Mongols were persuaded to seek easier targets to the west. In other respects, too, Iltutmish proved a capable ruler. His position as sultan was confirmed in 1229 when the caliph of Baghdad, the nominal head of the Islamic world, sent him a set of ceremonial robes.

By the time of Iltutmish's death in 1236, the Delhi sultanate was established as the largest, most powerful state in northern India. But a period of instability marked by a series of short reigns now followed, as a succession of his children and grandchildren tried to assume control. Even his daughter Razia briefly ascended the throne, reportedly 'equipped with all the necessary qualities of a sultan', only to meet with a violent death soon afterwards.

Stability was restored from mid-century onwards by Babur, who rose to become sultan in 1266.

By 1290, the Khalji dynasty had established itself in Delhi, and in 1296 the dynasty's greatest ruler, Ala ud-Din, set out on a career that took the sultanate's power far southwards. Ala ud-Din sent troops to capture the Rajput strongholds of Chitor and Ranthambor, then directed his attention to central India. The kingdoms of the Deccan Plateau had been in the hands of Hindu dynasties for centuries, and their forces proved no

Hard currency
These silver tanka coins, minted in Delhi, date from the time of Sultan Muhammad ibn Sam, also known as Muhammad of Ghur.

A sultan's burial-place
The tomb of Sultan Iltutmish rests in the Quwat al-Islam mosque in Delhi. Such mausoleums were unknown before the coming of Islam since Hindus practiced cremation.

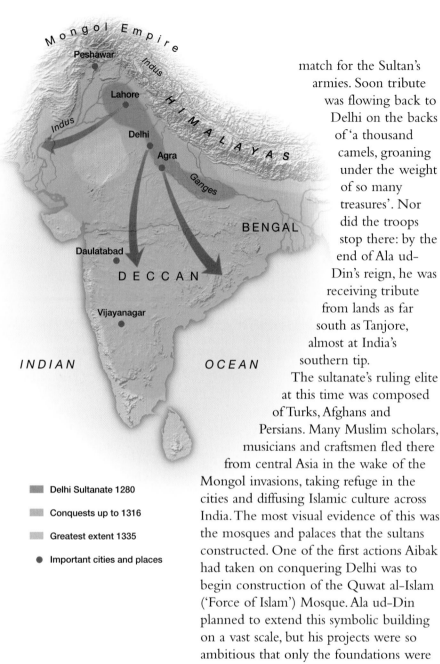

Mongol Empire
Peshawar
Indus
Lahore
HIMALAYAS
Indus
Delhi
Agra
Ganges
BENGAL
Daulatabad
DECCAN
Vijayanagar
INDIAN   OCEAN

■ Delhi Sultanate 1280

■ Conquests up to 1316

■ Greatest extent 1335

● Important cities and places

match for the Sultan's armies. Soon tribute was flowing back to Delhi on the backs of 'a thousand camels, groaning under the weight of so many treasures'. Nor did the troops stop there: by the end of Ala ud-Din's reign, he was receiving tribute from lands as far south as Tanjore, almost at India's southern tip.

The sultanate's ruling elite at this time was composed of Turks, Afghans and Persians. Many Muslim scholars, musicians and craftsmen fled there from central Asia in the wake of the Mongol invasions, taking refuge in the cities and diffusing Islamic culture across India. The most visual evidence of this was the mosques and palaces that the sultans constructed. One of the first actions Aibak had taken on conquering Delhi was to begin construction of the Quwat al-Islam ('Force of Islam') Mosque. Ala ud-Din planned to extend this symbolic building on a vast scale, but his projects were so ambitious that only the foundations were ever completed. He also envisaged doubling the height of the Qutb Minar minaret to over 140m (460ft), but this scheme, too, failed to bear fruit.

Meanwhile, India's indigenous Hindu traditions gradually infiltrated Muslim society. The sultans themselves adopted some habits of the Hindu kings, riding on elephants on ceremonial occasions and consulting astrologers for horoscopes. Some Hindus – particularly those from lower castes – chose to convert to Islam, but the bulk of the population remained loyal to their traditional gods. Their religious steadfastness suited the sultans,

for Hindu farmers and artisans not only generated much of the state's income but also had to pay a special tax, the *jizya*, levied on non-Muslims – good financial reasons for leaving them unconverted.

At first the sultans were tolerant of the peasantry, taking the view that they should not be overburdened with taxes. Official texts specified that 'the administration should be strict but fair… The peasants should have enough to live on, but not so much that they could support a rebellion'. Even so, Ala ud-Din demanded up to 50 per cent of all produce to finance his military campaigns in the south.

Expanding trade networks

Trade was vital to the economy. City markets thrived; travellers were particularly impressed by the market in Delhi, which catered to the enormous requirements of the sultan's court. The Arab traveller Ibn Battuta described Delhi as 'a mighty city that enjoys a worldwide reputation, and combines both beauty and strong fortifications. It is surrounded by walls the like of which exist nowhere else on Earth…'

Foreign trade also played an important role. Indian ships regularly sailed to Southeast Asia and the East African coast, calling at Hormuz, Aden and Jedda en route to unload cotton fabrics, precious stones, indigo and rice. Among the most prized imports were horses from central Asia and Afghanistan, coveted by the nobility and the army. The sultanate had a hard-currency policy and its rulers minted their own coins, notably the silver tanka, which encouraged international trade.

A place for Hindus

Although the highest offices of state were the preserve of Muslims, Hindus could make a career for themselves within the administration, and many skilled Hindu craftsmen received tax-free land grants and were exempted from paying the *jizya* tax. Hindus also served alongside Turks, Afghans and Persians in the army, forming the backbone of the infantry. Large units were stationed in Delhi and at other key strongholds around the country to ensure public order. On campaign, the army could increase to over 200,000 men, including servants, traders and support.

The troops were paid through the *iqta* system: soldiers were given a share of the income from a district that might be a small village or an entire province. The holders of the larger *iqtas* were expected to raise and provision troops for the Sultan's army in time of war. The granting of an *iqta* was in the sultan's gift; they could be revoked at any time and they could not be passed on to the holders' heirs.

Ala ud–Din's death in 1316 unleashed a fresh period of bloody conflict over the succession. Many of India's conquered Hindu states took the opportunity to declare their independence from the sultanate. One Muslim observer noted that the Hindus 'who before had been so oppressed that they could hardly

Force of Islam
The entrance to the Quwat al-Islam mosque in Delhi, which has been a UNESCO World Heritage Site since 1993. Twenty-seven Hindu temples were demolished to provide building materials for the complex.

find time to scratch their heads were now showing themselves off in new clothes, riding horses and practising archery'.

The sultanate at its peak

In 1320 the Tughluq dynasty assumed power in Delhi and under Muhammad ibn Tughluq, who came to power in 1325, the sultanate reached its greatest extent, embracing almost the whole subcontinent. Ibn Tughluq brought the last three independent Hindu states of southern India under his control, and in the north he advanced to the Himalayas. He even planned an expedition to Iran, but this was a venture too far. For finance he increased taxes on people farming the fertile land between the Yamuna and Ganges rivers, and triggered a full-scale peasants' revolt. Many tax collectors lost their lives and many peasants left the land, causing famine and a huge deficit of unpaid taxes.

The Sultan suppressed the uprising, but the Iranian expedition was indefinitely postponed and he turned his attention back to central and southern India to consolidate his power there. In 1327, he relocated his capital from Delhi to Daulatabad, some 40 days' journey to the south. A significant proportion of

Mixed influences
As this masonry detail suggests, many Hindu craftsmen were employed on mosque-building in India, and traditional Indian motifs were often worked into the decoration of the buildings.

TIME WITNESS

Ibn Battuta at the Sultan's court

'On feast days the palace is decked out with carpets and decorated in the most lavish manner… The highest throne, situated on the main facing wall of the audience chamber, is made of pure gold, and its feet are studded with jewels… The sultan sits on a cushion, while over his head a jewel-covered *baldachin* is stretched out to protect him from the sun. When he ascends the throne, the courtiers proclaim "Praise be to God!"…

'After the sultan has received his guests, they are served a meal commensurate with their rank… On this day, the great incense burner is also set up. It resembles a tower and is made of pure gold… Aloe wood, ambergris and benzoin resin are burned in it, and the fragrant smoke… fills the entire audience chamber.'

the population of Delhi was forced to move with him, at the cost of many lives and much discontent. People claimed that Muhammad had a grudge against Delhi's residents because they had circulated an open letter criticising his policies. Another rumour claimed that, on surveying the emptied city from his palace, he commented 'Now I am happy and at peace!' The whole enterprise proved a costly failure, and a few years later the court returned to Delhi.

The latter part of ibn Tughluq's reign was a time of deepening crisis. The expansion had left the sultanate militarily and financially overstretched. In an attempt to restore his depleted treasury, the Sultan tried minting copper and brass coins in place of the gold and silver ones in circulation, but the new coins proved easy to counterfeit, destabilising the currency and causing financial chaos.

The break-up of the empire

With the central administration in turmoil, the provinces rose in revolt. Rajput princes regained the important northern fortress of Chitor, while other Hindu rulers in central and southern India also took to arms. The situation deteriorated still further in 1338, when the Muslim governor of Bengal chose to secede from the sultanate.

When Muhammad ibn Tughluq died in 1351, the idea of all India under Muslim rule died with him. Most of the regions conquered early in his reign regained their independence, and the Delhi sultanate ceased to be the dominant power in the subcontinent.

Genghis Khan – the storm from the steppes

Genghis Khan united the Mongol clans under his leadership early in the 13th century. Soon afterwards his armies began their unstoppable advance across all Asia.

In 1206, a 'Year of the Tiger' in Chinese astrology, all the Mongolian steppe people who had been subjugated by Genghis Khan assembled their yurts, or felt tents, at the source of the Onon River and unfurled their nine-pointed white pennant. At this great *kuriltai* or clan gathering, the assembled tribal leaders gave the warrior, previously known as Temujin, the title of Genghis Khan – 'Universal Chief' – thus making him the leader of all the steppe nomads.

A hard start in life

Temujin had had a difficult childhood, and no one could have guessed that his name would one day be among the most famous in history. He was born the son of Yesugai, a leader of the Borjigid clan, probably in 1162. The Borjigids were part of a group of nomad clans known as the Mangchol, who grazed herds of sheep, cattle and horses on the Mongolian steppe between the Onon and Kerulen rivers. The region was inhabited by many other

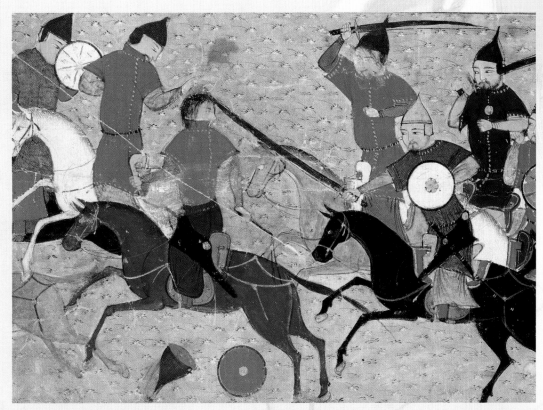

The universal chief (background) A portrait of Genghis Khan (c.1162–1227), founder of the great Mongol Empire. Although Genghis amassed vast quantities of treasure from his conquests, he had a personal aversion to luxury and extravagance.

The Mongol art of war
The Mongol armies were divided into heavy and light cavalry units. The light divisions weakened the enemy forces by unleashing a rain of arrows upon them from a distance, then the heavily armoured detachments would enter the fray to drive their opponents from the field. A 14th-century illustration from a book by Rashid-al-Din shows Genghis Khan in battle.

Sculpture from the steppe
In about 1220, Genghis Khan founded his capital at Karakorum in the Orchon Valley in what is now central Mongolia. This stone turtle is one of the few artefacts that have been unearthed at the site.

Mounted warrior
A ceramic tile from the Islamic lands shows a Mongol horseman at full gallop. Mounted Mongol warriors spread terror through the Middle East and Europe for much of the 13th century.

tribes who were closely related to the Mangchol in their language and way of life, among them the Merkits, Kereyits, Naimans and Tatars. Later, they all came under Mangchol sovereignty and in time referred to themselves as Mongols.

On the inhospitable steppes, the nomad's life was ruled by the harsh climate and the need to care for the herds, whose well-being was central to a tribe's survival. In addition, there were frequent raids and power struggles between tribes. The tribes had been briefly united at the start of the 12th century under Temujin's great-grandfather, Kabul Khan, but the confederation had collapsed into a welter of feuding clans.

Temujin's own father was murdered by members of the rival Tatar tribe. On his death, the Borjigid clan disintegrated and Temujin's mother was left to fend for herself and her sons as best she could. *The Secret History of the Mongols* – the only native source of information about Temujin, compiled in 1240 – dramatically recounts the many dangers and hardships that the family endured, struggling to feed themselves by hunting, fishing, and gathering wild berries and plants. They survived attacks by bandits, and on at least one occasion Temujin had to make a daring escape to evade capture by his enemies.

Throughout these harsh times, Temujin never forgot his noble origins or his hereditary claim to power. He soon won a reputation as a bold warrior, and thanks to his own diplomatic skills as well as the goodwill built up by his father, gradually attracted a military following. Eventually, he found himself at the head of a 20,000 strong force. One after another, the rival clans were forced to yield to him. By 1206 he was finally in a position to receive the homage of all the steppe peoples as Genghis Khan.

Mustering the hordes

Genghis first reorganised his army. It would no longer be composed of separate tribal contingents, but divided instead into permanent units of 10, 100, 1000 and 10,000 men. The troops were subject to strict discipline – severe punishment was meted out to anyone who tried to switch from one unit to another without permission. In Genghis's army a warrior's rank no longer depended on family background or status but rather on combat readiness and fighting ability. Any Mongol could attain a high leadership position solely through his own efforts.

Genghis gave command of the largest, 10,000-man units, known as *tums*, to particularly trusted men. One *tum* was assigned to Genghis himself. This complemented the 1000 hand-picked men who made up his personal bodyguard, and only saw combat when he himself was fighting.

To smooth relations between the different steppe clans, Genghis drafted a legal code known as the *jassa*. One of its provisions held that 'The khan can have no claim on the estate of a man who has died without leaving any heirs; rather, his property should go to the person who has been looking after it in the interim.' The *jassa* also established the principle of religious tolerance. For many centuries, the steppe nomads had been in contact with neighbours to the east and west via the Silk Road. As a result, some Mongols were Buddhists, while others adhered to various Christian sects, and Genghis left his subjects free to practise their chosen religions. While he took an interest in foreign religions, he always remained loyal to the pagan gods of his ancestors, believing that he was under the personal protection of the sky-god Tengri, the supreme Mongol deity. To ensure divine favour, he surrounded himself with shamans and soothsayers. His reverence for the supernatural did not stop him from ordering the execution of one of the court shaman when he learned that the man had been plotting against him.

Having established a position of unchallenged supremacy within the Mongol nation,

Genghis turned his gaze on the world beyond its borders. To the southeast lay China, a vast and prosperous land divided at the time between two separate empires. The rulers of the Jin dynasty, which governed northern China from Beijing, were themselves descended from steppe nomads, in their case the Jürchen people of Manchuria, to the east of the Mongol lands. Southern China was in the hands the indigenous Song dynasty, who had ruled the entire nation until driven from the northern lands a century before.

The onslaught begins

Genghis's first target was the Jin empire, whose ruler had angered him by demanding tribute. In order to gain access to Jin lands the Mongols had to overcome the intervening kingdom of Xixia, ruled by Tibetan Tanguts on land occupied today by the Chinese province of Gansu. In 1207 mounted hordes swept into the

A hardy life on the steppe
Genghis Khan's men were well prepared for the hardships of protracted military campaigning. From earliest childhood, riding, hunting and handling a bow were indispensable parts of the steppe nomad's way of life. In contrast with the sedentary peoples around them, whom they dismissively referred to as 'wooden-door people,' the Mongols lived in tents made of felt, as shown in a contemporary illumination (inset). Their descendants still live in similar yurts today (below).

region, quickly surrounding the Tangut capital, Ningxia. However, having no experience of siege warfare the Mongols were unable to take the city, and Genghis was forced to come to terms with the Tangut ruler. It was a weakness in his military skills that he soon dealt with.

Invasions east and west

In 1211, Genghis Khan and his sons, Chagatai, Zhotshi, Ogodei and Tolui, invaded northern China. Their forces swept aside the armies of the Jin, who took to the fortified cities. This time, Genghis had Chinese engineers in his service – men who understood siegecraft and gunpowder rockets. City after city fell to the Mongols and before long they were encamped before the gates of the capital, Beijing.

The Jin emperor negotiated a ceasefire and the Mongols withdrew laden with war booty including slaves, horses and huge amounts of treasure. But hostilities soon resumed, and in 1215 Beijing fell after a long siege.

Genghis now turned his attentions west. In 1217 he overran Kara-Khitai, a kingdom between Lake Balkhash and Tibet, which had come under the control of a Mongol rival of the Great Khan. The Mongols now found themselves on the borders of Khwarizm, a Turkic shahdom that covered much of central Asia east of the Caspian Sea, including parts of Iran and Afghanistan. The famed Silk Road cities of Bukhara and Samarkand lay within its borders.

Initially, Genghis had no plans to attack this powerful realm. He received trade envoys sent by the shah hospitably, and sent a delegation of his own to return the courtesy. When they were robbed and murdered at the frontier town of Otrar, apparently with the shah's consent, Genghis sent ambassadors to the shah's court to demand satisfaction. But they were sent back to their master with their heads shaved, a mark of shame.

Defensive walls
When Genghis Khan first launched his career of conquest, his armies had no means of overcoming solid defences like this fortified gateway at Bukhara. He relied on the expertise of captured Chinese military engineers to teach him the secrets of siege warfare.

The destruction of Khwarizm

For Genghis there was only one response to such provocation – war. In the spring of 1219 he crossed the shahdom's borders at the head of a force of 150,000 men. The individual units of the army struck rapidly from several directions, convincing the shah that he was surrounded. Rather than risk his troops in open warfare against the Mongol cavalry, he ordered a withdrawal to behind the walls of the fortified cities. But Genghis had 10,000 Chinese siege engineers in his train who were set to work. One by one, Nishapur, Merv, Balkh, Herat and Gurgan fell before the Mongol onslaught. When Bukhara's defenders tried to break through the besieging lines they were cut down beneath the city walls, and the city's inhabitants were mercilessly slaughtered. Samarkand met a similar fate.

In a three-year campaign Genghis devastated Khwarizm, in the process acquiring for himself a reputation for savagery that would echo down the ages. Possibly millions of civilians – men, women and children alike – were massacred as part of a deliberate campaign of terror. The shah was pursued to an island in the Caspian Sea, where he died.

The horde that had been hounding him subsequently continued westward, crossing the Caucasus Mountains to annihilate a Russian army at the Battle of the Kalka River in 1223. Although the Mongols then withdrew, the defeat gave the Russians a foretaste of what was to come when a fresh horde led by Batu, Genghis's grandson, invaded their lands 14 years later.

The shah's teenage son Jalal ad-Din tried to sustain Khwarizmian resistance but was defeated on the banks of the River Indus. He only escaped capture by making a daring horseback leap into the river, a feat later celebrated in fable.

With Jalal's defeat, the campaign was to all intents and purposes over. Genghis Khan returned at his leisure to Mongolia, taking time along the way to survey the lands he had conquered. Then in 1226 he set out once more, this time eastward against Xixia, which he had never fully subdued. It turned out to be his last campaign, for he died in his summer quarters in 1227, from injuries sustained in a hunting accident.

In 1229 a fresh *kuriltai* named Genghis Khan's favourite son, Ogodei, as his successor. Assuming the title of *khagan*, or great khan, Ogodei continued his father's aggressive strategy. In the first few years of his reign he completed the conquest of northern China and subjugated Korea, as well as campaigning further into western Iran. Then, in 1235, the *kuriltai* met again and resolved on an attack on the Christian West. Europe had little idea of the dark cloud that was about to descend.

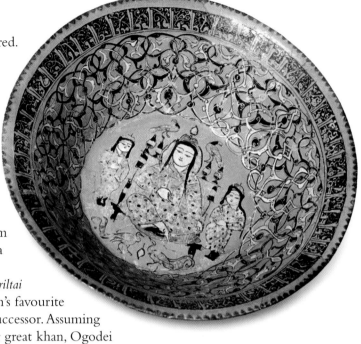

To the victor, the spoils
When Genghis Khan attacked China to the east of Mongolia and the Islamic world to the west, the Mongol armies looted treasures from both great civilisations. This finely decorated bowl was originally from Persia.

TIME WITNESS

Genghis Khan's grave

Persian historian Rashid ad-Din left this account of Genghis Khan's death while on campaign against the Tanguts of Xixia:

'Genghis's illness grew daily worse, until the ruler knew that his death was imminent. Accordingly, he issued the following order to his princes: "Do not announce my death or make any show of crying or lamenting, lest the enemy get wind of it. Rather, if the ruler of the Tanguts and the inhabitants of the city abandon it at the appointed time, kill them all."

'On the 15th day of the middle month of the Year of the Pig he departed this transient world, leaving his throne, his treasures and his command to his renowned lineage. Following his instructions, the princes kept his death quiet for as long as the Tanguts were still occupying the city. Then they slaughtered them to a man. Thereafter they took up his body and returned home. On the way, they killed every living being they encountered until they had brought his body back safely to their homeland…

'In Mongolia there is a great mountain called Burkan-Kaldun…where the Taidjigut people dwell. Genghis Khan had personally chosen this location for his burial with the order: "Here shall be the site for my grave and those of my clan."

'These words were now repeated by those who had heard them as the people began to mourn their leader. Thus did the princes and other leaders follow his directive in selecting this spot as the site of his tomb. It is said that, in the year when he was laid to rest, an enormous amount of trees and grass sprang up on the steppe. Now this forest is so dense that it can no longer be traversed, and the original wood and the site of his grave cannot be identified.'

The empire of the Mongol Khans

In its heyday the Mongol Empire stretched from western Russia to Korea. Yet it proved short-lived – within just a few decades the power of the Khans was already on the wane.

Most powerful ruler
A Chinese watercolour painting of Kublai Khan, the Mongol leader who completed the conquest of China. To speed communications across his East Asian empire he established a mail service that used 200,000 horses.

In 1236 an army of more than 120,000 men gathered on the Mongolian steppes. The troops, who had been assembled from all over the Mongol Empire, were under the command of Batu, a grandson of Genghis Khan, and his chief general, Subutai. Batu's destination lay far to the west.

In the course of their westward journey they destroyed the empire of the Volga Bulgars and subjugated the Turkic Kipchaks who lived on the southern steppes of Russia, forcing many thousands to seek refuge in Hungary. These victories cleared the way to their principal target – Christian Russia. One after the other, its principalities fell to the invaders.

By the winter of 1237 the Mongol forces were outside Ryazan, 300km (190 miles) southeast of Moscow. For five days they bombarded its defences with heavy catapults before they managed to force their way into the city. A contemporary chronicler reported: 'Not a single eye-witness was left to mourn the dead… people were impaled on stakes, while others had splinters of wood driven under their fingernails…priests were burned alive'. A similar fate awaited Moscow – not yet Russia's capital, just one principality among others – as well as heavily fortified Vladimir 200km (125 miles) to the east, upon which 'the stones hurled by the catapults fell like rain'.

A second Mongol assault breached the defences of the venerable city of Kiev on December 6, 1240. 'By day and night many battering rams hammered against the city walls,' a chronicler reported. 'The skies were dark with flying arrows, and a terrible slaughter ensued.' After the Mongols had pillaged and torched the city, all that was left of its former splendour was rubble and corpses. John of Plano Carpini, a Franciscan traveller, visited the site six years later and wrote: 'Journeying through that country, we came across innumerable skulls and bones of dead people strewn across the fields. For here once stood an extensive and densely populated city, which has now been almost completely destroyed.'

Modern archaeological finds from Kiev uphold contemporary reports of the destructive fury of the Mongols. Underneath one of the city's churches, investigators found the skeletons of a group of citizens who had made a last-ditch attempt to escape the invaders by tunnelling out of the city, but to no avail – all had been buried under rubble when the church collapsed.

The assault on Europe

News of the havoc the Mongols had wreaked quickly spread across Europe, prompting feverish defensive preparations. The invading horde divided into two. The main force headed for Hungary, whose broad plains provided a convenient springboard into central and western Europe. The other army struck north into Poland where, at Legnica on April 9, 1241, it met a combined force of Poles and knights of the Teutonic Order under the leadership of Duke Henry II of Silesia.

Although they fought bravely, the European knights were thrown into confusion at the start of hostilities when the Mongols lit fires that cloaked the battlefied in dense smoke. After unleashing a hail of arrows, the Mongol light horsemen then feigned a retreat. Duke Henry's army promptly fell into the trap and were struck down by the waiting heavy cavalry. The result was a resounding Mongol victory. Duke Henry was killed, along with 30,000 of his men.

The Mongol army then turned south, pillaging Moravia on its way to join the main force in Hungary. True to their motto of 'March separately, but attack in unison', the Mongol units already there had entered the country from different directions, converging on the cities of Gran and Buda (modern Esztergom and Budapest). King Bela IV of Hungary led his forces eastward to confront them at Mohi on 11 April, less than 48 hours after the battle of Legnica.

The Battle of Mohi

The two armies were separated by the River Sajo and the bridge across it was guarded by 1000 Hungarians. The Mongols attacked while it was still dark. Under the command of Koloman, Duke of Slavonia, the Hungarians grimly defended their position, even managing to knock a Mongol general and his horse off the bridge into the river. Yet the attackers kept pressing on under covering fire from catapult-like trebuchets and mangonels,

which could also deliver explosive rounds. Meanwhile, a detachment of Mongol heavy cavalry had secretly crossed the river downstream. They now charged the Hungarian flank. Caught completely unawares by the move, the Hungarians and their allies were slaughtered. An estimated 40,000 men died, and an eyewitness reported that 'their bodies lay all around, thick as rocks in a quarry'.

Desperate defence
An illustration from chronicles written in the mid-16th century, in the reign of Ivan the Terrible, shows Mongol forces beseiging Kozelsk, southwest of Moscow. The town held out for seven weeks against Batu Khan's forces in 1238. By the time it fell, almost all its defenders were dead.

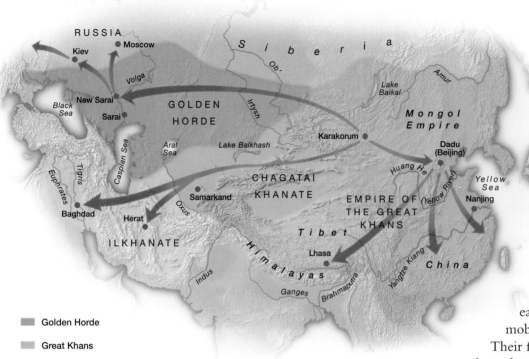

Golden Horde
Great Khans
Ilkhanate
Chagatai Khanate
● Important cities and places

Ornamental saddle
Raised in the saddle from early childhood, the Mongol warriors were peerless horsemen. Some boys were tied to the backs of ponies even before they learned to walk.

King Bela himself escaped, although the Mongols pursued him relentlessly.

After the victory Batu was preparing to invade Austria and Germany when news reached him of the death of the Great Khan Ogodei. Batu decamped at once with his army and hurried back to Mongolia for the *kuriltai*, the assembly of chiefs that would nominate Ogodei's successor. Europe waited in fearful anticipation, but the mounted hordes that had appeared from nowhere disappeared equally mysteriously back to the Central Asian steppes.

Winning at war

The Mongols owed their many victories not just to their well-practised fighting skills but to an ingenious grasp of tactics that evolved through the inter-tribal conflicts that had formed a regular part of steppe life. As they showed at Legnica, they were masters of the feigned retreat, a device that they called 'dog tactics'. When the enemy broke ranks in pursuit, the supposedly fleeing Mongol horsemen would turn on them and take advantage of their disorder. At the same time other units that had been kept in reserve would

burst upon the enemy's rearguard, trapping the foe. Another well-practised manoeuvre was to leave an obvious line of escape for surrounded adversaries, which encouraged them to try to use it rather than stand their ground in a fight to the death. Once they broke ranks to take advantage of the potential escape route, they could be picked off easily by the supremely mobile Mongol horsemen.

Their formations also exaggerated the real strength of their forces by such ruses as placing dummy soldiers on horseback or around campfires at night.

By the time of their assault on Europe, the Mongols were masters of siege warfare, having learned the necessary skills from captured Chinese military engineers. Since the most dangerous operations always had to be carried out within range of enemy fire, they forced prisoners taken captive on campaign to undertake this part of an attack. Other factors in the Mongols' success were the speed with which their horseborne troops advanced – this regularly took less mobile opponents by surprise – and the strict discipline of the army. Mongol commanders could execute rapid, precisely coordinated troop movements faster than any foe. Signal arrows, flags or flares were used to issue commands. Kettle-drummers on camelback usually gave the attack signal.

The impact on Europe

The death of the Great Khan Ogodei in 1241 saved Europe from disaster. Had Batu not broken off his invasion in order to attend the election of the new great khan, the history of the continent might have been very different. Yet ironically, the first reports about the Mongols to reach

Europe at the start of the 13th century had been seen as grounds for hope. Kings and popes alike were obsessed with the struggle against Islam, and when word filtered through of a new power that was inflicting catastrophic defeats on the Islamic nations of the Middle East, it seemed that Christian Europe might have found an unexpected ally. It was even widely believed for a time that Prester John, the legendary Christian priest–king of the East, had emerged with his army to crush the Muslim menace.

Such euphoria was rapidly dispelled by the murderous campaigns that Batu's armies conducted in Russia, Poland and Hungary. The new view spread that the mounted hordes had come straight from Hell to herald the end of the world. A coincidental play on words encouraged this belief, for one of the better-known Mongol tribes were called Tatars, a word inevitably linked with Tartarus, the Latin name for the infernal regions. So the Tartars, as Mongols in general came to be known in the West, were regarded more as devils than as men. Yet at the same time they inspired widespread curiosity. Within four years of the Christian defeats at

Legnica and Mohi, Pope Innocent IV was dispatching envoys, including John of Plano Carpini, to travel to the court of the Great Khan in the hope of converting the Mongols to Christianity.

A taste for luxury
This ornately decorated silver cup was discovered in a khan's grave. Ruling over long-established civilisations, the Il-Khans of Persia and the Yuan rulers of China lost the Mongol habit of simple living and acquired a love of fine things.

Dividing the empire

Before his death Genghis Khan had divided his empire up among his sons. The central *ulu* or khanate covered Mongolia, and its capital of Karakorum was the great khan's seat. The rulers of the other *ulus* accepted his overlordship and were obliged to provide troops for campaigns at his request. The borders of the different khanates were not clearly defined, and tensions between rulers came to a head on the death of Ogodei. His son Guyuk was chosen as the next great khan, but his election was contested by Batu of the Golden Horde.

Civil war threatened, until Guyuk's sudden death in 1248 resolved the situation. Mongke, a grandson of Genghis, was subsequently appointed great khan to universal approval.

VIEWPOINT

The Mongols – slaughterers or statesmen?

Chroniclers of every culture that came into contact with the Mongols vied to outdo one another in their depictions of the atrocities that the hordes had committed. Unarguably, the Mongol way of war caused more death and devastation than the military tactics typically employed in medieval times. It is also generally accepted that the massacres were a matter of deliberate policy.

One reason for the merciless killing was to avoid leaving potential enemies behind the advancing hordes who could later attack them from the rear. Another was to spread fear and panic, particularly among civilian populations: the brutal cruelty

that the Mongols regularly displayed was an integral part of their psychology of warfare. Terror was intended to weaken the enemy even before an actual encounter with the invaders, and to persuade people to surrender without putting up a fight. Cities that did surrender promptly without a struggle were exempted from the slaughter.

In the wake of their victories, the Mongol khans mostly ruled with skill and tolerance. As foreigners, they had to rely on the help of non-Mongol advisors and officials – Genghis Khan himself followed the advice of a Chinese aide, Yelü Chucai, to levy taxation at a reasonable rate on his new subjects rather than plunder them

without restraint. Even so, the fact that the Mongols remained deeply attached to their nomadic culture ensured that subject peoples were never really integrated into the running of the state.

Khan of the Golden Horde
Batu Khan led the Mongol invasion of the west and ruled the western Mongol Empire for 20 years (1235-55).

Conquerors tamed
As this plate from the Il-Khan lands illustrates, the Mongols learned new techniques and adopted artistic motifs from the civilisations that they conquered, blending them with features of their own. Background image: By the end of the 13th century the rulers of the Il-Khan realm in Persia had adopted the Islamic religion of their subjects, worshipping in buildings like the Jameh Mosque in Yazd, shown here.

Metropolis on the steppe

In Mongke's reign, the steppe city of Karakorum experienced a flowering that reflected the diversity of the rapidly growing empire. The capital expanded over many hectares, surrounded by a defensive wall. Captive craftsmen from across Asia and Europe – Chinese, Tibetans, Russians, Hungarians, Frenchmen, Persians and Germans among them – inhabited different quarters of the city. In contrast to the fate of other prisoners their lot was tolerable, since their Mongol masters valued their work.

Chinese and Muslim citizens lived in stone-built houses, but most Mongols preferred their traditional felt yurts. Each religious community had its own dedicated places of worship, so there was a Nestorian Christian church and two mosques, alongside a dozen or so Buddhist temples distinguished by enormous terracotta statues of the Buddha.

The Mongol nobility lived in mansions built in the Chinese manner, whose splendour was only overshadowed by the residence of the Great Khan himself. A Western visitor noted: 'This palace, which is laid out on a north–south axis, is built like a church, with a central nave and two side aisles behind rows of columns. The Khan sits at the northern end on a raised dais two steps high, so that everyone can see him.'
A marvellous device in an inner courtyard of the palace attracted the admiration of visitors. Guillaume Bouchier, a Parisian master craftsman labouring with the help of 50 Tibetan, Chinese and Mongolian assistants, had created a silver tree crowned by an angel with a trumpet. Four pipes were concealed within the trunk, and at a blast from the trumpet, attendants would pump wine and other alcoholic drinks out from the mouths of four sculpted snakes' heads. The fermented mare's milk known as kumiss, a favourite Mongol drink, flowed from lion's heads.

Envoys to the khan's court

Some of the most vivid reports of the lifestyle of the Mongol rulers came from the pens of European envoys. Two of the best-known were the Franciscan monks John of Plano Carpini and William of Rubruck. John arrived in Karakorum as a papal emissary in 1246, while William visited Mongke's court in 1254, travelling in the name of France's King Louis IX. Both men bore instructions to find out as much as possible about the Mongols and to sound out whether they could be converted to the Christian faith.

The Mongols were not particularly impressed by the European emissaries, since envoys from many lands were a common sight at court. For the most part the Mongols received the visitors graciously, although they expected them to show fitting humility in return.

A Dominican monk named Ascelinus who was dispatched to the Mongol lands at the same time as John of Plano Carpini found his way to the Caucasus region, where he succeeded only in antagonising the local Mongol commander, Baiju. He was lucky to escape with his life, for Baiju is said to have considered skinning him and his companions and stuffing their hides with straw.

Even successful legates like John of Plano Carpini failed to make much impression on their hosts. The Great Khan – it was Guyuk at the time – made his attitude clear in a letter that he gave John to take back to Pope Innocent IV.

In it Guyuk demanded that the Pope and all the crowned heads of Europe should come to Karakorum to pay him homage, or they would be treated as enemies.

Besieging Baghdad

Under Mongke's leadership the Mongols continued their campaigns of conquest. In 1252 he started the assault on the Song dynasty lands of southern China. Three years later Mongke's brother Hulegu prepared a major invasion of the Islamic heartland in the Middle East. Assembling a vast army at Samarkand, he thrust westward through Iran into what is now Iraq, aiming for Baghdad, the seat of the Abbasid caliphs. The city fell after a 50-day siege, during which it 'was filled with the thunder and lightning of smashing stones and burning naphtha missiles'. The victory brought almost all of the Middle and Near East into Mongol hands.

The empire breaks up

Mongke died in 1259, triggering a new bout of wrangling over the succession. His brother Kublai proclaimed himself great khan in 1260, violating the elective principle laid down by Genghis Khan. The empire was never truly united again, because after this time the individual Mongol *ulus* went their own ways, effectively transforming themselves into independent kingdoms.

In the fresh division that followed Mongke's death, Kublai Khan took Mongolia, Tibet and China as his domain. A new realm, the Chagatai Khanate, arose in the Central Asian lands now occupied by Kyrgyzstan, Tajikistan and the western Chinese province of Xinjiang. Hulegu's successors continued to rule the Il-Khanate in Persia and the Near East, while Russia remained under the control of the Kipchak Khanate, which soon became better known as the Khanate of the Golden Horde.

The name derived from the gold-decorated yurt of the state's first khan, Batu. Supplicants were only allowed to

A khan's tomb
Built between 1305 and 1313, the domed mausoleum of the Il-Khan ruler Oljeitu is all that remains of the Mongol city of Sultaniya in Iran. Another lasting legacy of the period was historian Rashid ad-Din's unsurpassed history of the Mongols, which was written during Oljeitu's reign.

enter the tent with the Khan's express permission; once inside, they had to kneel before the ruler, who received them on a raised podium where he sat with his favourite concubine. An attendant scribe noted down all that was said.

Batu ruled over his Russian realm from the city of Sarai on the River Volga. There he would receive the tribute of the Russian princes, who had by now come to terms with Mongol sovereignty in return for confirmation of their own positions and the understanding that they could retain their own culture. Even so, centuries of Mongol rule had major drawbacks, effectively cutting Russia off from developments in the West – a handicap that would later prove extremely difficult to redress.

The great trade routes brought considerable prosperity to the lands of the Golden Horde. Merchants converged on its capital, Sarai, from all over Eurasia. Ibn Battuta, the Arabian traveller, called the city 'a very beautiful town inhabited

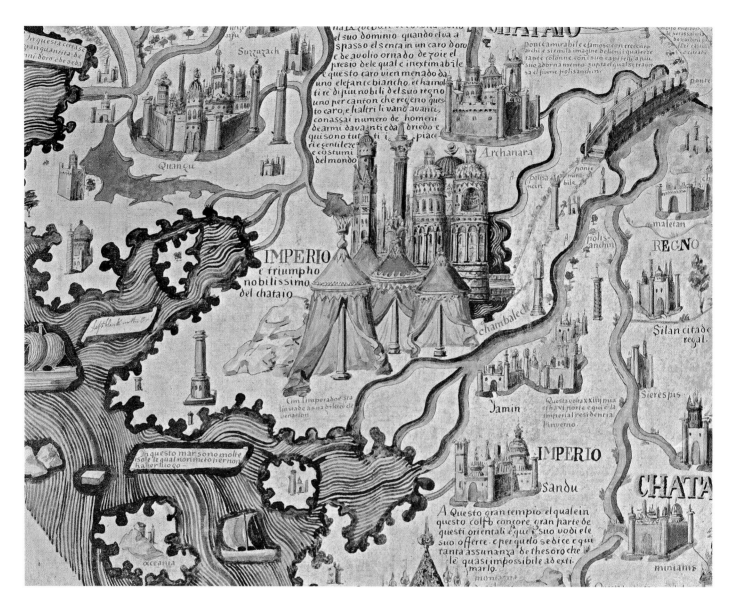

Land of wonders
A map from medieval Europe shows Cambaluc or Khanbalik, Kublai Khan's capital, plus a portion of the huge region that he ruled.

by many different peoples', noting that 'each nationality lives in its own quarter and holds its own special bazaar'.

The realm of Kublai Khan

Kublai Khan's rule in China has entered the realm of legend in the West, largely thanks to Marco Polo's famous account of his travels there. Kublai himself gradually shifted the focus of his attention from the old Mongol heartland to China, moving his capital from Karakorum in Mongolia to Cambaluc, close to the modern city of Beijing, in 1274. Following Chinese tradition, he called the dynasty that the Mongols established there the Yuan dynasty, meaning 'first origins'.

Five years later Kublai managed to bring the war against the Song dynasty to a successful conclusion, reuniting north and south China under his rule. Further military ventures such as planned naval invasions of Japan and Java failed, however, as did overland expeditions to Burma and Vietnam. Seaborne operations conducted over long distances and lengthy marches through humid jungle regions tested Mongol military capabilities beyond their capacity.

Perhaps surprisingly, China experienced a great cultural flowering in Kublai's reign, and many foreign travellers and merchants were drawn to his cosmopolitan court. Great opportunities awaited them there, for much of the civil administration of the state was delegated to foreigners, particularly Muslims from central Asia, who even made Persian the language of Chinese officialdom for a time. Marco Polo served Kublai Khan as a special envoy during a 17-year stay in his lands. The account of his travels that he gave on his return to Italy painted a picture of the Khan's magnificence and wealth that astonished the whole of Europe.

According to Polo, 'all the emperors and kings of the world combined cannot match the power wielded by Kublai, who is lord over all the Tartars on Earth'. He described the Khan on campaign and on hunting expeditions having himself carried in a litter borne on the backs of four richly caparisoned elephants.

A divided society

The Mongols introduced a rigid system of social segregation into China that prevented intermarriage between people of different racial groups. The Mongols took pride of place at the apex of the social pyramid, followed by the foreign officials brought in to run the country's bureaucracy. Among the country's indigenous inhabitants, the Han of Northern China were preferred to the peoples of the Song lands to the south. Social discrimination ensured that few native Chinese held official positions in the administration, and they also got unequal treatment in the law courts – if a Mongol killed a Chinese, he was only liable for a fine, but a native who killed a Mongol faced the death penalty.

Kublai himself never fully mastered the Chinese language. Even so, he took a keen interest in Chinese culture, promoting scholarship and ensuring that the imperial princes received a Chinese education.

The Mongol peace

For all the tensions that divided the different khanates, the Mongol Peace that the khans imposed ensured East–West connections via the trans-Asiatic trade routes flourished as never before. Seaborne trade to Southeast Asia, India and Persia was also thriving. In addition to spices and silk, novelties such as paper, printing, the compass and gunpowder all found their way from China to Europe at this time. China itself experienced an economic boom, partly thanks to the Mongols' introduction of paper money to create a currency that was valid throughout the whole empire.

The collapse of Mongol China

Yet for all the general prosperity, resentment festered among the native Chinese, who bore a disproportionate share of the taxes the Khan imposed and were also burdened with compulsory military service and forced labour duties on state building projects. Living conditions were particularly bad in the salt mines, and it was there that the first insurrections against Mongol rule took place early in the 14th century. Secret societies such as the White Lotus played a leading role in the unrest, drawing a steady stream of recruits through the increasing poverty of the general population. The misery was compounded by a general economic downturn that saw the paper currency devalued and corruption mushrooming among government officials.

From 1327 onwards, a succession of floods along the Huang He (Yellow River) compounded the situation, as devastating famines followed. Kublai's successors eventually lost control of the situation, and in 1368 a peasant uprising installed a new, indigenous dynasty, the Ming, bringing Mongol rule in China to an end.

Song-and-dance man
This terracotta figure, 37cm (15in) high, represents an actor from the Yuan (Mongol) period in China. Under Kublai Khan's rule, theatrical entertainments of various kinds were a popular feature of court life.

The great trade routes

The exchange of goods is one of the oldest and most important human activities. Its origins go back to the Stone Age, for from the earliest times people around the world have sought to obtain commodities that they were unable to produce for themselves or that were not available where they lived. In the centuries before the European discovery of America, a network of short and long-distance trade routes grew up linking Europe, Asia and Africa by land and be sea.

Rulers profited from a smooth flow of trade, both directly via taxes and indirectly through the prosperity it brought to their lands. The trade routes and the merchants who travelled on them enjoyed special protection, and in return, governments imposed high tariffs on the passage of goods through their territories.

Transcontinental trade

The longest transcontinental route was the Silk Road linking China in the Far East with the Middle and Near East. From there, goods were shipped over the Mediterranean to Europe. Stretching some 6500km (4000 miles) overland, it was complemented by a sea passage that ran from the ports of southern China via the islands of Southeast Asia to India and on to Arabia and the Persian Gulf.

The lands of the Near East – Asia Minor, Syria, the Levant – formed a hub from which goods headed south to Africa, radiating out along the North African coastal region then across the Sahara Desert, or by ship through the Red Sea then down the East African coast. Following the great sea voyages of discovery of the 15th and 16th centuries, most European trade with Asia and Africa went by sea and the old overland routes became largely obsolete.

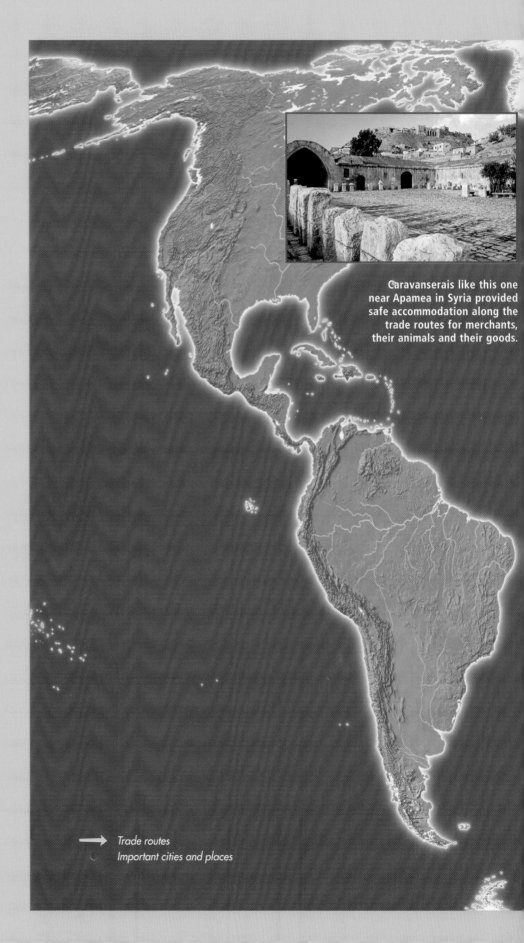

Caravanserais like this one near Apamea in Syria provided safe accommodation along the trade routes for merchants, their animals and their goods.

→ Trade routes
○ Important cities and places

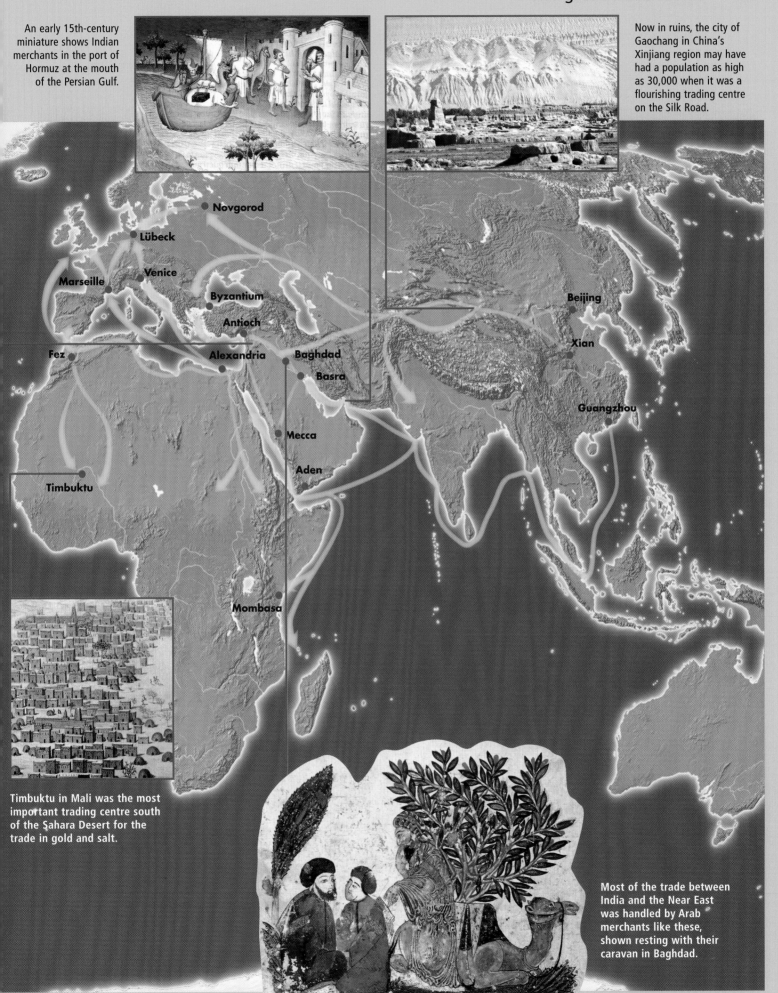

An early 15th-century miniature shows Indian merchants in the port of Hormuz at the mouth of the Persian Gulf.

Now in ruins, the city of Gaochang in China's Xinjiang region may have had a population as high as 30,000 when it was a flourishing trading centre on the Silk Road.

Novgorod

Lübeck

Venice

Marseille

Byzantium

Antioch

Fez

Alexandria

Baghdad

Basra

Mecca

Aden

Timbuktu

Mombasa

Beijing

Xian

Guangzhou

Timbuktu in Mali was the most important trading centre south of the Sahara Desert for the trade in gold and salt.

Most of the trade between India and the Near East was handled by Arab merchants like these, shown resting with their caravan in Baghdad.

All the world's luxuries

An illumination from a 14th-century manuscript shows merchants bartering in a fancifully imagined version of the Spice Islands. The profits of the East Indian trade were high enough to compensate for the many dangers involved.

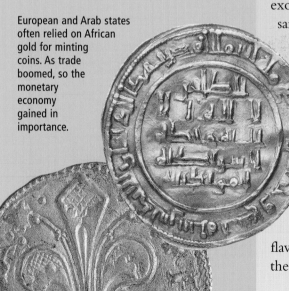

Imported into China from the Central Asian steppes, horses were expensive luxuries for the wealthy.

European and Arab states often relied on African gold for minting coins. As trade boomed, so the monetary economy gained in importance.

The caravans and ships that plied the world's trade routes carried every conceivable kind of cargo, but the greater part of the traffic catered to the luxury market. Goods had to have a high resale value to justify the costs of the long, perilous journeys involved. Usually they were intended for elite customers ready to pay astronomical mark-ups, yielding correspondingly fat profit margins for the traders who risked their lives transporting them.

Silk, spices and weapons

Silk had long been one of China's most valuable export commodities and it continued to be so in the Middle Ages, even though the Chinese lost their monopoly of the product in the 6th century AD. Subsequently, silk was produced in Byzantine Asia Minor and around the Mediterranean. Other Chinese exports that found ready markets in Europe and the Near East included porcelain, medicaments and salt.

The arms trade also flourished along the Silk Road, for the cities of northern Iran and western Central Asia were widely renowned for the fine steel weapons they produced. Southeast Asia's chief exports were exotic woods, spices and medicinal plants, especially sandalwood, nutmeg and cloves. In exchange, Indian ships brought textiles and high-grade items made of steel. The chief Indian exports to the West were gems and pepper.

African riches

Gold, ivory and slaves moved from the interior of Africa to the continent's east coast, where Arab traders took charge. In West Africa, caravans regularly travelled south over the Sahara Desert carrying salt – an essential commodity for preserving as well as flavouring foods. The salt was exchanged for gold in the lands of the Sahel.

Silkmaking was introduced into the West after silkworm eggs were smuggled out of China concealed in the walking-staffs of two Nestorian Christian monks.

In medieval Europe, exotic spices were prized not just as flavourings but also as preservatives and for their supposed medicinal value.

Caravans and ships

Arab ships used triangular lateen sails which made them better adapted to sailing into the wind than square-rigged vessels. Ships similar to this one in the Persian Gulf can be seen in the Red Sea to this day.

The development of the trade routes was shaped by the transport available to travel them. On the Silk Road, no single caravan ever covered the enormous distance from China to the Mediterranean coast. Rather, goods moved in stages, with different groups of merchants carrying them from one trading centre to the next. Even so, the distances involved could be considerable.

Beasts of burden

Overland routes often went through inhospitable terrain, so traders depended on reliable beasts of burden that could subsist on very little yet had the strength and endurance to carry loads for long periods. Merchants in Central Asia mostly used Bactrian (two-humped) camels, although yaks were sometimes called into service. They had horses too, but usually either chose to ride them themselves or provided them as mounts for the guards who accompanied the caravan. In North Africa, dromedaries (single-humped camels) were exclusively employed on the trans-Sahara route, carrying both the merchants and their goods; mules were also available, but they were only used to carry small loads over short distances. In the rainforest and savanna regions of Africa there were no suitable beasts of burden, so long columns of human porters took their place.

On the high seas

Given the many dangers and pitfalls that attended the land routes, traders with access to harbours generally found it quicker and safer to send goods by sea. Arab merchants in lateen-rigged dhows dominated the maritime trade of the Indian Ocean, but Indian and Chinese merchant ships also plied the routes.

Astrolabes that enabled voyagers to take their bearings against the stars were essential navigational aids both in the desert and at sea. Early travellers navigated with the help of the sun's position and notable landmarks in daylight hours and by the sky at night.

Constructed in the 14th century and restored from the 1970s on, the Khan Mirjan caravanserai in Baghdad is an unusually large and finely built example of the hostels that greeted travelling merchants in the big cities of the Middle East in the Middle Ages.

Caravans like the one shown in this Chinese ink drawing (below) had plied the Silk Road for centuries. They often employed native guides to lead them through unfamiliar sections of the route.

Wagons like these Chinese examples (left) were used mostly for local journeys. They were too cumbersome for the long-distance transcontinental routes and required constant repairs.

Trade, religion and science

Monumental columns – one supporting the Lion of St Mark – rise in front of the Doges' Palace in Venice. Thanks to its trading activities and connections with the Eastern Mediterranean, the Adriatic port was one of the main channels by which oriental culture reached Europe.

The secrets of gunpowder may have reached Europe via Arabic manuscripts like this one. The Arabs referred to the saltpetre used in the process as 'Chinese snow'.

The trading networks linking Europe, Asia and Africa did more than speed the flow of goods. They also served to disseminate knowledge, such as religious ideas and scientific discoveries. Pilgrims and missionaries travelling along the Silk Road helped to spread Nestorian Christianity, Persian Manichaeism and, above all, Buddhism far into Central Asia and China – Buddhist shrines and temples arose in all the major trading cities of the region. Writing systems that had originated in India and the Near East found their way to Central Asia. Meanwhile, Arab traders carried the message of Islam across North Africa, down the East African coast, and as far as the island states of Southeast Asia.

Technology transfer

Knowledge of technological innovations also spread out along the trade routes. New methods of steel production reached India from the Islamic world, while in sub-Saharan Africa iron manufacture – an indigenous development dating back deep into antiquity – experienced a major upswing.

Europe also profited from the ongoing cultural exchanges. News of many Chinese technological innovations reached the continent through Arab and Turkic middlemen. It was from China that the Western nations originally learned of paper manufacture, book printing, gunpowder and the compass, while Chinese metalsmiths had pioneered cast iron and the blast furnace even before the start of the Christian era. Europe's later rise to technological pre-eminence owed much to such borrowings.

Stupas in the town of Dunhuang in northwestern China bear witness to the Buddhist culture that flourished along the Silk Road.

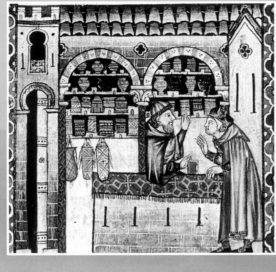

A Jewish apothecary plies his trade in Spain. The Moorish civilisation of the Iberian Peninsula was a major conduit for the transmission of Arab medical knowledge.

Solid receptacles like this medieval Persian jar stored costly herbs and medicinal plants from far-off lands in dried or powdered form.

The call of distant lands

Shown here in a 14th-century manuscript, Marco Polo travelled to the court of Kublai Khan, the Mongol ruler of China, in company with his father and uncle. Kublai employed Marco as an envoy, sending him to Vietnam, Burma and southern India.

World maps like the one prepared by the 12th-century Moroccan cartographer al-Idrisi helped broaden the ethnological and geographical horizons of Europe.

William of Rubruck (right), a Flemish Franciscan monk, travelled to the Mongol capital of Karakorum in the hope of converting them to Christianity.

Travellers, envoys and pilgrims followed in the footsteps of merchants along the great trade routes. Some left extensive descriptions of their adventures, their accounts painting vivid pictures of the conditions and customs they found in distant lands, stimulating other intrepid souls to set off on a journey.

Perhaps surprisingly to us today, the Mongol conquests of the 13th century opened a window for East–West travel. The peace imposed over the great empire by the victorious khans guaranteed safe passage on the principal roads through their realms, enabling people to travel in relative security. Even so, the threat of illness, extreme weather conditions and difficult terrain still presented significant hazards to the voyager.

Ruins on an island off the Tanzanian coast are all that remain of the great trading city of Kilwa Kisiwani, visited by ibn Battuta in the course of his travels.

On the road in the Middle Ages

Two churchmen, William of Rubruck and John of Plano Carpini, took advantage of the settled conditions to make their way to the court of the Great Khan himself at Karakorum in Mongolia. Mongol delegations similarly journeyed westward, reaching France and England, where they excited great curiosity. Such treks were not new: many centuries earlier, the Chinese pilgrim Faxian had travelled as far as northern India via the Silk Road before returning home by ship by way of Southeast Asia.

The account that most fired European imaginations was that of the Venetian merchant Marco Polo, who spent 17 years at the court of Kublai Khan in China. Yet the Arab traveller ibn Battuta actually went even further afield. Setting off from his home in North Africa in 1325, he spent almost 30 years on the road, exploring large parts of Africa, Arabia, Central Asia, India and Southeast Asia as well as China and leaving a compelling record of his travels in the work known as the *Rihla* ('Journey').

Cartography developed in response to the practical needs of merchants and other travellers. The detail below is from a medieval Arabic map of the Red Sea. The map is oriented with south at the top, and the turrets to the left of the sea represent the Arab cities of Mecca and Medina.

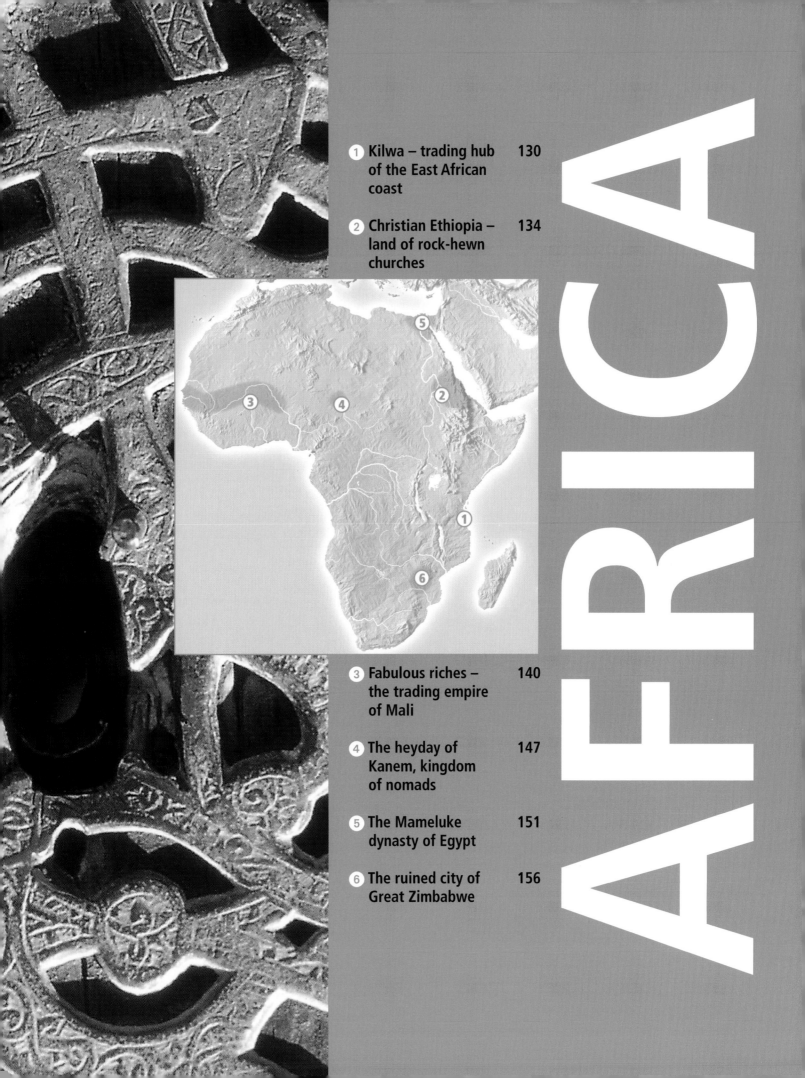

AFRICA

Kilwa – trading hub of the East African coast

A small island off what is now Tanzania developed into an economic giant in the course of the Middle Ages. Its sultans amassed great riches from their position as middlemen between Africa and the eastern and Islamic worlds.

Far Eastern import
This graceful 13th-century Chinese vase was found in the ruins of the sultan's palace in Kilwa. It is a relic of the extensive trade contacts that existed between East Africa and Song China.

A splendid sight awaited sailors approaching the Indian Ocean coast of what is now Tanzania in the 13th and 14th centuries. From afar they would have seen, on a small offshore island, the walls of a thriving city with houses built of stone, dominated by the dome of its mosque and sultan's palace. The palace contained more than 100 rooms and was probably the biggest building in sub-Saharan Africa in its day.

Island metropolis

Arriving at the port's harbour, they would have been swept up in the non-stop bustle of activity. The markets and squares teemed with merchants and traders from all corners of the earth – indigenous Africans, Arabians, Persians, Indians, even Chinese. The prosperity of the city showed that trade was booming. Ivory, incense, exotic spices and valuable tropical woods were all on sale – as were slaves. There was a brisk trade in metals, including iron ore from mines to the north and tin from Shaba (in what is now the Democratic Republic of the Congo). Above all, the city was a key trading centre for gold, brought up the coast from mines in the territory ruled from the walled city of Great Zimbabwe, far to the south.

The port's citizens called their home Kilwa, but because there were other towns of the same name in the vicinity, over time it became known to outsiders as Kilwa Kisiwani, 'Kilwa on the Island'. Only ruins now remain to testify to its former greatness, but 700 years ago it was internationally famous.

An Islamic trading network

Given the extent of Kilwa's fame in the Middle Ages, surprisingly little is known today about its development and growth. The scant information that is available comes from Arab and Portuguese chroniclers and from archaeological finds made at the site.

The spark that transformed the island's destiny was struck by the Islamic expansion of the 7th and 8th centuries. Warriors inspired by the Prophet Muhammad carried their new faith through North Africa, the Middle East and beyond. In time, Islamic rulers took control of the entire North African coast, and Arab merchants established a trading network that stretched down the Red Sea to ports in the Persian Gulf, the Indian Ocean and even far-off Indonesia. Inevitably, some traders turned their attentions to East Africa as the natural western terminus of the Indian Ocean trade, and so Kilwa's fame began.

Persian connections

Over the years, Arab entrepreneurs established a chain of settlements stretching from Mogadishu, in what is now Somalia, as far south as Sofala on the coast of Mozambique. In between were other ports that would have long and illustrious histories, among them Mombasa (in present-day Kenya) and Zanzibar. Like Kilwa, both grew up on offshore islands, which had obvious defensive advantages for maritime traders.

Tradition has it that the founder of Kilwa was Ali bin al-Hasan, a native of Shiraz in Persia. He is said to have arrived on the East African coast in the year 956, with his father and five brothers in a fleet of seven ships. The story goes that the family went on to found seven separate cities, Mombasa being another of them.

Whatever truth there may be in the story, archaeological evidence indicates that there was, indeed, an early ruler of Kilwa named Ali bin al-Hasan. Thousands of copper coins bearing his name have been excavated on Kilwa itself and on the neighbouring island of Mafia, which the sultans also ruled. The coins have been dated to the 11th century, putting Ali's reign a century later than the legendary account suggests.

Another story tells how the first Muslim settlers purchased Kilwa by giving its former African ruler enough rich clothing to encircle the entire island. The king took the garments with

Relics of past glory
The fortress at Kilwa (bottom) was built by the Portuguese, who occupied the city in 1504. Subsequent additions were made by the sultans of Zanzibar, who ruled the island in the 18th century. The Great Mosque (inset below) was built on the orders of the Mahdali sultans early in the 14th century. It was the most important sacred building in Kilwa, and also one of the largest in East Africa.

the unspoken intent of coming back at low tide a few days later to drive the foreigners off his land. When he eventually did return at the head of his troops, however, he found that the newcomers had deepened the channel separating the island from the mainland coast so that his men could no longer cross by foot. Outwitted, the king was left with no option but to abide by the agreement he had made. The story is most likely legend, but excavations have confirmed the existence of a settlement at Kilwa before Ali bin al-Hasan's time, dating back at least to the 9th century.

Rich on gold

However Kilwa was won, it developed into a thriving commercial centre. A major boost came from the late 13th century onwards, when the Muslim rulers of the Delhi Sultanate extended their rule down the coasts of India, stimulating a rapid expansion in Indian Ocean commerce. At the same time, the growing wealth of Europe was stimulating an increasing demand for gold that peaked in the 14th century. Kilwa's sultans helped to feed the market by developing close commercial links with the port of Sofala, 1750km (1000 miles) to the south. Sofala served as the coastal terminus for trade routes that lead inland to the gold-producing region of Great Zimbabwe. Boats carried the precious metal up the coast to Kilwa, where it was sold on to merchants from across the Islamic world. In exchange they provided not just hard currency but also trade goods that included cloth from India and porcelain from China.

Kilwa's position at the heart of the gold trade survived a transfer of political power from the Shirazi to the Mahdali dynasty, of Yemeni origin, at the start of the 14th century. Like their predecessors, the island's new rulers were happy to flaunt the wealth that flowed into their coffers from the tariffs they charged on all goods passing through the island. Their palace of Husuni Kibwa, built from the local coral stone, had four separate reception courts and amenities that included an octagonal bathing pool. As for the city itself, the celebrated Arab traveller ibn Battuta, who visited in 1331, declared it to be 'one of the most beautiful and well-constructed in the world'.

Swahili – a shared language and culture

Despite its relatively small size and insular situation, Kilwa had a powerful cultural impact on the surrounding region. Within its walls Africans lived cheek by jowl with Arabs, Persians, Indians and even some Chinese. Its cosmopolitan atmosphere, like that of the other Arab settlements that dotted the Indian Ocean coast, encouraged the intermingling of different traditions. The result was the development of a distinctive coastal culture that became known as Swahili, from the Arabic term for the people of the East African coast. The culture found expression in the KiSwahili language, which developed as a lingua franca in the ports and then spread into the hinterland. KiSwahili derived

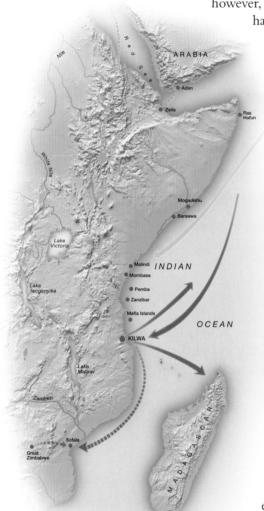

Muslim cities and settlements

┄┄▶ Arab trade routes

───▶ Chinese trade routes

───▶ Indian trade routes

┄┄▶ African trade routes

from the Bantu tongues of the local African peoples, mixed with Arabic, Indian and Persian elements. Some 50 million people speak it to this day.

Father of Gifts

The sultans of Kilwa never sought to make their state a major political power. Their rule never extended beyond Kilwa and Mafia, even if their influence stretched at times as far as neighbouring Zanzibar and the Comoro Islands. For the most part, they were content to enjoy the wealth that trade brought them without getting involved in risky foreign ventures.

Within their small domain the sultans exercised absolute power, but their position was rarely challenged because the population at large shared in the benefits of the islands' prosperity. Successive rulers relied on munificence to bolster their support. Ibn Battuta reported that al-Hasan bin Sulaiman, the sultan at the time of his visit, was known for his generosity as the 'Father of Gifts'. On one occasion he was said to have agreed to surrender the clothes on his back at the request of a visiting Yemeni holy man, only to buy them back for a substantial payment of slaves and ivory.

Centuries of decline

Kilwa's position weakened with the decline in the gold trade from Great Zimbabwe. From the 14th century onwards it came under increasing pressure from the ports of Mombasa and Malindi further north. The arrival of the Portuguese on the East African coast in the early 1500s dealt it a fatal blow. The city was occupied and plundered, and its trading importance was undermined.

The memory of Kilwa's great days lingered on. The island even enjoyed a commercial revival in the 18th century, when it came under the control of the sultans of Zanzibar to the north. It finally fell into insignificance in the late 19th century, when East Africa became a German colony. Today, Kilwa Kisiwani is no more than a village, but the ruins of its great mosque are preserved as a UNESCO World Heritage site.

Copper coins
The sultans who ruled Kilwa minted their own currency from the 10th century onwards. Most of the coins were made of copper. These are from the reign of Sultan Sulaman ibn al-Hasan, in the 14th century.

Merchant vessel
Arab merchants transported their goods across the Indian Ocean in two-masted, lateen-rigged dhows, similar to this one still in use today.

Christian Ethiopia – land of rock-hewn churches

The Zagwe dynasty and the Solomonid rulers who replaced it revitalised the kingdom of Ethiopia as a Christian enclave in a region of Africa now largely under Islamic rule.

Between 1205 and 1209 several magnificently appointed delegations sent by Ethiopia's King Lalibela arrived at the court of the Fatimid sultan in Cairo, where they attracted much attention. The display was a matter of royal policy: through the envoys' finery, Lalibela wanted to demonstrate to the Islamic world that Christian Ethiopia had regained its former greatness.

The new sense of self-confidence in this ancient kingdom on the Horn of Africa was also reflected in a threat that the King made at the time to dam the flow of the Blue Nile, a move that would literally have left Sudan and Egypt high and dry. Although the Egyptian sultans may have doubted the feasibility of the plan, it must have warned them that there was a new force to be reckoned with in the south.

Nation under threat

Back in about AD 1000, the prestige of the once-powerful Ethiopian empire of Axum had sunk to an all-time low. Its power had waned as the might of Islam had grown, first on the Arabian Peninsula and then in North Africa and across the Middle East. By gaining control of Red Sea shipping, the Arabs broke Axum's commercial supremacy in the region. In the centuries that followed, the Ethiopians lost control of the coastal areas of their own kingdom and of the trade routes leading into the African interior. Hostile tribes even attacked the capital city of Axum itself, partially destroying it.

By the time the new millennium dawned, little remained of what had once been a mighty empire. Now its rule barely stretched beyond the immediate vicinity of the capital. Yet the memory of Axum's former greatness lingered and its ancient traditions continued to be cherished – so much so that, in the centuries to come, the coronation ceremonies of the rulers of Ethiopia were invariably held at Axum.

The Zagwe takeover

In the 11th century, the Agaw people of northern Ethiopia rose to become the foremost power in the land. Cushitic speakers from the Lasta region south of Axum, the Agaw had long formed part of Ethiopia and had adopted the prevailing Christian–Axumite culture.

In the mid-12th century, Agaw rulers of the Zagwe dynasty took control of the kingdom and laid the foundations for national revival. The most illustrious king of the Zagwe line was Lalibela, who reigned early in the 13th century. He

Old traditions
Ethiopia's Christianity absorbed elements of earlier African culture. This ceiling fresco depicting the Sun adorns the 12th-century rock church of Beta Mariam in Lalibela.

endowed the Church with rich estates and other gifts, and (along with other members of his dynasty) is remembered in Ethiopia as a saint. Legend has it that his name – meaning 'The bee recognises his royal nature' – was given to him because bees swarmed around at the time of his birth. The sign was considered propitious, for bees (together with lions) were associated with royalty in local tradition.

Churches in the bedrock

Shortly after his investiture, the King moved his capital from Axum to Roha, which lay some 300km (200 miles) to the

south; the town was later renamed Lalibela in the king's honour. Here, over the course of his reign, the king left an enduring monument to his rule in the form of 11 churches hewn directly out of the ground-rock.

The unique method of construction soon made these churches famous far beyond Ethiopia's borders. Some were hollowed out of the rock of natural

Hewn from stone
The extraordinary, semi-subterranean churches of Lalibela were carved out of solid rock. In most cases trenches were excavated into the bedrock to form a square around a solid core of granite, which was then shaped and hollowed out to create the church in the shape of a cross.

Negus Negesti

Ethiopian rulers bore the proud title of Negus Negesti – King of Kings – and so are often referred to as emperors. They traced their claim to power back to their supposed descent from the legendary Menelik I, son of King Solomon and the Queen of Sheba.

Legend tells that Menelik brought the Ark of the Covenant from Jerusalem to Ethiopia, going on to establish the country's ruling dynasty. The royal seal of the Negus Negesti alluded to this ancient tradition with the words: 'The Lion of the Tribe of Judah was Victorious'. The Solomonic kings made much of the connection, and under their rule in the early 14th century, the story of the royal descent from Solomon was first written down.

caverns; others were created by excavating directly down into the bedrock of the plateau on which the city stands. In each case, the buildings were monolithic; even the altars were carved in a piece from the same stone as the structures around them. The king's intention was to make Roha an African Jerusalem, a place of pilgrimage for the continent's Christians who were unable to travel to the Holy Land itself. Sites around the city were given suitably biblical names, and the river running through it was called the Jordan.

End of a dynasty

While Lalibela's churches amaze visitors to this day, much else about the Zagwe is shrouded in mystery. No reliable list of kings has survived, and historians still argue over whether the dynasty lasted for 133 or 333 years. However, in the mid-13th century, amid widespread popular unrest, a power struggle took place. The Church backed the opposition, because

even though the Zagwe kings had always championed the Christian cause, they had never fully won over the priesthood, who regarded them as usurpers.

In about 1270, the Zagwe line was toppled by a general named Yekuno Amlak. According to tradition, his mother was the slave of an Amhara chieftain, and he himself was brought up by monks. He is said to have escaped from captivity to raise the flag of rebellion in the Amhara provinces. Amlak defeated and displaced the last Zagwe king, whose name was subsequently erased from the historical record – he is referred to only as Za-Ilmaknun, 'the Unknown One'.

The change of dynasty marked a shift in the balance of power within Ethiopia. The new dynasty came from the mountainous region of Shewa in the centre of the country, north of modern Addis Ababa. Henceforth, the Semitic-speaking Amhara were to replace the Cushitic Agaws as the nation's rulers.

The link to Solomon

Yekuno Amlak, who ruled from 1270 to 1285, traced his ancestry through his father to the last king of Axum, whom the Zagwe had dethroned. He and his successors made much of the connection, claiming to represent the true Ethiopian royal line tracing its origins all the way back to the biblical King Solomon, in whose name they established their Solomonid dynasty. The Solomonid kings remained in power for 700 years, right up until the death of the last emperor, Haile Selassie, in 1975, and the coup that ended the monarchy.

Emperors on the move

Kingship in Yekuno Amlak's time was a feudal affair. The Zagwe rulers had divided the country into a number of fiefdoms that were entrusted to vassals who answered to the king. In practice, however, the degree of power that any ruler wielded depended largely on his own personality.

Once a year the king would embark on a journey through his realm in order to assess the state of the different regions and the performance of their governors, as well as to pass legal judgments and settle disputes. In time the annual tour evolved into a lifestyle that saw the ruler, accompanied by his entire court, moving perpetually from place to place.

City of tents

The rugged mountainous terrain of Ethiopia made this mobile style of rule necessary, for it was only by constant travel that the Emperor could maintain control over the different parts of his realm. The Solomonid emperors maintained and extended the tradition, travelling amid great pomp and

Dynasty's founder
The coronation of Emperor Yekuno Amlak, founder of the Solomonid dynasty, took place in 1270. The ruler ordered the construction of the Church of Gennata Maryam near Lalibela, which contains the first dateable Ethiopian wall paintings. Here he is seen with slaves and Muslim ambassadors.

Visible sign of faith
A processional cross dating from the 13th or 14th century (left). The Ethiopian craftsman who forged this iron crucifix decorated it with gold insets. Devout believers carried such crosses at important Church festivals.

The influence of Egypt
The Ethiopian Church had close links to the Coptic Church of Egypt, which is clearly evident in the nation's religious art. This 14th-century manuscript illustration shows the entombment of Jesus.

Gifts from the godly
The Ethiopian people expressed their religious devotion in lavish ritual offerings that furnished the churches. These bronze oil lamps, found only in churches around Lake Tana in Ethiopia, would have been devotional offerings.

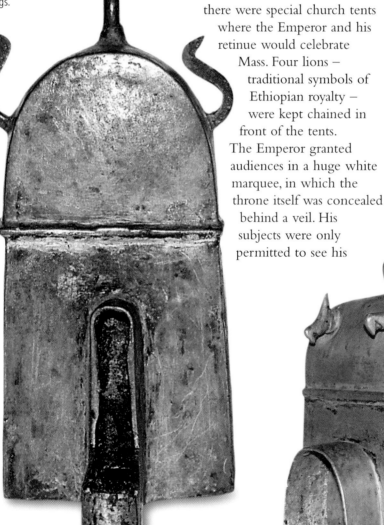

circumstance. A vast tent city several kilometres wide would rise up at each of their halts. At its centre was the Emperor's royal enclosure, surrounded by a belt of thorn scrub to screen it off from the rest of the compound. Soldiers stood guard at 12 narrow entry points to the enclosure, granting access only to courtiers and other privileged individuals.

Within the enclave there were special church tents where the Emperor and his retinue would celebrate Mass. Four lions – traditional symbols of Ethiopian royalty – were kept chained in front of the tents. The Emperor granted audiences in a huge white marquee, in which the throne itself was concealed behind a veil. His subjects were only permitted to see his face at the festivals of Christmas and Easter.

The arrival of the royal tent city put a heavy strain on the resources of the surrounding region, which had to provide huge quantities of grain, firewood and animals for slaughter, to cater for the king's retinue, his high officials and their followers. Their numerous draught animals and beasts of burden also had to be provided for.

The power of the Church

Next to the ruler, the Church was the chief power in the land. At its head was a metropolitan or *abuna*, a word meaning 'Our Father'. He was answerable to the patriarch of the Coptic Church in Alexandria who, at the emperor's request, would choose candidates for the post from among the holders of high ecclesiastical offices in Egypt.

The Egyptian connection went back to the early days of Christianity in Ethiopia almost a millennium before, when missionaries from Egypt had spread the faith in the time of the early Axumite kingdom. Monks translated Coptic works on Christian and Jewish history into Ge'ez, an ancient Ethiopian language that, like Latin in the Catholic Church, continued to be used as an ecclesiastical tongue after it ceased to be used in common speech. One of the most politically significant works was the *Fetha Negast* or 'Law of the Kings', a Coptic work that was translated from Arabic in the first half of the 14th century. Drawing on biblical precedents, this legal code laid down basic principles, including the divine right of the Emperor and the right to keep slaves. Over the ensuing centuries, the emperors would refer back to this text when administering justice.

Rights to land

The country's prosperity was based on its good geographical position as a trade centre linking the African interior, Egypt and the Red Sea. Agriculture was the other main prop of the economy. Ethiopia's volcanic soils ensured that the land yielded good harvests.

Most of the cultivated land, as well as the taxes and tithes that flowed from it, were in the hands of the imperial family, the Church or the nobility. Theoretically, all land belonged to the Emperor, who allowed his vassals the use of it on a temporary basis. In practice, though, such grants were rarely revoked, especially those made to the Church and the monasteries, and new rulers would confirm them as a formality. Only a small proportion of the land available for agriculture was owned by ordinary farming families, and this was passed down from father to son.

High agricultural yields enabled Ethiopia to maintain a large standing army, which in time of war might comprise over 100,000 men. The emperors needed a substantial fighting force because a permanent state of war existed with the Islamic sultanates on the Red Sea coast to the east. Ethiopia's mountain terrain offered some protection from attack, and the country also profited from the sultans' disunity. Frequently, Islamic rulers who had come off worst in conflicts with their neighbours would seek refuge at the Ethiopian court.

Time of trial

At the beginning of the 14th century Ethiopia found itself hard-pressed by the sultanate of Ifat, which had established regional supremacy from 1285 onwards and whose armies had advanced into the eastern Shewa mountains. At the same time, the Mameluke rulers of Egypt were openly hostile to Ethiopia They colluded in the murder of Ethiopian envoys and in preventing a new *abuna* from taking up his post, with the result that the country was without a spiritual ruler for several years at a stretch.

A new emperor

The situation changed with the accession of Amda Seyon I in 1314. He brought stability to the realm and ushered in a time of economic prosperity and a cultural flowering. When the sultan of Ifat ordered the torture of an imperial envoy on his way back from Cairo, Amda Seyon responded by launching an attack on the sultanate that resulted in its defeat in 1328.

The sultan's successor, Sabr ad-Din, tried to renew the struggle, but was no match for Amda Seyon. Having captured one of the sultan's allies, Amda made the man send the sultan a false report of an Ethiopian defeat. Sabr ad-Din promptly dispatched troops to take advantage of the situation, but an elite Ethiopian force, known as the Emperor's Wolves, successfully held up their advance until Amda Seyon himself arrived at the head of the rest of his army. The ensuing battle, which took place in 1332, ended in a devastating defeat for the Muslims.

Amda Seyon and his successors succeeded in consolidating Christian Ethiopia's position within a region otherwise dominated by Islam.

Sacred language
The Semitic language known as Ge'ez was the common tongue of the ancient Axumite Kingdom of Ethiopia. Scribes used a unique script derived from a southern Arabian model. Ge'ez disappeared from popular usage in the 13th century, but exists to this day as an ecclesiastical language. The sample above is from a 14th-century parchment text.

Fabulous riches – the trading empire of Mali

A combination of able rulers and access to gold made Mali one of the most important empires of medieval Africa.

In the 13th and 14th centuries, Europeans knew little about Africa. For most people, the lands south of the Sahara Desert were a mystery. Only one name made scholars, merchants and crowned heads take note: Mali.

Rumours of Mali's huge size were well-founded – it stretched for 2000km (1250 miles) inland from the West African coast. After 1324, stories began to spread of an immensely rich king who reigned over the empire. In that year Mali's ruler, Mansa ('Emperor') Musa, made a

spectacular pilgrimage to Mecca, the holy city of Islam. News of his journey, filtered westward from Cairo in Egypt, where it was said that the Malians spent so much gold they destabilised the local currency.

In contrast, the Muslim world had known about Mali and its predecessor, the Empire of Ghana, for a long time. Arab warriors had conquered North Africa in the great expansion inspired by Muhammad, reaching the Straits of Gibraltar within 50 years of the Prophet's death in AD 632. The Islamic message spread rapidly to the peoples and tribes on the southern side of the Sahara, as well as to the nomadic desert tribes and the people along the coast. The Arabs called the region 'Sudan', meaning 'the land of black people'.

The rise of the Mandinka

The Mandinka people, who later founded the Empire of Mali, adopted Islam in the mid-11th century, long before they rose to historical prominence. At that time they inhabited a small homeland on the upper reaches of the Niger River, in the southwest corner of the present-day state of Mali. No-one could have guessed then that this backwater would one day be the nucleus of a major African power.

For the next 150 years the Empire of Ghana held sovereignty over the region.

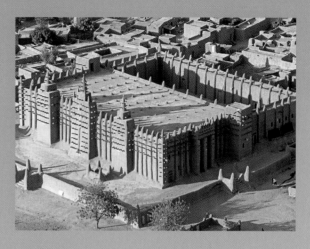

Bird's eye view
The huge extent of the Great Mosque at Djenné, with walls 150m (500ft) long and 20m (65ft) tall, becomes apparent only when seen from the air.

The Great Mosque of Djenné
Djenné was part of the Mali Empire from the reign of Mansa Musa onwards. The Great Mosque is a visible symbol of the importance of Islam in the empire. The mosque is built of adobe and the protruding poles are an integral part of its structure, serving as scaffolding for essential restoration work after each year's autumnal rains.

Ibn Battuta in Mali

In 1353 the Moroccan traveller ibn Battuta spent eight months in Mali, and the description he left of his visit is the earliest first-hand account of life in the West African kingdoms. His first experiences were not encouraging: 'Ten days after our arrival there we ate a thick soup that was made from the [root of the] taro plant and was favoured by the people of this place over all other dishes. On the following day, however, all six of us fell ill, and one of our number died.'

He was more impressed by the principles of the kingdom and its people: 'They are seldom unjust and have a greater abhorrence of injustice than any other people,' he wrote. 'There is complete security here. Neither the traveller nor the native citizens need fear robbers, thieves or high-waymen. The black people do not confiscate the goods of whites who have died there, even when great riches are at stake.'

African emperor

A Spanish map shows the Mali Empire as it was thought to look in 1375. A merchant riding a camel approaches Mansa Musa, whose throne sits between Timbuktu and Gao, the two main cities of his realm.

Ghana's prosperity was based on its control of the southern end of the Saharan caravan routes and the lucrative trade in salt from the north in exchange for southern gold. Its heartland straddled modern Mali and Mauritania, in the Sahel region south of the Sahara – nowhere near today's republic of Ghana, which lies far to the south.

In time, Ghana was weakened by attacks from the north – Almoravid Berbers held its capital for 20 years, from 1076 onwards – and eventually its power crumbled. Vassal kings broke free of the emperors' control to challenge their power. The old imperial heartland came under pressure from Susu peoples to the south and

from the independent kingdom of Takrur, based in Senegal to the west. The stage was set for a new power to come to the fore and impose its will.

A dynasty's legendary founder

The Mandinka people's rise to imperial greatness was inextricably bound up with the figure of Sundiata Keita. The son of a local ruler of the Keita clan, he grew up to become a figure of heroic legend. It was said that he spent eight years in his mother's womb, and was then born

crippled as the result of a rival wife's curse. He was magically cured at the age of 7, and as a young man spent years in the wilderness gathering his strength before returning home to reveal his new powers. On reaching adulthood he wrested the leadership of the Mandinka from relatives who had conspired against him. The historical record shows that he laid the foundations of his future rule by defeating the Susu ruler, Sumanguru, at the Battle of Kirina in 1235, subsequently razing the Susu capital to the ground.

Within a few years of victory at Karina, Sundiata's forces had conquered much of the land between the headwaters of the Gambia and Niger rivers. In the north, his influence extended as far as the important caravan city of Oualata (now in south-eastern Mauritania). By 1240 he had erased the last relics of the Empire of Ghana and was on the way to establishing the Empire of Mali in its place.

Tolerance and gold

Sundiata showed himself to be a wise ruler as well as a successful general. Early in his reign he moved the seat of government from Jeriba in the Mandinka homeland to Niani, in present-day Guinea, closer to the gold mines that were the economic bedrock of his realm. Although he took large tribute payments from the peoples over whom he ruled and required that their traditional rulers swear allegiance to him as Emperor of Mali, he left their other freedoms intact.

He also showed respect for their religious beliefs. A Muslim himself, he made little or no attempt to force Islam on his subjects. He performed the traditional rites of kingship expected of rulers in West Africa, even though these were associated with paganism and the ancient belief that kings had semi-divine powers. As a result, he had few problems with his vassal peoples, who generally proved willing to accept his overlordship so long as they were allowed to regulate their own affairs as they saw fit.

The peace that Sundiata imposed allowed Mali to flourish, much as Ghana had done in its heyday two centuries earlier. Mali's prosperity was even greater, however, as it had more direct control over the gold-fields on which its economic well-being depended. The mines at Galam, Bambuk and Bouré-Mali had lain beyond the borders of the old Empire of Ghana, but were firmly within the heartland of the Mandinka rulers. Niani quickly became a hub of trade, attracting merchants from North Africa and even distant Arabia, winning for itself the nickname of 'the world's navel'. In Niani's markets, gold, ivory and slaves were exchanged for salt, cloth, glass, ceramics and horses.

Sundiata's death

The nascent empire suffered a severe shock in 1255, when Sundiata drowned in the Sankarani River near Niani. His death set off a prolonged struggle over the succession to the throne that might have destroyed a less stable realm. But Sundiata had put down firm roots and Mali survived despite the fact that his successors possessed neither his authority nor the personal qualities he had shown as leader. Even so, the state was beset by intrigues and recurring rivalries.

The taking of Timbuktu

Thirty years after Sundiata's death, a former slave

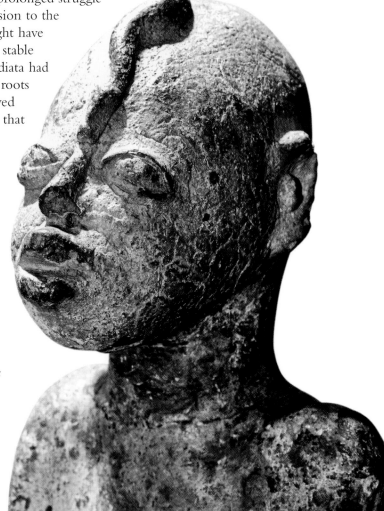

Serpent head
A terracotta figure, from 14th-century Djenné, of a man with a snake on his brow. The inland city was a major centre for trade with the lands of the Atlantic seaboard and local artists may have been exposed to the influence of famous Benin bronzes from that region, but the figure shows that Mali had a sculptural tradition of its own.

Malian horseman
Figures like this rider astride a serpentine horse were used as ornaments for altars and shrines in ancient Mali. The image may relate to the myth of Nommo, a traditional Malian deity.

was succeeded by Abu Bakr II, who had audacious plans to turn Mali into a sea power. With that in mind he dispatched a fleet of 200 ships to 'the farthest ends of the Atlantic', as one Arabic account put it. Only one vessel returned. Abu Bakr was not discouraged, however, and a second expedition, reportedly involving 2000 ships, set off under his command. This one failed even more completely than the first, for no-one ever set eyes on the ships or the Emperor again.

The greatest ruler

Abu Bakr's disappearance, presumed dead, ushered in Mali's greatest age for Mansa Musa now stepped onto the stage of history. He ruled for 25 years, from 1312 to 1337, and was the most important monarch in sub-Saharan Africa in medieval times. Malian and Arab chroniclers vied to outdo one another in their praise him. He was described as a 'virtuous, pious and god-fearing king', who was said to free one of his slaves each day in order to satisfy a resolution he had made to perform a daily good deed.

A growing hunger for gold

Mansa Musa further extended the empire, which by the time of his death stretched from the Atlantic coast of what is now Senegal and The Gambia to the bend of the Niger River, in modern east-central Mali. The realm's prosperity also increased, over the same period, mainly thanks to the Emperor's promotion of the trans-Saharan trade. One of the principal forces driving the boom was the ever-growing market for gold, stimulated by rising demand from Europe. Ever since the city of Florence had started minting gold coins in the mid-13th century – introducing the first gold currency since classical times – Europe's appetite for the precious metal had increased exponentially.

Musa met the challenge by opening up fresh sources of supply. He annexed the city of Djenné, located on a southern

of the royal household named Sakura got the ship of state back on an even keel. He even managed to increase the area under Mali's control, extending it as far as Timbuktu, a Berber-held trading city on the northern loop of the Niger River that was one of the principal termini of the trans-Saharan caravan route. Goods arriving from North Africa were exchanged there for commodities shipped along the Niger or carried overland from Central Africa or from the coastal lands bordering the Bight of Benin on the Atlantic.

Doomed explorers

Sakura was murdered while returning from pilgrimage to Mecca in 1300. He

tributary of the Niger, which controlled gold production in the region now occupied by the Ivory Coast and modern Ghana. The gold was transported across the Sahara by camel caravan, and then shipped to Europe from Venetian and Genoese trading settlements on the North African coast.

Despite the booming trade with Europe, Mali's long-established mercantile connections with the Muslim nations of North Africa remained even more important. By the time of Musa's rule, fresh links had been forged with the Mameluke rulers of Egypt. The Arab writer and diplomat, al Omari, resorted to superlatives to describe the King, noting that: 'The ruler of Mali is the most important of the kings of the Sudan. His realm is the largest and his army the strongest. He is the most powerful, the richest, the best provided, the most feared by his enemies, and the most well-placed to do good deeds wheresoever he chooses.'

A fabulous journey

Al Omari could hardly but be aware of Mansa Musa's largesse, for all Egypt had talked of little else during the Emperor's famous pilgrimage to Mecca. He was not the first Malian ruler to undertake the hajj. Sakura had made the pilgrimage, and a ruler named

Ule had done so within a few years of Sundiata's death. Musa's pilgrimage, however, was a spectacle that would be remembered for centuries to come.

Contemporary accounts of the size of the Emperor's entourage range from 8000 to as many as 60,000 people. Observers reported that when the expedition set off, in 1324, Mansa Musa was still in his palace at Niani when the advance party had reached Timbuktu, some 800km (500 miles) away. The route that the imperial train followed led through Timbuktu to Teghaza (now Terhazza in northern Mali) and Tuat (in modern Algeria), then along the North African coast to Egypt and its capital, Cairo.

The Emperor was accompanied by a personal retinue of up to 12,000 slaves, all dressed in brocade and Persian silk. Five hundred men preceded him, each one carrying a gold-adorned staff weighing about 2.7kg (6lb).

Sacred hut at Kangaba
The Mandinka town of Kangaba was the home of the Keita dynasty and the base from which Sundiata led them to conquer an empire. This hut was built as a shrine where people could venerate the ruling family. Its thatch is still renewed every seven years.

His baggage train included 80 camels, each bearing trunks containing 140kg (300lb) of gold.

If Egyptian observers were overwhelmed by his wealth, they were equally impressed by the lavishness with which he spent it. Al Omari reported that the Emperor 'poured forth waves of generosity over Cairo'. An unwelcome side effect of all this generosity was that the Emperor's gold flooded the market. As a result, the value of the precious metal became so depressed, it still had not recovered its former value by the time al Omari was writing, 12 years after the Emperor's visit. Al Omari also noted the inflationary effects of so much new wealth, reporting that, a dozen years after Musa's passage, 'a person will buy a shirt or a coat or cloak or some other garment and pay five dinars for it, while in fact it is not even worth one dinar'.

The pilgrim's return

Quite unaware of any negative effect his riches might be having on the Egyptian economy, Musa continued on his way to Mecca. There he fulfilled the Muslim obligation to give alms to the poor – to the tune of some 20,000 gold pieces. His largesse was so great that even his fantastic resources eventually ran out, and he had to borrow money on his return to Cairo to finance his return journey to Mali.

Meanwhile, the empire continued to manage its affairs so well it could afford its ruler's profligacy. While Musa was away, one of his generals captured the important trading city of Gao, capital of the neighbouring Songhai people. On his return

Musa stopped there to survey this latest conquest and during his stay he commissioned an Arab architect in his company to build a mosque there of burnt bricks, a building material previously unknown in West Africa. The pilgrimage also inspired him to take other initiatives to spread Islam's influence through his realm. He came back with a retinue of poets and scholars in his train who helped to turn Timbuktu, where he also built a new mosque, into a centre of Muslim learning.

Mansa Musa's patronage had a lasting effect on the chief cities of his realm. But it is doubtful that his proselytising efforts had much effect on the masses living in farming communities in the countryside. For the most part they continued to follow their traditional beliefs, untouched by the cosmopolitan culture of the great religious centres.

The years of decline

Mansa Musa died in 1337, but his empire was still flourishing 15 years later, at the time of ibn Battuta's visit. In the second half of the 14th century, Malian generals managed to expand its borders even further, conquering fresh lands to the east, as far as the shores of Lake Chad.

Thereafter the empire went into decline, as a result of dynastic feuding and attacks from the Tuareg nomads of the Sahara Desert. In the mid-15th century what was left of the empire fell to the Songhai of Gao, former subjects of the Emperor. The new rulers retained much of Mansa Musa's administrative structures but did away with the last scions of his ruling house.

Thirty-eight years after Musa's death, the first European map of North Africa was published on the Spanish island of Majorca. Mansa Musa is clearly shown, labelled in Latin as '*Rex Melli*' or 'King of Mali.' In the most literal sense, he had put his empire on the map and, in the centuries to come, the memory of its former greatness would not fade.

Ancestor worship
To Mali's non-Muslim inhabitants, bronze sculptures such as this embodied the spirits of revered ancestors. People made contact with their forefathers through magic rituals.

The heyday of Kanem, kingdom of nomads

The kings of Kanem created an enduring empire in the lands around Lake Chad. They ruled over nomads and farmers and controlled the trade in salt and slaves.

In 1257 the Hafsid sultan of Tunis, al-Mustansir, received a memorable visit from a delegation from Kanem, a region that lay to the south of the Sahara. Such embassies were by no means unknown – North Africa's rulers had been aware of the famous kingdom of Kanem for centuries past, reflecting its crucial economic role as the southern end of the east Saharan trade routes. A similar party from Kanem had visited Tunis itself 20 years previously.

Even so, the Sultan must have awaited the appearance of these particular envoys with considerable curiosity. Greeting the sultan with the dignity expected of representatives of a powerful kingdom, they showered him with presents – valuable fabrics, exotic woods, slaves – that had been chosen to exhibit the munificence of the Great King whom they served. Yet one gift above all the others captured the Sultan's attention and

found its way into the chronicles of the day: a live giraffe, described by one observer as 'an animal of very irregular appearance'. The Sultan's thoughts on what to do with his ungainly new acquisition are not recorded.

The long-lasting Sef dynasty

The giraffe was a gift from Dunama Dubalemi, the 17th *mai* or king of Kanem's ruling Sef dynasty. This line of monarchs proved extraordinarily enduring, governing Kanem from the kingdom's foundation in the 8th or 9th century AD right up until 1846, when its last representative died without leaving an heir. By that time it had become possibly the longest-lasting dynasty in the world.

The kingdom that Dunama ruled was centred on Lake Chad, which stretches over some 25,000km² (10,000sq miles) and straddles the borders of the modern African states of Chad, Niger, Nigeria and

Desert journey
A caravan moves slowly across the desert. Camel trains were the main trading outlet for the kingdom of Kanem, which controlled the eastern routes across the Sahara to the North African coast.

Cameroon. Kanem lay on the Sahara's southern fringes, a region where nomadic herders exploiting the grazing land of the semi-arid tropical zone came into contact with settled farmers, growing millet, maize and okra in the fertile soils around the lake.

Kanem also lay at the intersection of many trade routes. Its people owed much of their prosperity to the ancient trails leading northward through the area of the Sahara known as the Fezzan, now in southwest Libya. Like the Kawar region to its south, the Fezzan was dotted with oases where desert travellers could find water and fresh dates from the palm groves that grew so well there. The chief caravan route ended at Tripoli on the Libyan coast, where it connected with the main east–west routes that traversed the Mediterranean coastal region.

The different zones that made up Kanem gave the kingdom a mixed population. Black farming people lived alongside Berber nomads from the North African coastal lands who had moved south when the Arabs invaded in the 7th century. There were also more specialised groups, like the fishing communities along the shores and islands of Lake Chad and the isolated Tubu cliff people from the Tibesti Mountains in the central

The blacksmith's art
An ornamental horse harness plate created in the medieval era by a blacksmith of sub-Saharan Africa. Mounted warriors drawn from Kanem's ruling clans formed the elite of the armed forces.

EVEYDAY LIFE

By caravan across the desert

Nomadic herders and traders in North Africa spent much of their lives on the backs of camels. In the desert wastes of the Sahara, the camel was so indispensable as a means of transport it was known as the 'ship of the desert'. The camel's great advantage over other beasts of burden lay in the fact that it could subsist on very little and go for days without water, so it could cross arid regions where horses, donkeys and oxen could not go.

Traders and pilgrims might cover over 300km (200 miles) in a week. Because of the many dangers on the route – of bandit attacks as well as thirst and heat exhaustion – they would join up to travel together in camel trains, or caravans.

The desert was arduous for both men and beasts. Unbearably hot days were followed by bitterly cold nights. But the caravans could find welcome food and, above all, fresh water at the oases that dotted the eastern Sahara.

Sahara. The latter were known to the ancient Greek historian Herodotus as the Troglodytes.

The longevity of the Sef dynasty was all the more remarkable given the diverse nature of the people whom they ruled and the fact that many of their subjects were nomads, traditionally a politically unstable group given to fragmentation along clan lines. The Sef themselves probably originated as an aristocracy of animal herders and traders from the lands on the desert's fringes. As rulers, they had their capital at Njimi to the north of Lake Chad, but they retained their wandering habits and the ruler and his chief advisers travelled constantly in the exercise of their administrative duties.

The Sef kings had long been Muslims, like their counterparts in the sultanates of the North African coast. The first Sef king to convert to Islam was Hume, who ruled in the late 11th century, almost three centuries before Dunama Dubalemi's day. Hume's conversion probably followed naturally from Kanem's close trading connections with the Maghreb, although in later years a tradition circulated that the dynasty was itself of Arab stock, tracing its origins to Yemen across the Red Sea. This story, which reflects the prestige of the great Muslim civilisation of the Middle East at the time, clashes with the fact that contemporary observers generally agreed that the nation's rulers were from a black African background. As devout Muslims, however, they regularly undertook the hajj or pilgrimage to Mecca, and also ensured that Islamic scholars visited their realm.

Dunama and a warrior elite

The power and wealth of the Kanem kingdom grew over the centuries and reached a peak under Dunama, who ruled from 1221 to 1259. He pursued a policy of military expansion that stretched the borders of the realm further than they had ever reached before. To the north, his troops extended Sef control into the Fezzan, previously controlled from North Africa. The King established the walled settlement of Traghen as a new capital of the region.

In the west, meanwhile, Dunama's forces successfully repelled the troops of the Hausa states. In the east they advanced as far as Wadai, now in eastern Chad. Under Dunama's rule and the rule of his immediate successors, Kanem's influence was felt all the way from the Nile to the Niger and from the Fezzan to the Adamawa Plateau on the borders of Nigeria and Cameroon.

On the domestic front, Dunama, like his predecessors, relied on retaining the loyalty of the clan chiefs to secure his hold on power. In time of war, these local potentates and their close kin formed elite mounted units; in peacetime they were responsible for the administration of the areas where their people lived.

The King appointed 12 members of this ruling group to a supreme council that met to take decisions on any political and military matters that affected the state as a whole. One of the chief duties of a strong king was to keep the members of this council under control and working in harmony, making sure that their deliberations and decisions did not run against the policies that he himself had set for the kingdom.

Salt caravan
Salt was one of the chief commodities transported by Kanem's travelling merchants. Among the main sources were the oases of Kawar, located in what is now Niger near the borders with Libya and Chad. Salt destined to be carried by camel was packed into flat slabs (inset) that would hang neatly by the animals' flanks.

To maintain law and order across his lands, the King relied on the warriors at his command. When the state was in danger, he could call up most able-bodied men of military age. In times of need, he could put as many as 100,000 horsemen in the field, alongside twice as many foot soldiers. Not surprisingly, Kanem was a much-feared regional power.

Kings like gods

One aspect of life in Kanem that shocked outside Muslim observers at the time was the semi-divine aura that surrounded the King – this tradition harked back to ancient pagan beliefs and did not sit well with orthodox Islamic views. The monarch rarely allowed himself to be seen in public, except on important ceremonial occasions. Even in private, guests or envoys granted an audience were not permitted to cast their eyes upon him, for he would receive them seated behind a veil that screened him from their gaze. His subjects believed that he had the power to confer sickness or health on chosen people. The rulers themselves no doubt encouraged such beliefs as a way of maintaining their status and binding the people to them, so reducing the risk of rebellion. The more their subjects venerated them as gods, the less likely they were to judge them critically as fallible human beings.

Trading salt and slaves

Dunama's long-term goal seems to have been to cement relations with the Islamic states at the northern end of the trans-Saharan routes, helping to secure Kanem's trading position and guaranteeing the main source of its prosperity. It was with this goal in mind that he dispatched the embassy to Tunis in 1257. His efforts evidently paid

Enigmatic figure
This terracotta image of a female figure with scarifications was found in an archaeological site at Tago near Lake Chad. It is thought to have had religious significance.

off, for the last decades of the 13th century saw traffic across the desert at its height, with caravans carrying cotton, cola nuts, salt, spices and slaves to trade for northern copper and luxury goods.

Kanem's traders played a major role in the trans-Saharan traffic in slaves, which also involved the Hausa kingdoms to the south. The slaves themselves were mostly captured in warfare or in raids on villages beyond the borders of the kingdom. The trade fed a constant demand for cheap labour, not just in the Islamic states along the North African coast but also much further afield. Many slaves were shipped out of Kilwa on the East African coast to the Middle Eastern slave market.

The move to Bornu

Kanem was at its peak in the late 13th century, then in the 14th it went into a decline. New nomad incursions put pressure on its borders, and reverses in battle caused growing discontent among the ruling elite. Subject peoples who had suffered in the past took the opportunity to rise up against their nomadic rulers. The Tubu, the So and, above all, the Bulala from the region around Lake Fitri, east of Lake Chad, all took up arms and the kingdom was badly shaken by the uprisings and bloody clashes.

Eventually, pressure from the Bulala forced the Sef kings to abandon their old capital of Njimi and move to Bornu on the opposite, western, side of Lake Chad. The region here offered good grazing land, and many of the nomadic herdsmen who had always provided the core of the kingdom's military strength were happy to follow the court westward. There, *Mai* Omar established a new capital in the city of Birnin Ngazargamu, now in north-eastern Nigeria. In time the kingdom, which would thereafter become known as Kanem–Bornu, found a new lease of life. In the 16th century, the Sef dynasty kings recovered control of Kanem itself, further to the east, and went on to rule the kingdom for a further 300 years.

The Mameluke dynasty of Egypt

Originally brought to Egypt from southern Russia as military slaves, the Mamelukes eventually seized power in their own name and proved effective, if brutal, rulers.

On May 2, 1250, Turan Shah, the Ayubbid sultan of Egypt, was about to negotiate the release of the French King, Louis IX, who had been captured on Crusade – the seventh – in Egypt. Suddenly, a group of Turan's own soldiers burst in and attacked him. Breaking free, he fled for refuge to a wooden tower on the banks of the Nile. His pursuers set the building alight. The Sultan leaped into the river in a final desperate attempt to escape, but was cut down as he stood in the water.

Slave warriors from the steppes

Turan Shah's assassins were high-ranking officers from his own army. They came from the elite ranks of troops known as Mamelukes, who were not Egyptians at all but the offspring of Turkic peasant families, mostly Kipchaks settled in the Crimea and the steppe-lands of southern Russia. The Ayubbids, like the rulers of many Muslim dynasties, relied on foreign-born warriors for the defence of the realm. The Mamelukes were bought as children to be trained single-mindedly for military service.

Elite troops
Long years of training, discipline and a strong sense of fellowship made the Mamelukes superb warriors. Even the sultans who commanded them were true soldier-kings and in battle were to be found in the thick of the action. This illustration shows a mounted Mameluke archer.

Luxury goods and currency
The art of metalworking during the Mameluke period was stimulated by an influx of Persian and Iraqi smiths driven south by the Mongol invasions. Skilled craftsmen produced magnificent artefacts like this goblet with a coat of arms. The Mameluke sultans minted gold, silver and bronze coins, on which each ruler displayed his own heraldic symbol. This dinar dates from the reign of Baybars I, whose symbol was a lion rampant.

The word *mamlukun* means 'servants who belong to a master', yet the Mamelukes were far from ordinary slaves. Taken into the households of the sultan and his entourage, they were raised as Muslims and received a military education in riding and combat skills. Torn from their families when young, they usually developed a deep sense of loyalty to their master and to their fellow Mamelukes. Conversion to Islam opened up the possibility of advancement to the top ranks of the army.

The pick of the troops and the sultan's own elite force were the Bahris, so called because they were stationed on the island of Bahr al-Nil just outside Cairo. The Bahris expected to be favoured by their master above others, but Turan Shah let them down, favouring Sudanese soldiers for promotion over them. They took their bloody revenge on him in 1250 and this left a power vacuum that they were well equipped to fill. But one person stood in their way – the dead sultan's mother.

A woman in power

Shajar al-Durr had been the favourite wife of Turan Shah's father, who had died the year before, in 1249. She had been instrumental in securing the throne for her son, keeping his father's death secret until the new ruler had time to return to Cairo to press his claim. But Turan ungratefully demanded the return of property that had once belonged to his father. Outraged, she appealed to the Bahris for protection, and so indirectly helped to bring on her son's death.

In the wake of the assassination there was no obvious successor to the throne, and fear and unrest spread across Cairo. The Bahris ran wild in the streets – they were even accused of raiding the women's public baths – and outlying provinces of the Ayubbid Empire took the chance to break away from Egyptian rule. Shajar al-Durr herself stepped in to restore order, briefly becoming the first woman ruler of Muslim Egypt.

A blood-stained marriage

Shajar realised that the country was not ready to accept a female monarch, so to strengthen her position she took as husband an emir named Aybuk from the non-Bahri Mamelukes. In 1250 Aybak ascended the Egyptian throne as the first Mameluke sultan, officially sharing power as co-regent with his wife. Aybak's promotion was challenged, however, by the populace at large, who feared and distrusted the Mamelukes as over-powerful foreigners. Angry protests broke out across the country, and the riots were suppressed with bloody severity.

Trouble also bubbled on within the ruling family itself. As time passed, Shajar grew increasingly apprehensive of Aybak's ambitions, fearing that he intended to install another woman as his chief wife. In 1257 she resolved to be rid of him once and for all. On April 15 of that year, as the unsuspecting sultan relaxed in his bath, his wife's eunuch servants strangled and drowned him.

The assassination backfired badly on Shajar, however, for Aybak's own supporters came seeking vengeance. The queen held out for a time in Cairo's citadel, until hunger forced her into the open. Seventeen days after her husband's murder, she was caught and beaten to death by her dead husband's concubines. Her body was left out in the street for the dogs to eat.

Kutuz seizes power

The new sultan, a son of Aybak by his first marriage, was only 15 years old and he proved unable to hold onto the throne. Just two years later his Mameluke regent, Kutuz, staged a coup and set himself up as sole ruler. Kutuz's action caused little protest because events abroad were suddenly threatening Egypt's security. The land on the Nile found itself in mortal danger and needed to show a strong and energetic leader at the helm.

The Mongol menace

The threat came from the Mongols who, from the early 13th century onwards, had spread terror across Asia under the leadership of the mighty Genghis Khan. The empire he created had been divided on his death, and the south-western portion had fallen to the Il-Khan dynasty, based in Persia. In 1258 the Il-Khan leader Hulegu, a grandson of Genghis, struck westward and captured Baghdad, the capital of the Islamic caliphate. The victors pillaged and burned their way through the city, massacring many thousands of citizens including the caliph and most of his family. The sack of Baghdad spelled the end of the Abbasid caliphate and left the Islamic world without its titular head.

The capture of Baghdad did not sate Hulegu's ambitions. He swept on into Syria, taking Aleppo and the capital, Damascus, early in 1260. Egypt was next on his list, and its fate seemed to be sealed. Then destiny intervened. News reached Hulegu that Ogodei, the Mongol Great Khan, had died and he at once hurried eastward, with much of his army,

Mameluke mausoleum
The Mamelukes ruled Egypt for over 250 years, until the Ottoman conquest of Egypt in 1517. During that time, many new mosques and other buildings were put up in Cairo, among them this mausoleum, the final resting-place of the Mameluke sultans.

Manuals for training warriors

The success of the Mamelukes was based on the military skills they acquired through intensive training, including the study of manuals devoted to the art of warfare. These hand-illustrated manuscripts contained information on such subjects as diverse as the correct use of swords and spears, the best way of treating wounds, and the execution of battle tactics like the feigned retreat.

The Mamelukes regularly practised and performed military manoeuvres on public display at the Cairo hippodrome, and the sultan himself would often come to watch the spectacle. By the time warriors had completed their training, they were not only accomplished soldiers who, thanks to long practice, had no difficulty wielding their heavy swords all day long, but were also knowledgeable in the theory of warfare.

Incense ball (background) This finely worked brass censer for burning incense was created in Damascus in about 1280, during Mameluke rule in Syria.

to attend the ensuing succession dispute. Even so, he left behind a considerable force under the command of his general, Kitbugha, who soon showed his intention of resuming the assault on Egypt. No Mongol force had yet been defeated in open battle, and even though Kitbugha's troops were depleted, he still expected them to be more than a match for the Mameluke army.

Triumph at Ain Jalut

Cairo was in a state of panic but Kutuz kept a cool head, quickly assembling an army that greatly outnumbered Kitbugha's force. Marching at its head, he met the enemy at Ain Jalut, near Nazareth in Palestine, on September 3, 1260.

The Egyptian army was the first in the field and took the opportunity to prepare an ambush. Hiding the main body of his forces behind hills, Kutuz sent an advance guard of Mamelukes forward to employ one of the Mongols' own favourite tactics: the feigned retreat. Duped into pursuing the fleeing troops, Kitbugha's men found themselves surrounded. The ensuing battle produced an unequivocal Mameluke victory. Kitbugha himself was captured and beheaded and the remaining Mongol forces were put to flight in a disorganised rout.

The victory of Ain Jalut saved not just Egypt but also what was left of the Islamic heartland from Mongol control. Yet Kutuz did not have long to enjoy his triumph: on the way back to Cairo he became involved in a dispute with Baybars, one of his most gifted field commanders and the man who had cut down Turan Shah. Hungry for power, Baybars demanded the governorship of the city of Aleppo as payment for his services. When Kutuz refused, Baybars secretly vowed to take his revenge. His chance came when the army reached the Nile Delta. He and his fellow conspirators waylaid the Sultan on a hunting trip, and while one held Kutuz's hand as though in supplication, Baybars ran a sword through the Sultan's back.

A brutal but effective ruler

Baybars then took the throne to the unanimous approval of his fellow Mamelukes. As one reportedly said at the time: 'He who kills the ruler should himself rule.' Once installed in Cairo, the new Sultan quickly consolidated his position, gathering around him a loyal force of guards.

One of his first acts was to appoint a new caliph, as the Islamic world had been lacking a supreme spiritual leader since the Mongols had sacked Baghdad two years earlier. Baybars entrusted this high office to an Abbasid prince who had fled Baghdad at the time. Since the city itself remained in Mongol hands, Cairo became the new seat of the caliphate and there-after the position lost what little remained of its earlier political significance.

Baybars quickly showed himself to be an effective if singularly ruthless and unscrupulous ruler. With single-minded determination he set about the task of destroying all threats to Mameluke power. He persecuted the long-established Jewish and Christian communities within his lands, forcing them to wear distinctive dress and closing down many of their places of worship. He also set up an elaborate internal surveillance system to nip possible coups in the bud.

Most of his energy, however, was directed against Egypt's foreign enemies. First, he subdued the Assassins, a long-established terrorist network linked to the minority Shi'ite branch of Islam. Then he brought to heel the remaining Abbasid princes of Syria, who had survived the attacks of the Mongols. Above all, he renewed the struggle against the surviving crusader enclaves on the eastern Mediterranean coast.

In 1268 he captured the great port of Antioch, which had been in Christian hands for 170 years. To prevent any possibility of the victory being reversed, he closed the gates of the city and ordered a general massacre of its inhabitants; those who were not killed were sold into slavery, flooding the market for years to come. He was less successful in his attempt to win back the Sultanate of Rum, in what is now Turkey, from Mongol overlordship. Although initially victorious, he was eventually forced by an Il-Khan army to retreat to Damascus.

There, in 1277, the 54-year-old Sultan became ill and died. His death was caused by drinking a draught of the fermented mares' milk known as kumiss. According to one account, the concoction had been prepared on his own orders to poison a rival, but he drank it himself by mistake.

The capture of Acre

Baybars' successors pushed on with the policies he had set in train. Two years after his death a new ruler, Qalawun, won another decisive victory over the Mongols at the Battle of Homs and this secured the Mamelukes' hold on Syria. Qalawun also dealt another blow to the crusader states by taking the port of Tripoli in 1289. That left only Acre in Christian hands. This formidable stronghold was set on a peninsular and so was defended on three sides by the sea; on its landward flank it had triple walls. Qalawun died of a fever in 1290 while planning an attack on this last Christian bastion, leaving the task of taking it to his son and successor, Khalil.

The young Sultan launched the assault in April 1291. The city's defenders held out desperately for six weeks, but they could do nothing to prevent the Muslim

forces from undermining the land walls. The city finally fell on May 18, bringing the age of the crusader states to an end. Khalil's forces sacked the city then razed it to the ground.

The capture of Acre marked a high point for the Mamelukes. Over the ensuing centuries the dynasty would be weakened by infighting, much of it between new Circassian elements in the Mamelukes' ranks and the original Turkic core. The result was that most of Khalil's successors had short reigns that ended in violent death. Even so, the slave warriors retained their hold on power in Egypt for a further 226 years. When they finally lost control, in 1517, it was to another great Muslim dynasty – the Ottomans.

Oasis in the desert
Some merchants relax while others prostrate themselves in prayer in this manuscript illumination showing one of the many caravanserais that lined the major trade routes of Mameluke Egypt. The nation prospered as a commercial crossroads between Europe and the Far East, where goods from India and the Spice Islands were sold on to merchants from Genoa and Venice.

The ruined city of Great Zimbabwe

On the southern plains of Zimbabwe stand the stone remains of a city steeped in legend – all that is left of a wealthy yet enigmatic civilisation that flourished 700 years ago.

Tower of mystery
No-one knows the purpose of this stone-built conical structure in the Great Enclosure at Great Zimbabwe. One theory is that it represented a granary, symbolising agricultural fertility.

The Great Enclosure
The wall surrounding Great Zimbabwe's Great Enclosure is 250m (800ft) long and 10m (30ft) high. The enclosure probably contained thatched huts (now lost) belonging to the ruler's family, alongside a number of ceremonial stone structures.

The land of Zimbabwe in southern Africa occupies a plateau whose central region, now known as the highveld, stretches for 500km (300 miles) and reaches heights of up to 1500m (5000ft). This raised tableland holds a secret that lay silent and undiscovered for centuries: the ruins of a stone-built city, overlooked by a mountain temple set on a rocky outcrop crossed by deep ravines. The stone buildings of this mysterious settlement have stood for more than 700 years, built by masons skilled in construction without the use of mortar.

Historians now think that from the 13th century on, the stone enclosures of Great Zimbabwe lay at the heart of a powerful kingdom that grew rich first on cattle-rearing and later on the trade in gold and ivory. Yet the origins of this city that would one day be dubbed the 'African Acropolis' lie still further back in southern Africa's turbulent and still obscure history.

Settlers of the tablelands

At the end of the 1st millennium, people migrated from the north into the land between two great rivers – the Zambezi in the north and the Limpopo in the south. These rivers form Zimbabwe's northern and southern borders to this day. The newcomers belonged to the Bantu-speaking Shona people, who still inhabit the area now, making up over 80 per cent of modern Zimbabwe's population. They were particularly attracted by the mild climate and regular rainfall of the area.

The plateau was blessedly free of the tsetse fly, a lowland scourge of the region they had come from, that infected both cattle and humans with sleeping sickness. In addition, there were rich mineral resources that could be extracted easily, promising a rich yield. It is thought that the Shona were mining iron, copper and chrome in the region as early as AD 1000, forming the metals into tools and weapons and selling both ores and metal goods in the neighbouring areas.

Cattle and gold

The settlers quickly learned that the climate of the grassy plateau was well suited to livestock grazing, particularly for the long-horned cattle indigenous to the region. Before long, cattle-rearing had become the economic foundation of their society, and a man's wealth was measured by the number of beasts he owned.

Of equal importance for the long-term prosperity of Great Zimbabwe were the substantial gold deposits in the region. The Shona had little use for the gold themselves, but they soon became aware of its value among traders operating along Africa's eastern coast. Shrewdly, they took care to keep secret the location of the veins that yielded up the precious gold and the places where alluvial gold was washed from the mountains into Zimbabwe's streams and river beds.

They also spread terrifying legends intended to deter gold-hunters. One tale told of a four-legged pot that ran around an enchanted mountain, filled with burning embers that glowed golden-yellow. Whoever dared approach the site was said to risk losing all his hair; those who went too close either came back mad or else were swallowed up by the earth and were never seen again.

Trading with the coast

Before long the Shona had established regular trade connections: merchants were bartering gold – along with ivory, cattle, millet, cotton, iron, salt and other commodities – for cloth and glass beads from India, Arabian glassware, Persian faience and Chinese porcelain. Arab and Indian traders imported these sought-after luxury items into the Swahili port of Sofala in what is now Mozambique, 400km (250 miles) to the east of Great Zimbabwe. The African ivory was supplied by native hunters, who brought it from the surrounding hills to sell in Great Zimbabwe itself.

Zimbabwe's prosperity grew throughout the 13th century, and the Shona became a wealthy and powerful people. The wealth was not, however, equally shared. An elite who had more cattle and greater access to the profits of

trade came to the fore, eroding the old egalitarianism of village society. This new ruling class sought to separate themselves from their fellow-citizens, and apparently they chose to do so behind stone walls.

A capital built of stone

By the 10th or 11th centuries, walled enclosures had made an appearance across the high plateau. Traces of at least 150 of these survive to this day. None, however, compare in size or splendour with Great Zimbabwe, which evidently emerged as the capital of the Shona kingdom and the seat of its ruling dynasty.

Building without mortar
Great Zimbabwe's builders constructed the city's walls and other structures from the granite of the surrounding hills. Wide fluctuations between day and night temperatures helped them to split the rock into slabs, a process that could be aided by heating the stone with a fire built against a rockface, then dousing the stone with water. Undressed stone was used at first, but by the 14th century masons were chipping the blocks to the required shape and size.

Bird's-eye view
An aerial view of Great Zimbabwe gives some idea of the city's extent. The entire site covers an area of over 40 hectares (100 acres). The Great Enclosure can be seen in the foreground, with the area known as the Valley Complex adjoining it. The Hill Complex, an oval area measuring about 100m (300ft) by 45m (150ft), stands on high ground overlooking the other structures.

Female figure
The gods of Zimbabwe were anthropomorphic. This soapstone female figure is now in the British Museum.

In the Shona language, the words *dzimba dza mabwe*, from which the name derives, mean 'great structures built of stone'. The ruined city lies near Masvingo, some 240km (150 miles) south of Harare. The first Portuguese seafarers, who reached the area early in the 16th century, were amazed to hear reports of its stone buildings, for at that time the vast majority of Africa's people lived in wattle-and-daub huts with thatched roofs. Writing in 1531, Viçente Pegado, one of the first Europeans to record

Great Zimbabwe's existence, wrote that: 'Among the goldmines of the inland plains between the Limpopo and Zambezi rivers is a fortress built of stones of marvellous size, and apparently with no mortar joining them… The natives of the country call these edifices Simbaoe, which in their language means "court".'

Building houses of stone was unknown in southern Africa at the time, and it has remained a mystery to this day how the Shona acquired their knowledge of stoneworking. To compound the puzzle, by the time European contact was renewed they had lost the skill, choosing instead to build their villages of wattle and daub. When the city was rediscovered by the outside world in the late 19th century, even the local Shona themselves found it hard to imagine that their ancestors had possessed such skills, stimulating the promulgation of outlandish theories about the origins of the ruins.

Legends of a lost city

The first European to visit and describe the ruins in modern times was Karl Gottlieb Mauch, a young German adventurer who had travelled to southern Africa in search of Ophir, the Biblical land of gold. Mauch believed that he had discovered the home of the Queen of Sheba – an idea that later influenced the Rider Haggard adventure classic, *King Solomon's Mines*. Subsequent archaeological investigations have shown that Mauch was mistaken. The ruins of Great Zimbabwe developed out of indigenous African traditions and date back no further than the 11th century AD.

The Great Enclosure

Scholars still argue over the exact purpose of the various buildings and complexes that make up the site. The most impressive is the Great Enclosure, surrounded by a wall about 250m (800ft) long and 10m (30ft) high. Archaeologists now think that the wall served less as a defensive bulwark than as a sign of status. The wives and children of the king may have been housed within it, living in traditional round huts that have since disappeared. Other members of the royal retinue lived in similar, smaller walled enclaves, whose circular remains can still be seen clustered outside the Great Enclosure.

King and high priest

The king himself probably spent much of his time in the Hill Complex, perched 80m (260ft) up on a high ridge overlooking the city. As both high priest and secular ruler, he was responsible for his people's spiritual well-being and would have been expected to remain in contact with the spirits of dead ancestors.

Not much remains of the Hill Complex to indicate the exact function or purpose of its various stone structures. Archaeologists assume, however, that at least some of the structures were temples where the king and other priests prayed for rain and agricultural fertility, and where sacrificial offerings were made to tribal ancestors. Marks scratched on a polished stone that may have served as an altar have been interpreted as representing the souls of deceased rulers. After his supplications, the king, with his musicians and retainers, would have descended to the valley via a narrow set of steps.

Traditions of craftsmanship

There is also controversy over how many people may have lived in Great Zimbabwe in its heyday. It seems likely that the vast majority of the population lived outside the stone enclosures in thatched wattle-and-daub huts jammed so tightly together that their eaves almost touched. Huddled together in this way, well over 10,000 people might have lived at the site. The residential quarters also housed craftsmen's workshops, and many locally produced artifacts have been uncovered in the ruins.

One striking artistic tradition was the carving of soapstone sculptures. The most famous pieces are eight delicately carved birds, thought to represent the

white-headed fish eagle, which is native to the region. No-one knows the precise significance of the figures, but they probably served as cult objects; one theory is that they may have represented the spirits of dead rulers. Traditionally the Shona are known to have venerated a spirit known as Shiri ya Mwiri, the 'Bird of God', which interceded between the human and divine worlds. The Zimbabwe bird is used as a symbol of the nation to this day.

An unexplained decline

Great Zimbabwe was at its peak around the turn of the 15th century, but buildings put up after that time show signs of decline, and the entire complex seems to have been abandoned around 1450. In the absence of written records, scholars can only speculate over the causes of its downfall.

A new kingdom called Monomatapa had appeared on the scene by the time of Portuguese contact and had apparently taken over the trade routes that had earlier made Great Zimbabwe rich.

It may be that the city's inhabitants were defeated in battle. It is equally likely, though, that they were victims of their own success, and that the population of the area simply grew too large for local resources to support, causing a downward ecological spiral that ended when the exhausted soils of the region could no longer sustain either cattle or people. Whatever happened, Great Zimbabwe's glory was eclipsed, and the city vanished from history for the next four centuries.

Zimbabwe bird
Eight separate sculptures showing stylised representations of fish-eagles have been found in the ruins of Great Zimbabwe, where they may have served as sacred guardians set on the outer walls. One such image appears on the national flag of modern Zimbabwe.

AMERICA

The Chancay and Ica-Chincha cultures

In the centuries before the Incas, a number of small states flourished in the valleys along the coast of central Peru, in places where long-dead civilisations had earlier existed.

Hungry monkey
A Chancay carver fashioned this monkey with a corncob in its paws to decorate the top of a wooden staff. Chancay craftsmen often used motifs from the natural world.

Throughout Peru's early history, a succession of small but distinctive cultures arose in isolated river valleys that drained into the Pacific Ocean. They owed their individuality and their political independence to the unique geography of the area. The Atacama, one of the world's driest deserts, runs along the coast of Peru, occupying the strip of land between the Andes mountains and the sea. A barren sandbelt between 20km and 150km (12 and 100 miles) wide, it is broken at irregular intervals by some 30 rivers that carry meltwater down from the mountains. The valleys created by these rivers form ribbons of greenery, and it was in these riverine oases that many of the pre-Inca Amerindian civilisations developed.

Most of these cultures were restricted to a single valley, but a few expanded to include their immediate neighbours to north or south. So, in the mid-12th century, several settlements in the valleys of the Chancay and Chillon rivers – among them Pisquillo Chico, Lumbra and Zapallán –

banded together to form what would become a small state. At its head stood an elite of noble families under the overall leadership of a prince named Cuismancu.

By the end of the century, Chancay was the most significant political entity in the central section of the coast. Its temple city of Pachacamac was home to a famous oracle that pilgrims came from all across Peru to consult. Chancay's influence extended to the neighbouring Huara and Rimac valleys, and its culture dominated the region of central Peru where Lima now stands. In the north, the Chimú, centred on the Moche Valley, were the dominant people at this time, while further to the south the Ica-Chincha valley culture was flourishing.

Of potters and weavers

The Chancay had no need of armed forces as military expansion was not on anyone's agenda. Cocooned within their valleys and cut off from neighbours by the desert, the people had neither obvious lands to conquer nor fears of invasion.

Chancay's rulers set little store by ostentatious displays of power. Their architecture was modest in comparison with that of other parts of Peru. Most people lived in small adobe huts with roofs thatched with reeds. Public buildings consisted of unremarkable temples set around ceremonial squares. The largest town in the area at the time may well

In the Chancay culture magnificent feather head-dresses and fine fabrics were symbols of a person's status.

Woollen doll
In addition to clothing and wall-hangings, Chancay's weavers made textile dolls, sometimes even creating tableaux composed of several figures. They were probably intended as toys, although they may also have been used for ritual purposes.

have been Cajamarquilla in the Rimac Valley, now located on the outskirts of the Lima conurbation, which was mainly a creation of the earlier Huari Empire.

The inhabitants of the region, like those of Peruvian cultures before them, were extraordinarily skilled in the making of textiles. Their fabrics dramatically illustrate the richness and inventiveness of Amerindian culture at the time, and have made the Chancay culture famous.

Raw materials were plentiful because cotton was cultivated in the valleys on a grand scale. It was converted by weavers and dyers into tapestries, brocade work and embroidery.

Two techniques in particular reached a high standard in the Chancay cultural region: the manufacture of gauze and the production of colour-fast dyes. To make gauze, cotton was woven in an open mesh that was far lighter and more pliable than more coarsely made fabrics. Dyes were prepared in over 120 different shades from natural materials such as minerals and plant extracts. Moreover, the dyes fixed so firmly that the colours can still be clearly distinguished from one another even after the passage of more than 500 years.

The fabrics produced by the Chancay weavers were put to many uses, from clothing for the living to shrouds for the dead. Some were used as wall hangings to adorn homes. Traders peddled the textiles up and down the coast, stimulating a market in the neighbouring valleys.

Chancay's pottery was also much in demand. Typically, it was made in only two colours, featuring blackish-brown designs painted onto a porous cream-coloured base. The Chancay potters were in fact less adept technically than some of their counterparts in earlier Peruvian cultures, but they made up for any failings in this regard by the vitality and humour in their work. Their favourite motifs seem to have been apes, fish, rodents and birds, but they often gave their pots human features and cartoon-like limbs. They also made egg-shaped jugs with loop handles and comic faces modelled on their broad rims.

The cult of the dead

Like all of the Peruvian valley states, Chancay society had a cult of the dead which they honoured with elaborate rituals. Prominent people were buried with a carefully chosen selection of grave goods, particularly pottery vessels, piles of plates and valuable textiles.

Sometimes animals were sacrificed at burials: the skeletons of dogs, guinea pigs and even llamas have been found interred alongside human corpses. The bodies were buried in shrouds that were invariably painted or dyed red. Sometimes they were given false heads made of cotton and other textiles, painted with facial features and even occasionally adorned with actual human hair.

For almost 200 years the Chancay culture developed at its own pace. At the beginning of the 14th century, however, it came under threat from the north, where the Chimú empire was extending from its capital of Chan Chan and threatening to encroach on Chancay territory. With no written records from the time, the relationship between the two cultures remains obscure, but the Chancay seem to have preserved their independence and staved off the challenge until the mid-15th century, when both cultures were overtaken by the expanding Inca Empire.

The Ica-Chincha culture

The two valleys of Chincha and Ica lay more than 300km (200 miles) to the south of Chancay and were the most highly developed in southern Peru at the time. The area had earlier formed the heartland of the extinct Nazca culture, famous for its 'lines' etched on the desert floor. Later it had been part of the Huari Empire, which collapsed toward the end of the 1st millennium AD. From around 1000 onwards, a number of different communities in the valleys came together to form a distinctive culture of their own and, by about 1160, several urban centres had developed in the Chincha valley. The largest of these, Tambo de Mora, had up to 20,000 inhabitants,

VIEWPOINT

Graves or storage chambers?

A number of subterranean chambers have been excavated in the vicinity of Chancay, ranging from deep rectangular shafts to shallow depressions. These chambers were long assumed to be graves, but for some time now scholars have taken the view that the pits might have been used as cool rooms for storing perishable goods. Chancay was an important centre for trade between the coastal valleys and Peru's mountainous hinterland, and storage facilities would have been essential. The finds made in the chambers – pieces of fabric and pottery, fragments of tools, weapons and jewellery, as well as mummified human remains – could support either theory.

mostly tradesmen, fishermen and farmers. The town was the largest commercial centre in the region and merchants set out from it by sea and by land. Other significant centres included Lurin Chincha, La Centinela and Las Huacas, whose principal activities were agriculture, silver-working and textiles. The towns had sizeable temples and palaces that the Spanish would later call *huacas*, decorated with superb carved friezes in bas-relief.

The nearby Ica valley and its chief town of Ica Vieja ('Old Ica') came to be similarly adorned with public buildings. The bulk of the population, however, lived as farmers in villages in the surrounding countryside.

The Ica-Chincha culture also stretched to the adjoining Pisco and Nazca valleys.

It took many generations for the separate valleys to come together politically under a shared ruling elite. By about 1150, however, Chincha and Ica had emerged as the dominant centres of the confederation. In time, Chincha gained the upper hand thanks to its greater size and its broad sphere of influence, which extended all the way up to the Andean highlands. In its heyday in

Burial oar
This paddle-like wooden object was carved in Ica and destined to be buried with its owner. It probably represents one of the oars used to paddle and steer the rafts that traders used on the local rivers and along the coast. The topmost sections of ceremonial pieces were often ornately carved. This one is decorated with a row of tiny, intricately carved figures (above).

the 14th century, the combined state had a population of around 150,000. As much as a fifth of the valleys' population may have been employed in trade. They had devised a sophisticated system of weights and measures, and even used currency to conduct some transactions.

Today, the Ica-Chincha culture is probably best remembered for its pottery. At first, this took its imagery and inspiration from the wares of the Huari Empire that had preceded it. Soon, however, a distinctive style had developed. After centuries of using only two colours, the Ica potters suddenly began to use up to five different hues in the vessels they produced. The Huari figurative motifs gradually became stylised into ornamental geometric patterns, partly, it seems, in response to growing demand and the need to increase production.

A regulated industry

Similar trends were at work in Ica-Chincha's textile production, which was tightly regulated. Most of the fabrics were made from alpaca wool, although vicuña or even bats' fur were used for exceptionally

fine garments. The animals that provided the wool were communally owned, and state officials handled the distribution and sale of the goods produced by the weavers, who worked from their own homes. The coarsest cloth, known as *cosi*, was used to make blankets, while that of medium quality, *ahuasca*, was used for clothes. The very finest material, called *cumpi*, was reserved for the colourful tunics of the elite.

Trade flourished along the coast as merchants ventured out of the river mouths on rafts to journey north to the ports of the Chimú Empire and the coast of what is now Ecuador. There they bartered salt and copper for emeralds, gold and Spondylus mussel-shells, used as jewellery and to decorate costumes. Sometimes the valleys' rulers went on similar raft-borne expeditions, and on their return were greeted on the riverbank by the foremost dignitaries of the realm dressed in all their colourful finery. Ceremonial rowing regattas were held to mark festivals.

The Inca takeover

The Ica-Chincha culture, like the Chancay, expanded through trade rather than force of arms, extending its influence along the coast and inland up into the Andean highlands. Llama caravans regularly ventured into the mountains to exchange fish, cotton, maize, pottery and guano (seabird droppings, used as a fertiliser) for gold, silver, copper and coca, a sought-after stimulant.

In the mid-15th century the strategic balance of the region changed when the highland Inca imposed their rule on the inhabitants of the valleys. Like the Chancay to the north, the Ica-Chincha people put up little resistance to the conquerors from Cuzco, and in return were granted a privileged position within the Inca Empire.

The Inuit – hunters of the far north

A thousand years ago, the ancestors of today's Inuit travelled from Alaska westward as far as the coast of Greenland, always on the lookout for seals and whales to hunt.

In winter in the Arctic Circle the sun disappears below the horizon for three months at a time and temperatures drop far below freezing. The lands of the American far north are transformed into a snowscape stretching as far as the eye can see. This is the time when Inuit hunters search for food among the ice. For thousands of years they have followed essentially the same lifestyle, devoting themselves single-mindedly to the task of finding food.

Crossing to America

The earliest predecessors of the Inuit arrived on the Siberian shores of the Arctic Ocean about 4500 years ago. They were hunting for seals and migrating whales. Climate change in the form of shortened summers and ever-longer winters forced the hunters to migrate eastward from their original home in the far north of the Asian landmass. Driven by hunger, these wandering nomads from Siberia eventually chose as their new home the coasts of Alaska and northern Canada, which were teeming with wildlife.

The Bering land-bridge

Prehistorians argue over the way in which these immigrants from Siberia crossed from Asia into America. They were not natural seafarers, and even once they developed the kayak, they only ever used them to hunt in calm waters.

One possibility is the appearance of a land bridge across the Bering Strait in the last Ice Age, when freezing conditions caused sea levels in the region to drop by more than 100m (300ft), exposing the sea bed. However, this overland link is reckoned to have disappeared by about 9000 BC – too early for the wave of settlement in the far north, although it was used by earlier waves of immigrants who then headed south towards Central America. Most scholars now take the view that the settlement of Alaska from Asia must have been via the sea route, with the incomers gradually advancing further west by island-hopping along the Aleutian chain in crudely constructed boats.

Whatever route they took, common linguistic features shared between

Craft skills
The Inuit were fine carvers, using whatever materials they could find in the absence of wood (other than driftwood) north of the treeline. This handle was fashioned from the tooth of a walrus.

Sea-going kayaks
In summer the Inuit ventured out into the open sea in their water-tight kayaks, fishing or hunting for seals and small whales. This carving shows a kayak built for two, but some kayaks were single-seaters.

Inuit lands

→ First journeys 1000-1200

┅┅► Second journeys from 1200

● Inuit settlements from 1200

the nomadic peoples of Siberia and the indigenous population of the North American Arctic confirm that the early settlers originated in Asia. Researchers also claim a genetic link between the two populations in the epicanthus or Mongolian fold – a fold of skin extending vertically over the inner angle of the eye that is characteristic of the Arctic inhabitants of both continents.

The Dorset culture

Some 3000 years ago, a first wave of migration took the settlers from Alaska along the northern coast of Canada and around the shores of Hudson Bay as far as

the Atlantic. The lifestyle they developed became known as the Dorset culture. Finds dating from 900 BC or earlier indicate that Dorset culture hunters were by that time already making simple kayaks out of leather and bones and using them for hunting seals. They were also using sleds, although these were apparently pulled by humans. In summer they constructed houses from rocks and grasses. Coastal communities lived mainly off the flesh of seals and whales, which they killed with harpoons tipped with stone. In the forested regions, they used bows and arrows to hunt caribou and moose.

The Thule people

In a second wave of migration between about AD 1000 and 1200, the people of a new culture travelling in small groups journeyed right across the Canadian Arctic and beyond to Greenland. Their name – the Thule – comes from the settlement in Greenland where their culture was first identified. They are generally regarded as the direct forebears of today's Inuit.

Thule culture shared many traits with the Dorset people, including semi-subterranean houses, toggle-headed harpoons, lamps and ivory carvings. In addition, however, they brought new features, including dog sleds, bone arrow-heads and lip ornaments. The Thule culture eventually replaced the Dorset.

The Thule migrants shared the same extreme northern habitats as the earlier Dorset culture, and had only limited

BACKGROUND

Snow goggles: guarding against the sun

The slit glasses that the Inuit fashioned from wood or caribou bones are some of the earliest known devices designed to protect the eyes from the sun. The narrow eye-slits enabled hunters to see without being dazzled as they trekked after polar bears across the ice, sometimes for weeks on end, or waited for long hours at seals' breathing-holes.

It is hardly surprising that inhabitants of the Arctic should have invented such objects, since snow and ice in the far north reflect as much as 80 per cent of the sun's glare. Sunlight at such an intensity can cause serious damage to unprotected eyes.

At the same time, the Inuits' snow goggles functioned as visual aids in the modern sense of the term. The slits cut

out peripheral glare, concentrating the light that did enter them directly on the centre of the retina. This narrow focus enabled hunters to maximise their vision and spot their prey faster in the white Arctic wastes.

Elegant eye-protectors

Goggles like these, which were made between AD 600 and 800, were carved from bone or driftwood and held in place with thongs. They were vital pieces of equipment for hunters on the ice.

contact with other, more southerly peoples, who called them *esqimantisk* – 'eaters of raw meat'. This word eventually became Anglicised as 'Eskimo', a term that modern Inuit consider insulting. 'Inuit', meaning simply 'human beings', is how they prefer to call themselves.

A fragmented community

Life in extreme conditions encouraged the development of self-supporting local communities that recognised no wider political allegiance. Dialects developed naturally, given the intense local focus of Inuit life and the absence of writing in earlier times. The Inuit language has a great variety of dialects. Yupik is spoken to the present day in the coastal regions of the Bering Sea, while on the Arctic coast Inupiat is predominant; the two are so different as to be mutually unin-telligible. An allied people, the Yuit, inhabit eastern Siberia and St Lawrence Island in the Bering Strait. Although they are culturally related to the Inuit and share the same ancestry, they speak a completely different language, Aleut.

Living off the sea

Inuit groups settled mainly around the coasts, as the sea provided their main sources of food: seals, walruses, whales and fish. Finding food presented few problems in summer and autumn, so communities lived in settlements near good hunting grounds. Some lived in permanent dwellings, others in tents improvised from driftwood, whalebones, willow saplings and reindeer pelts, sometimes partly sunk into the ground for better insulation. Life in winter was different, since hunters had to leave their homes and follow their prey over the ice in order to survive, sometimes taking their families with them.

By 1200, the Thule takeover was virtually complete and the Dorset people had been displaced almost everywhere, except perhaps on Southampton Island at the mouth of Hudson Bay where what may have been a remnant Dorset

community survived until 1904. The Thule immigrants had brought new skills with them, particularly in whale-hunting, which they practised communally in open boats called umiaks. For greater efficiency in exploiting the Arctic's scant resources, Thule families banded together in small hunting communities of 20 to 100 individuals.

Tactics for survival

With the coming of winter, cold and hunger became the factors that bound the various communities together. Shared hardship and the challenges presented by the environment gave the groups a strong communal spirit. Each individual took on responsibility not just for himself and his own immediate family but for the survival of the whole group. Hardly any distinctions were drawn between private and joint property. Everything – above all food – was shared. The only personal possessions were clothes, hunting tools, kayaks, sleds and small items such as amulets.

The women were in charge of cooking utensils and lamps which provided heat and light. The fuel came from the blubber of marine animals. When a woman left her husband, which happened often, she simply packed up her utensils and took them with her, as they amounted to her dowry. The Inuit frequently swapped wives, with little conflict or jealousy. For example, a hunter with a pregnant wife could not take her with him on a long hunting trip, so instead would entrust her to another man's care while he was gone. Such practises tended to strengthen bonds of friendship between men.

The Thule people took an equally pragmatic and unsentimental approach to the question of survival. If starvation

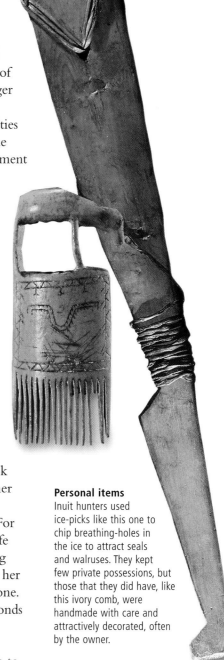

Personal items
Inuit hunters used ice-picks like this one to chip breathing-holes in the ice to attract seals and walruses. They kept few private possessions, but those that they did have, like this ivory comb, were handmade with care and attractively decorated, often by the owner.

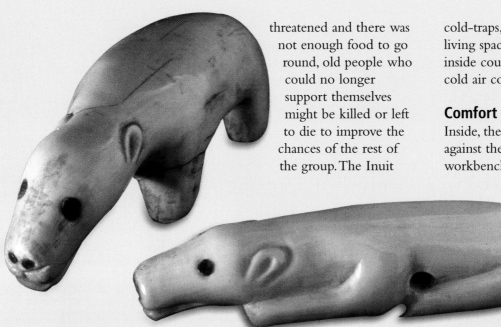

Polar-bear playthings
The Inuit had a flair for sculpture, showing a preference for rounded shapes and polished surfaces, as demonstrated by these elegant bears. The materials they most often used were soapstone and walrus ivory.

threatened and there was not enough food to go round, old people who could no longer support themselves might be killed or left to die to improve the chances of the rest of the group. The Inuit also practised infanticide as a form of population control in times of scarcity. Girls were more often killed than boys, as boys would soon grow up to be valued hunters, going out with adults from as young as 11. New-born babies might be smothered or left in the snow to die of exposure. Children were more likely to be spared once they had been given a name, for names were believed to have spiritual power. If a woman died in childbirth, her newborn was also killed if no-one could be found to adopt the child.

Building an igloo
The constant battle against the cold forced the Inuit to be inventive. For shelter on long-distance hunting trips, they learned to make dwellings from snow. The first step was to cut blocks of impacted snow, leaving a central pit where the blocks were removed. The builder then laid a foundation layer in a circle around the pit. Successive courses of snow blocks were placed one on top of another, each sloping slightly inwards and spiralling up to form a dome. Finally, the cracks between the blocks were sealed with loose snow.

Hunters took advantage of the fact that warm air rises to insulate their igloos. The tunnel-like entrances were designed as cold-traps, set at a lower level than the living space so that the warmth generated inside could not escape to the outside and cold air could not easily blow in.

Comfort zones
Inside, the builders left a wide ledge against the back wall to serve as a workbench by day and a sleeping platform at night. If the igloo was to be inhabited for days or weeks, the women would line it with animal skins. Light was provided by small blubber lamps with wicks fashioned from twisted strands of moss. Cooking utensils were made from soapstone until the time of European contact, after which the stoneware was largely replaced by iron pots obtained through trade. Heated by the burning lamps and the body warmth of the occupants, the temperature inside an igloo could be as much as 50°C higher than the air outside.

As in most other hunting societies, the women were responsible for cooking, looking after the household and caring for the children. They also maintained the tallow candles used for lighting and sewed and repaired the hunters' clothes. To make trousers and coats they used double layers of sealskin. The pelts were naturally stiff, so the women first had to chew them to make them soft and pliable. They used similar methods to produce boots and anoraks (a word that derives from *anora*, the Inuit term for the wind). They were skilled at weaving baskets from grasses and showed considerable artistic flair in the elaborate designs with which they decorated weapons and household items.

Kayaks and umiaks
Occasionally the women would paddle the umiaks. These were sturdy open boats, about 9m (30ft) long and more than 2m (6ft 6in) across the beam, with a frame

covered with walrus skins. They were manoeuvrable vessels that could carry several people, on whale-hunting expeditions, for example, or to transport cargo. With the women paddling, the men could concentrate on directing their harpoons or lances.

Whale-hunting was one of the ancient traditions of the Inuit. Legends told of a primeval bond of brotherhood between humans and whales. People had good reason to feel grateful to the great beasts, as the meat from a dead whale could provide food for an entire community for several months. Believing in reincarnation, the hunters held that the dead creature's spirit returned to the water to be reborn.

In summer the Inuit hunted seals and narwhals – small, tusked Arctic whales up to 5.5m (18ft) long – from kayaks. These small, light hunting boats were made from seal skins stretched over a wooden frame. An opening was left in the centre of the craft. In Greenland and Alaska, the skin of the boat came right up to the waist of the person paddling, so the whole craft was practically watertight.

In winter, when the Arctic ice covered the sea, the Inuit used sleds for transport. Men fashioned the chassis from caribou antlers and animal tendons. To provide seating, they stretched strong skins over the frame, and the runners were made of walrus tusks or fishbones. Metal runners were only used after foreign traders had brought in iron.

Dogs and bears

All the Thule Inuit groups – with the exception of those inhabiting southern Greenland – used husky dog teams to pull their sleds. The animals, which the Inuit simply called *qimmiq* ('dogs'), were descended from Arctic wolves and were well suited to life on the icy wastes. Their coats gave them excellent protection against the bitter temperatures. Because pure-bred huskies were considered to have innate hardiness, no cross-breeding with other species was allowed.

EVERYDAY LIFE

Inuit hunting strategies

The Inuit used different hunting methods depending on their prey. For seals, they would lie in ambush at breathing holes that the seals made by butting their muzzles against the forming ice. In autumn, when the ice was forming, the Inuit hunters could simply follow the noise seals made to find their prey. For the rest of the year they had to scan the ice closely to find the holes, which are surrounded by a ring of rime formed by the seal's breath. Having found one a hunter would wait, harpoon in hand, sometimes for hours on end, until a seal approached the hole and the opportunity came to strike.

Intriguingly, Arctic polar bears use a similar technique, waiting motionless for hours by ice holes for seals to surface for air, then seeking to kill them with a lightning-fast blow of the paw. Bears are also known to stalk seals when they come across a group resting on the ice. They show great cunning in the hunt, sometimes even using a forepaw to cover their black noses to help them pass unnoticed against a backdrop of ice.

The Inuit's favoured prey in summer were caribou and moose. They would drive great herds of the animals towards the sea and then follow them along the shore in their kayaks until they could kill them with spears. Sometimes they would drive the caribou into specially built enclosures where they could shoot them down with bows and arrows.

A comparable method was used to catch fish. When trout and salmon ran upstream in the summer to spawn, the Inuit would wait for the ebb-tide to block the mouths of the rivers with stones. They could then spear the fish trapped behind the temporary dams.

Effective hunting tools
Inuit hunters developed a formidable armoury of weapons including harpoons, throwing sticks and lances.

The Inuit also valued their dogs as hunting companions, especially when tracking polar bears. On such occasions, the hunter would free a chosen husky from the team to follow the bear's scent. Polar bears were known respectfully to the Inuit as *nanook* ('great hunter'), and they were only killed in times of need. Hunters instinctively avoided wasting meat from a kill, and they rarely needed the 600kg (1300lb) of raw flesh that a fully-grown bear could supply. As a result, they would often leave the bears unmolested.

The bears themselves were not always so mindful of the Inuit, and one of the huskies' other jobs was to guard winter quarters from attacks by these fiercest of predators of the Arctic world.

Placating the spirit world

The division of hunting spoils followed a strict set of rules. The hunter himself was allowed to keep small animals and small to medium-sized seals, as long as he gave a share to the old and sick. Large seals, walruses and beluga whales were shared among the community as a whole.

According to a time-honoured tradition, everyone was granted a share of the first whale caught at a new hunting ground or of an especially large whale. If a hunter killed a caribou, he was entitled to its innards and head, as well as the fat from the fore and hindquarters, but the meat was common property.

All these rules had to be followed to the letter, or the wrath of the dead animals' spirits might be incurred. It was particularly important not to upset the marine goddess, Sedna, who dwelt on the seabed tending the prey animals on which the Inuit relied for their survival. From there, she watched over the mammals of the deep, admonishing hunters not to take more than they could eat and deploring senseless slaughter of her animal charges. Sedna's spirit was present in every drop of water, and so hunters would pour a few drops into the mouth of every marine animal they killed to give thanks to the goddess and show their respect to the dead animal.

Shamans communicated with the supernatural world and the souls of dead ancestors. As mediators between humans and the invisible spirit realm, they were responsible for healing the sick, banishing malign forces and persuading the gods to send prey to feed the community. An Eskimo shaman was not required to wear any special clothing, but he would often conceal his face behind a mask when embarking on a psychic voyage so as not to be recognised subsequently by the spirits he encountered. In that way he hoped to avoid any revenge they might be planning.

To enter a trance state the shamans beat drums or tambourines, the only musical instruments the Inuit possessed. Shamans

Shaman's mask
Inuit shamans wore masks like this one to go on spirit journeys to the divinities they believed controlled human health and natural phenomena such as the weather. Most were made from driftwood. This one is painted, and was made by Yupik Inuit.

were also responsible for handing down their people's creation myths from generation to generation. Whereas the Inuit of Greenland held that the first humans emerged from under the earth, other groups believed that they had fallen from the sky. One Alaskan myth claimed that a raven had created the human race and taught them to survive by hunting. Some groups believed that the Northern Lights, the fantastic light-shows to be seem in Arctic skies, were the souls of the dead playing ball with the walrus's skull.

Warm gatherings on cold nights

In the icy nights of winter, whole communities in some parts of the Arctic would gather in large, permanent buildings, where they danced, sang and played games involving animal bones and string that gave them the chance to show off their manual dexterity. Men sang songs about their hunting exploits to the beat of hand-drums, and the women would practice the throat-singing called *kattajait*, creating rhythmic sound patterns deep in the gullet. Later, families would sit in a circle around the shaman to hear him recount the legends of their ancestors. The gatherings provided brief spells of sociability and cheerfulness before the unending search for food began once more, the following day.

For a long time, the Inuit were totally unaffected by outside influences. Over centuries they maintained their traditional ways, nurturing their cultural legacy and handing down time-honoured hunting methods, dances and songs through the generations. Their world began to change when foreign explorers entered their lands, the first being the British mariner Martin Frobisher, who unsuccessfully sought to find the Northwest Passage on three voyages in the 1570s. Although these first contacts had only limited impact, they marked the start of the long, slow process that would eventually wrench the northern hunters out of their harsh but splendid isolation.

Nomad invaders of Central America

The Tarascans and Chichimecs entered Central America from the north as unsophisticated nomads and cave dwellers, but eventually made a niche for themselves in the region.

In about the year 1200, three nomadic tribes, whom the Spanish would later call 'Tarascans', made their new home on the banks of Lake Pátzcuaro. The lake lay 2200m (7200ft) up in a mountain valley in the highlands of western Mexico and it teemed with fish. The Tarascans consequently christened the region Michoacán, or 'Land of Fish'. There were three distinct groups – the Pátzcuaro, Tzintzuntzán and Ihuatzio – and at that stage they were enemies, so they founded separate settlements at a distance of a few kilometres from one another.

The origins of these people is a mystery. Their language was not related to any of the other language families of Mesoamerica, but it did have remarkable similarities to ancient tongues that had once been spoken in Peru and in the southwestern USA. They called themselves the Purépecha, or 'working people'.

Like all nomadic peoples, they accorded greater importance to hunting and fishing

Fire temple
In comparison with the works of some of their neighbours, and even with their own handicrafts, the architectural achievements of the Tarascans were relatively modest, but they were still impressive. The platform of the temple complex in Tzintzuntzán was 425m (1400ft) long and 250m (820) wide. On it the Indians built their *yacatas*, or temple pyramids.

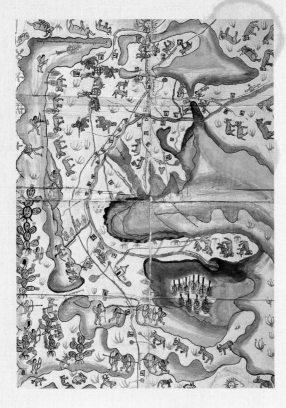

Land of lakes
An ancient map portrays the lakeland landscape of Michoacán. The abundance of wildlife in the region is clearly shown.

Aztec image (background)
The Aztec codices make frequent references to the gods and customs of the inhabitants of the high-lying valleys of western Mexico. This scene from the Codex Vaticanus tells of the Chichimec god Mixcoatl and his deeds.

than to agriculture. They were excellent fishermen using large nets, and they hunted geese and wild ducks with spears hurled from slings, so it was natural enough that Lake Pátzcuaro attracted them. All three tribes arrived on its shores within a short time of one another. After decades of restless wandering they had found a home.

Their first ceremonial act on reaching the lake would have been to light fires in honour of the fire god Curicáveri, their principal deity. The pyres that they created were supposed to burn for ever. They also built temples in honour of the god. The complex at Tzintzuntzán comprised five separate buildings erected on a raised platform 425m (1400ft) long by 250m (820ft) wide. Platform and temples alike were made of large stones fitted together without the use of mortar, covered with a cladding of smooth stone slabs.

Fire worship provided the main focus of the Tarascans' religious beliefs – the name Curicáveri meant 'Great Bearer of Fire'. The main duty of their high priest, known as the *cúriti-echa* or 'firestarter', was to construct pyres, set them ablaze and keep them burning. A newly married man could only move in with his wife once he had built a pyre in front of her wooden house. The Tarascans even sacrificed prisoners of war to the sacred fire. Before they were

consigned to the flames, they were adorned with the symbols of Curicáveri, tall peaked hoods and golden sun-disks.

Gods of fire and water

The Tarascans' most important annual festival was held in honour of the goddess of the rainclouds. In autumn, when dense clouds hung over the region, they would go up into the mountains to the Zinapécuaro thermal springs, situated close to the shores of Lake Cuitzeo. During the ceremony, the priests would cast the hearts of human sacrificial victims into the hot geysers. This caused the steam rising from the springs to condense and, sometimes, precipitate an artificial 'sacred rain' to honour the raincloud goddess.

In the course of a few generations, Tzintzuntzán became the largest and most imposing of the three lake cities, and in the 13th century the first recorded Tarascan ruler, Hiretican, came to power there. By that time the three cities were already linked through a single ruling elite. Their rulers enjoyed absolute power, and each designated a son or nephew to succeed him. In the second half of the century, the leader of Tzintzuntzán, Tariácuris, finally managed to unite the warring cities in a tripartite confederation. It was from this point on that the Tarascan kingdom truly arose.

The ruler not only wielded absolute civil and military power, but was also both the highest judge in the land and its senior religious official. His duties included guarding the statue of Curicáveri that was thought to embody the god's spirit in earthly form. Even the priests who supported the *cúriti-echa* did not have access to the sacred effigy, and they accepted the king's role as the supreme authority in spiritual affairs. A committee of advisors supported the ruler. Each member had a clearly defined area of responsibility – military affairs, the administration of justice, religious rituals, or guardianship of the state treasury, a hoard comprising gold, precious and semi-precious stones, and the feathers of rare birds. The treasure was kept in a specially designated building and was frequently augmented with booty taken on military campaigns into neighbouring lands.

Initially, the aim of the raids was simply to plunder. To guard their own frontiers, they constructed forts made from the trunks of whole trees. These served as the residences of the provincial governors, each of whom had authority over a number of local village chiefs.

The Tarascan kingdom expanded significantly in the second half of the 15th century under the leadership of Tzitzi-pandácuri, a strong ruler who was a great-nephew of Tariácuris. In 1478 his forces won a famous victory against the Aztecs at a time when the Aztecs were otherwise sweeping all before them. By the end of his reign, Tzitzipandácuri's sphere of influence stretched across all of western Mexico and far to the north and south.

The Tarascans' skill in metalworking played a part in their military success, for their warriors benefited from the superior quality of the copper weapons they wielded. Tarascan smiths employed highly sophisticated techniques to work gold and silver as well as copper. They were familiar with the lost-wax process for moulding metals, as well as with filigree work, chasing and even welding. In addition to weapons and jewellery, they produced tools such as knives, pincers and tongs.

The Chichimec – 'dog people'

While the Tarascans were establishing themselves in western Mexico, other northern nomads found their way to the Valley of Mexico where Mexico City stands today. This heavily populated region

was the heartland of Mesoamerican civilisation, with a tradition of urban culture stretching back more than a thousand years. In its prime, the city of Teotihuácan, which had flourished there in the middle of the 1st millennium AD, may have been the largest in the world outside of China. The sophisticated inhabitants of this highly developed region had a word for the uncivilised immigrants who found their way there from the north. They called them Chichimecs – the 'dog people'.

The Chichimecs probably started their wanderings in the wide plains of what is now the southern USA. They travelled in clans, but they shared a common tribal history that was handed down from generation to generation. A king list covering 28 generations of rulers was pieced together from oral history by later Spanish scholars.

Their culturally advanced neigh-bours considered the Chichimecs to be barbarians, and in many ways they lived up to their reputation. They sought shelter in caves, went naked or dressed in animal skins and pursued a primitive hunter-gatherer lifestyle. They were also frequent users of hallucinogenic drugs in the form of the peyote cactus. To quote a post-conquest Spanish chronicler: 'The peyote ... has an effect akin to that of certain fungi on those who eat it or drink it in solution. Under its influence, people see things that terrify them or make them laugh uncontrollably. Its effect can last for one or

Sacrificial bowl
This sculpture of a crouching man holding a basket on his head is one of the finest surviving testaments to the artistry of Tarascan stonemasons. Its purpose is uncertain – it may have held a sacred fire.

two days before it finally wears off".
The Chichimecs used peyote to prepare
for battle and to put themselves into a
trance for rituals.

The Chichimecs arrived in the
highlands of central Mexico at a time
when a power vacuum had
opened up following the
collapse of the once mighty
Toltec empire. The
newcomers squatted among
the ruins of the Toltecs'
former capital, Tula, and
intermarried with Toltec
survivors, adopting several
of their customs and usages.
They were soon restless
again, however, and were
tempted by the riches of the Valley of
Mexico immediately to the south. They
first established a presence there under
the leadership of a legendary commander,
Xolotl, who brought them to the shores
of Lake Texcoco, a shallow body of water
rich in fish. There he founded first the city
of Xoloc, and soon afterward Tenayuca,
close to where the Aztec capital of
Tenochtitlan would one day rise.

In the east Xolotl's conquests took
him all the way to what is now the state
of Veracruz on the Gulf of Mexico. In
the west he encroached upon the
neighbouring kingdom of the Tarascans,
who recorded his expansionist drive in
their histories.

Nomads find a home

Sometime early in the 14th century, under
Xolotl's great-grandson Quinatzin, the
Chichimecs moved the capital of their
empire to the newly founded city of
Texcoco. Quinatzin encouraged the
growth of an artisan class. As Chichimec
society became more settled, demand was
growing for artworks to adorn temples
and for fine clothes and jewellery to dress
the nobility, so their handiwork
was needed.

Central temple
The central temple complex at
Tenayuca was constructed by the
Chichimecs between the 12th
and 15th centuries.

Tenayuca – a shrine with a history
The Chichimecs built their shrines on top of the
ruins of a Toltec temple. In all, there had been
seven previous structures on this same site.

Two shrines topped the temple pyramid at
Tenayuca, which measured about 50m by 30m
(165ft x 100ft) at its base. Chichimec priests
are thought to have practised astronomy and a
cult of the Sun here. The snakes' heads –
known as *teccalli* – on either side of the
sanctuaries may have demarcated the limit
of the shadow cast at the winter and
summer solstices.

The double set of steps ascending to the top
of the pyramid plinth was the work of
Chichimec builders, indicating that this
architectural feature was already known on
the shores of Lake Texcoco before the advent
of the Aztecs, who adopted it.

The temple was surrounded on three sides by
a wall decorated with carved serpents, known
to the Aztecs as *coatepantli*. The Chichimecs
brought this architectural feature with them
from Tula. Over the next 200 years it was to
form the model for other, similar sacred
enclosures around the lake.

Quinatzin's most enduring legacy may have been to bring literacy to his people by importing Mixtec teachers from the Pacific coast region to the south. The Mixtecs taught his subjects reading and writing and helped to familiarise them with the long-established Mesoamerican calendrical system. The Chichimecs had adopted the language of the Toltecs, which eventually entirely replaced their original tribal tongue.

Quinatzin also sent envoys to the Chichimec homelands to encourage groups that had stayed behind to migrate south as his ancestors had done. After the ruler's death, however, the hard-won unity of the realm he had built up crumbled once more. In this fresh power vacuum, a whole series of independent, competing city-states sprang up around the shores of Lake Texcoco. In time they would become easy prey for fresh incomers – the Aztecs, one of the last Chichimec groups to answer Quinatzin's call.

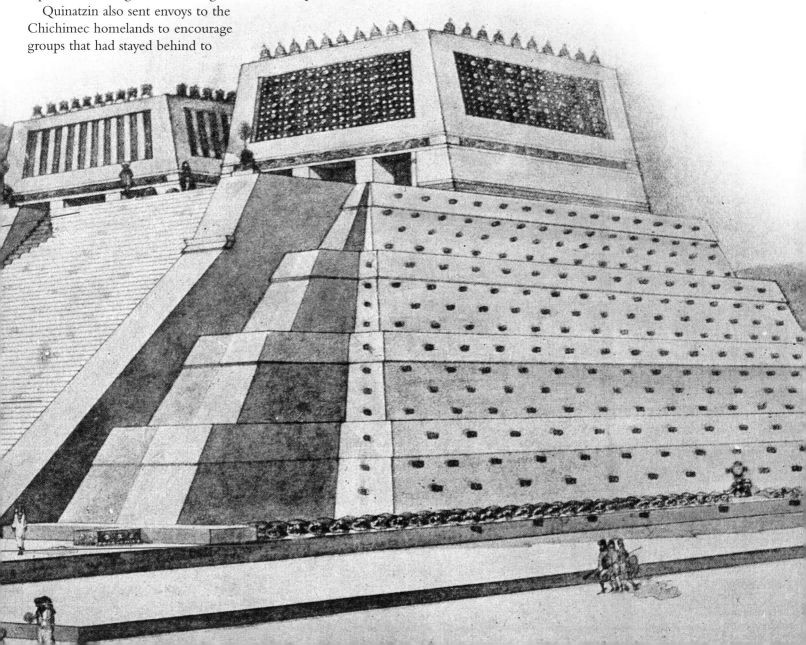

Divine serpent
Snakes played a major role in the religion of the Chichimecs. Numerous statues of snakes and snakes' heads such as this one adorned the temple complex at Tenayuca.

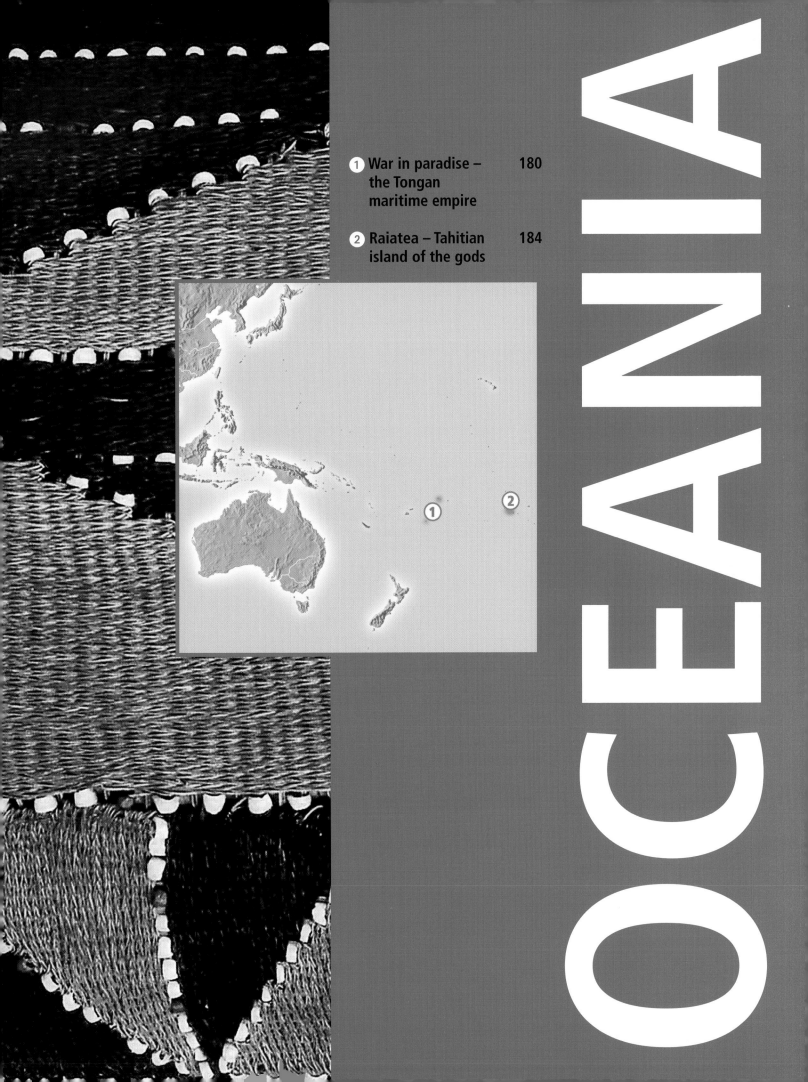

OCEANIA

War in paradise – the Tongan maritime empire

Tonga's rulers were surrounded by a semi-divine aura enjoyed by no other Polynesian kings. They erected massive ceremonial monuments and, for a time, extended their sway to cover Samoa, Fiji and other islands.

Ivory figurine (background)
A huge pantheon of gods and demigods featured in Tonga's mythology. Many of the stories of their deeds were linked to actual historical events, and so have become important sources for scholars researching the history of the Polynesian islands. This ivory figurine is from a later century.

Craft-masters
Baskets woven from strips of bark were reserved mainly for important ceremonies such as weddings and religious festivals. Tonga's basket-makers were masters of their art, which survived through the centuries – this example was made in the 18th-century.

Sometime at the start of the 13th century Tu'itatu'i, the 11th king of Tonga's ruling Tu'i Tonga dynasty, took possession of a new royal residence. In the space of just a few years his subjects had built him an entirely new capital, Heketa, located on the northeast coast of the island of Tongatapu, the largest in his realm. The settlement was endowed not just with a prestigious palace for the ruler and fine houses for the island group's aristocratic elite, but also with a number of massive stone monuments. To build them, the islanders had dragged into place large masonry blocks weighing up to 40 tonnes and raised them upright with little but muscle power to help them.

The first settlers

Tonga is an archipelago of about 150 South Pacific islands, divided into three main groups: Vavau, Haapai and Tongatapu. Some of the islands are volcanic, high and mountainous; others are low-lying coral islets.

It seems likely that humans first reached the islands in about 1300 BC, travelling from Fiji, the farthest outpost of Melanesia, which lies some 750km (450 miles) to the northwest. The settlers were of the Lapita culture, easily recognisable by the distinctive pottery found on all the sites that its people settled, and they

needed new lands to colonise in the South Seas. Landing at a sheltered bay (now an enclosed lagoon) on Tongatapu, the new arrivals soon realised that conditions on the tropical island were highly favourable for settlement. Word spread, and soon Tongatapu and then the entire island group was colonised.

The lifestyle of the new settlers revolved around fishing and agriculture. When need arose, the ruler would conscript them to help on major building projects or to perform military service. It seems that a society organised along rigidly hierarchical lines had developed on Tonga at least as early as the beginning of the 1st millennium AD. A king exercised supreme authority from Tongatapu, while high-ranking chiefs ruled the individual island groups that made up the archipelago, and local tribal leaders administered the smaller islands.

It was in about 950 that the Tu'i Tonga dynasty made its entrance onto the historical stage. The dynasty's name would also become the title of its rulers.

Legends of kingship

Legend has it that the Tu'i Tonga rulers were directly descended from the gods. Once, when the sky deity Tangaloa came down to Earth, his path led him to Tonga. There, he fell in love with a beautiful young woman and conceived a son with her, called 'Aho'eitu. Thereupon, Tangaloa went back to heaven. When the boy grew older, he felt a burning urge to know who his father was. Scrambling up the intricate branches of the casuarina tree, he ascended to heaven to meet him. But although his father was overjoyed at 'Aho'eitu's visit, his divine half-brothers reacted with anger and jealousy. They lured poor 'Aho'eitu into an ambush, killed him, and began to feast on his corpse.

Tangaloa caught them in the act and flew into a rage, ordering them to spit out the body of the dead youth and piece it back together again. When they had completed the task, Tangaroa breathed life into the boy once more and sent him back down to Earth. His half-brothers had to accompany him, and Tangaloa ordered them and their descendants to serve the newly appointed King 'Aho'eitu and his family for all eternity. Mindful of their rulers' divine ancestry, the Tongan people thereafter venerated every Tu'i Tonga as a demigod, especially since, in addition to their role as kings, they were also the high priests of their island kingdom.

The mysterious Trilithon

The Tu'i Tonga were at the height of their power in the year 1200, when the city of Heketa was commissioned. The new capital

was intended to reflect the monarchs' majesty, and with that in mind King Tu'itatu'i ordered the construction of the so-called Trilithon as the architectural jewel of the capital. This massive stone monument consisted of two vertical columns, each about 5m (16.5ft) high and 1.4m (4ft 6in) thick, topped by a huge lintel just under 6m (20ft) in length. The monument stands to this day. The upright sections are thought to weigh 30 to 40 tonnes each and researchers have estimated that it must have taken at least a thousand strong men to move and erect these enormous megaliths – in other words, a quarter of the island's entire male population of working age.

Another local legend recounts how the Polynesian trickster god, Maui, carried this mysterious stone edifice on his shoulders from Wallis Island to Tonga, thus

Camel rocks
Tama Tuma, or 'Camel rocks' are a distinctive feature on the neighbouring island of Samoa, which was conquered by the Tongans in the 13th century. Lush vegetation meant that crops could be grown easily to support the islanders. Tonga's main crop was yam, but other Polynesian islands grew mainly taro roots on irrigated terraces.

explaining why the Tongans called the monument Ha'amonga'a Maui – 'Maui's burden'. A separate tradition suggests that King Tu'itatu'i wanted to demonstrate to his two sons the great things that they and the community at large could achieve if they worked together in pursuit of a common goal.

The Trilithon may have been a monumental arch framing the king's throne, or possibly a ceremonial gateway giving access to the royal residence. A third theory suggests that it was intended to serve as a calendar in stone. Research has shown that a notch cut into the stonework points exactly in the direction of the rising sun at dawn on June 21, the shortest day of the year. Moreover, three paths that lead from the Trilithon to the coast are aligned with sunrise on three highly significant days of the year: the summer and winter solstices and the spring equinox. Some observers have suggested that the king, in his capacity as high priest, used the information provided by this gigantic sundial to determine the correct time to sow and harvest crops.

The role of ceremony

Religious ceremonial played an important part in the islanders' lives, and one of the most important of the annual celebrations was the *insasi*, or harvest festival. The people would file before their sovereign, bringing him gifts of newly harvested fruit and vegetables – yam and taro tubers, bananas and sweet potatoes.

The *insasi* is thought to have taken place in front of another mysterious stone monument. This monolith, known as *'Esi Makafakinanga* or 'the Stone for leaning against', stands 2.7m (9ft) tall

and was sited on a mound in the capital of Heketa. Like the Trilithon, it has also become the subject of legend.

According to one story, King Tu'itatu'i constantly feared assassination, and so used to sit against the monolith which, literally, protected his back. If any of his subjects approached too closely, the ruler would use his switch to rap the presumptuous individual on the legs as a warning to step back. Tongans use this story to explain the etymology of the king's name for, translated literally, Tu'itatu'i means 'Strikes the knee'.

Tu'itatu'i's reign was a high point in the Tu'i Tonga dynasty. His legacy was short-lived, however, for his son and heir, Talatama, chose not to rest on his father's laurels. He decided to move the capital once more, bringing to nought all the effort that had gone into the construction of Heketa.

The site Talatama picked for his new capital was Mu'a, just a few kilometres away. Legend claims that he made the move because his sister was disturbed by the sound of waves breaking on the coral reef off Heketa. In reality, his motives seem to have been linked to a new orientation in Tongan state policy. In spite of the vast expanses of open ocean that separated the archipelago from its nearest neighbours, its rulers now embarked on a period of expansion that briefly gave them a maritime empire.

The new Tu'i Tonga had ambitions to extend his rule over the other island groups with which it was in contact. Tu'itatu'i had built up a large naval force of war-canoes, each over 20m (65ft) long and equipped with outriggers for ocean navigation. Now Talatama

Seaborne empire (background) The Polynesians travelled to the Tongan archipelago in sea-going outrigger canoes. There, they found some 150 islands of varying sizes.

EVERYDAY LIFE

House-building in Oceania

Although they all share some basic elements in common, the wooden houses that were built throughout Oceania displayed an amazing variety of styles and techniques. Some were constructed on stone platforms, while others were raised above ground level on stilts. Dwellings were oval, rectangular or circular.

The roofs were covered with banana or sugarcane leaves. The side walls generally consisted merely of mats of woven coconut-palm fibres hung between supporting beams.

In Tonga and Samoa the houses of the ruling elite were built on low artificial mounds. Larger platforms were constructed to support ceremonial buildings.

determined to put the fleet to use. On the king's orders, heavily armed Tongan warriors put to sea to conquer the island groups of Samoa, Fiji and Uvea, which lay some 1000km (600 miles) to the north. The warlike Tongans drove the Samoans inland, taking the coast.

The Tongan kingdom had a particularly antagonistic relationship with Samoa, which had been settled by emigrants from Tonga many centuries before. As usual in Polynesia, there was a legend to explain the animosity, tracing it to a divine source. The story told how, in times gone by, there had been coconuts on Tonga but no chickens, whereas the opposite was the case on Samoa. The gods of the two islands agreed to exchange commodities, yet each fully intended to cheat the other on the deal. Thus, the Samoan god tried to deceive his adversary from Tonga by disguising an owl as a chicken. Meanwhile, the Tongan god secretly hollowed out a coconut, hoping to pass it off as a full one in the exchange. As they did the exchange, both gods secretly laughed at the gullibility of the other, but then realised that they had also been duped. Since that time, so the story went, there had always been trouble between Tonga and Samoa.

End of empire

The new capital at Mu'a had several advantages for a king bent on conquest. The coast at Heketa offered no proper anchorage for the Tongan fleet, and there was always a danger that the precious craft would be damaged in rough seas. In contrast, the new royal residence of Mu'a was on the eastern side of the Fanga Uta lagoon, at the site where Polynesian settlers were reputed to have first made landfall. The Tu'i Tonga ensured that the site was fortified and equipped with a well-defended harbour.

For centuries after Talatama's time, the Tongans prided themselves on being the foremost warriors of the South Seas. For

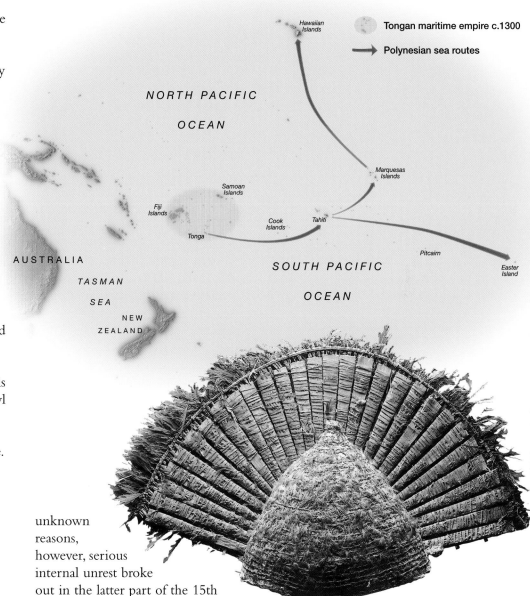

unknown reasons, however, serious internal unrest broke out in the latter part of the 15th century. In about 1470 the 23rd Tu'i Tonga, a ruler named Takalau, was assassinated and future Tu'i Tonga were restricted to a purely religious role as high priests, while a new line of kings drawn from the same lineage, the Tu'i Ha'atakalau, took secular power.

Sometime later the Samoans rose up and freed themselves from Tongan control. In about 1600, an indigenous ruling dynasty known as the Malieota came to power there, asserting their independence. After four centuries of imperial power, the Tongan kings were forced to be content with ruling only their own island kingdom.

Tu'i Tonga head-dress
The Tu'i Tonga was the absolute ruler of his kingdom. He owned all the land, which he granted in fee to his subjects. Farmers and fishermen paid him tribute in the form of a share of their livelihood.

Raiatea – Tahitian island of the gods

For a long time Raiatea, one of the Society Islands, was a centre of religious activity where Polynesians worshipped their creator-god Tangaroa and the war-god Oro.

Located 180km (110 miles) northwest of Tahiti, Raiatea is the largest of the Leeward Islands, the smaller of the two groups that make up the Society Islands, as the Tahitian archipelago is known. At barely 15km (10 miles) across, it is little more than a dot in the vast expanse of the Pacific Ocean. Yet in its day it had great prestige as a ceremonial centre. Pilgrims in canoes would travel to the island to take part in ceremonies in the temple complex of Taputaputea, where they would worship Tangaroa, the Polynesian sea god and, for the Tahitian islanders, the creator of heaven and earth.

Tangaroa began as just one of a multitude of minor gods peopling the Polynesian pantheon. The Society Islanders venerated him as the god of fishermen, imagining him in the form of a whale. Yet as early as AD 725, some 100 years after the islands were first settled, he began to grow in popularity after a powerful Tahitian chief claimed him as an ancestor. Tangaroa's cult gradually spread across the islands, which were dotted across a sea area of some 1600km² (600sq miles). In time, Tangaroa became a greater figure locally than the three deities who had hitherto been the principal gods of Polynesia – Tane, Tu and Ronga.

Sacred trees and sacrificial animals

In about 1250, the islanders built a major cult centre dedicated to Tangaroa, at Taputaputea on Raiatea's east coast. The complex consisted of seven *marae* or temples, each a rectangular courtyard with low stone walls, and often a sacred grove of trees planted within it. At the far end of the complex they built a stone platform or *ahu*, used to display effigies of the gods.

Facing the platform, the builders sank three or more large standing stones into the ground. These were said to serve as backrests for the gods who, invisible to human eyes, graced the ceremonies with their presence. Opposite the *ahu*, animal sacrifices were offered up – most often pigs, which were widely kept as domestic animals. Later in Raiatea's history, humans were sometimes sacrificed before wars or other major undertakings.

Ritual architecture
Over the course of centuries, many thousands of Polynesians found their way to the religious festivals held at Taputaputea on the island of Raiatea – the largest and best-known ritual site in the Society Islands.

Details of the religious ceremonies held at Taputaputea and similar *marae* have been lost, and soon after Europeans arrived on the islands in the 18th century, ancient customs fell into disuse – even the oral tradition recalling them was lost. It seems clear, though, that solemn rites were performed to appease the gods before important decisions were made or a new chief assumed power. In addition, there were fertility rituals at which the islanders would implore the gods to grant them a good harvest or a plentiful haul of fish.

Tangaroa – the creator

The shrines at Taputaputea lie close to the shore, for the Polynesians believed that the ocean breeze – which they called the 'sea's breath' – helped to keep the sacred places pure. There were also practical reasons: the ocean preserved the site from inquisitive eyes and also provided easy access for pilgrims arriving by canoe.

Pilgrims would have known the great myths of how the world was created. At the beginning of time there was an endless void populated solely by Tangaroa, who floated in a closed mussel shell. At some point he broke open the shell, lifting up the lid and thereby creating the heavens. From the lower half of the shell he made the Earth, fashioning its constituent parts from his own body. His backbone became a mountain chain; some of his entrails were transformed into clouds, while others were shaped into lobsters, shrimps and eels. Then he took the feathers that decorated his body and formed plants from them, and used his blood to colour sunsets and rainbows.

To put the finishing touches to his work, Tangaroa used his remaining bodyparts to create other, lesser gods and the first human beings. No ordinary mortals could boast of this honour, but only the Ariki – the aristocratic elite that dominated Raiatea's closed society. Legend had a much lowlier explanation for the emergence of lesser humans, who were said to have crawled out of a maggot

bitten in two by a bird dispatched by Tangaroa. The god used every part of his body in his great work of creation except for his head, which henceforth was venerated as a sacred being.

Tangaroa seems to have been, above all, the god of the Ariki, whose exalted social position he helped to legitimise. In return, the aristocrats spared no efforts in reinforcing their patron god's position, for by doing so, they were reaffirming their own hold on power.

In contrast, Tangaroa played a relatively minor part in the lives of the farmers and fishermen who made up the bulk of the population. They rarely attended the shrines at Taputaputea, instead using their own, smaller *marae* for important family occasions such as weddings, births or funerals. There they would honour the spirits of their forebears, for ancestor worship was a vital point of reference in the lives of Polynesians, and detailed knowledge of a family's lineage was passed down by word of mouth from generation to generation.

So the divine hierarchy venerated on Raiatea mirrored the structure of society on the island. At its head were Tangaroa and

Tahitian god
One of the many deities that populated the Polynesian pantheon is depicted in this carved wooden figure from Tahiti. Such statues were thought to embody the spirits of the gods at religious ceremonies, and so were stationed around the area where rituals took place.

Master mariners
Shown here in a European watercolour, native craft lie off a Polynesian island. Employing tools made of stone, shell and bone, Polynesian shipwrights shaped whole tree trunks into oceanworthy craft. Breadfruit gum was used to caulk the vessels.

Fisher god
The art of woodcarving was highly prized throughout Polynesia. The islanders placed figures like this one representing the god of fishing in the prows of their boats, and made offerings to the god before setting out to sea.

descended from him the Ariki, who thanks to their divine origins were endowed with a special spiritual power or *mana* – a mysterious combination of good fortune, courage and strength. It was an essential quality for a ruler, who had to be equal to all the tasks he faced and able to guarantee the well-being of his subjects.

Mana also helped to reinforce the social order by raising certain people above the common run of humanity and endowing them with status, authority and high esteem. Alongside rulers and high priests, artists and craftsmen such as woodcarvers, tattoo artists and shipwrights belonged to this privileged group.

The world of taboo

Closely allied with mana was *tapu*, the word from which the English term 'taboo' derives. For the Polynesians *tapus* formed an intricate framework of rules of conduct that had to be obeyed rigorously if ordinary people were to avoid danger in their dealings with people or objects possessing mana.

Strict *tapus* were attached to various foodstuffs, which were fit only for the island's ruler and were forbidden to ordinary mortals. Yet kings too were subject to restrictions on their behaviour. They had to take particular care not to touch any object that would later come into contact with any of their subjects. If even the royal shadow fell on some foods, the monarch alone could eat them; otherwise, they had to be thrown away. Intimate waste products such as the sovereign's nail clippings had to be disposed of with the utmost care because of the dangerous mana they contained. Similar taboos regulated most areas of contact between the different social classes. The islanders firmly believed that severe punishment would follow if a taboo was broken – generally illness or death.

So far as is known, the strict segregation of the upper and lower classes on Raiatea was never challenged. People accepted their place in society, and the bulk of the population toiled in the fields without complaint, tending lands that belonged exclusively to the Ariki.

Origins of the Arioi cult

Although the Polynesian islanders at this time had no metals and no knowledge of the wheel, they were highly skilled boat-builders and craftsmen, and their spiritual development was also impressive. They had a priestly class, the tahu'a, who not only conducted ceremonies at the *marae* but also served as teachers, instructing male and female pupils in subjects that ranged from religion and medicine to wood-carving and canoe-building.

Another class of individuals who claimed special religious authority rose to prominence in the 13th century. This was the Arioi, a cult dedicated to the worship of Oro, the god of war.

The earliest surviving written accounts of the Arioi date from the era of European contact five centuries later, by which time the sect included both men and women and venerated Oro in his pacific aspect as 'Oro of the laid-down spear'. By that time the Arioi had a function reminiscent of the mummers of medieval England, travelling from place to place and from island to island to stage public performances that combined pantomime, comedy and wild dancing and that were said to be notable for their lewdness. Wherever they went, they were greeted hospitably, feasted and treated as honoured guests.

The origins of the Arioi, however, may have been very different. In earlier times they seem to have been an all-male society devoted to war, and their rise may have been linked to a violent power struggle that broke out on Raiatea among the ruling elite.

Members of the cult were childless, not because they embraced chastity but rather because they practiced infanticide on any children born to them – a tradition that survived into the 18th century and shocked European observers.

The journey of the *Aotea*

Although the date is uncertain, the rise of the Arioi may have been linked to another event celebrated in oral tradition. This was the departure from Raiatea of a group of settlers under the leadership of an individual called Turi in a canoe named the *Aotea* ('White Cloud').

Maori legend describes how the group arrived on New Zealand's North Island, which they helped to settle. Supposedly, their exodus was triggered by a blood feud on Raiatea that started when a local chief killed Turi's son. Turi responded by killing the chief's own son, cooking the youth's heart, and serving it up to his father as part of a ritual meal. He then made his escape on the *Aotea*, in company with a second group in another canoe that was lost on the journey.

The *Aotea* legend undoubtedly seems to preserve genuine memories of a link between Raiatea in Tahiti and the Maori settlement of New Zealand. A monument to the canoe and its crew was erected by descendants of the early settlers in the east-coast town of Patea on New Zealand's North Island. Some people even associate the canoe with New Zealand's Maori name of Aotearoa, meaning the 'Land of the White Cloud'.

Ceremonial staff
This ritual stave or 'god stick' has been wrapped with bast, a fibrous material made from the inner bark of palm trees that was one of the South Sea islands' most useful and widespread products.

Page numbers in *italic* refer to the illustrations and captions.

Abbeviations: t = top, c = centre, b = below,
l = left, r = right, T = Timeline, B = Background.

AAA = Ancient Art & Architecture Collection
akg = akg-images
BAL = Bridgeman Art Library
RMN = Réunion des Musées nationaux
TAA = The Art Archive

Front cover: Genghis Khan – James L. Stanfield/
National Geographic
Back cover (top to bottom): TAA/Dagli Orti;
Ashmolean Museum, University of Oxford, UK, BAL;
akg/Gilles Mermet; TAA/Gabaldoni Collection
Lima/Dagli Orti; The Trustees of the British Museum.

1: TAA/Genius of China, Exhibition; 2-3: c 4: TAA/
Dagli Orti; 6 and T: Kirche St. Johannes, Cappenberg,
BAL; 7: akg; 8: Interfoto/Bildarchiv Hansmann;
9: Interfoto/Artcolor; 10 B: Interfoto/Artcolor; 10: picture-
alliance; 11: Interfoto/Artcolor; 12 t and b: akg; 13 and
T: Interfoto/Alinari; 14: Interfoto/Aisa; 15: TAA/Dagli
Orti; 16: akg/British Library; 16, 17 B: Interfoto/
Photos12; 18 t: akg; 18 b: Interfoto/V&A images;
19: Interfoto/AAA; 20: Schmidt/F1 online; 22:
Interfoto/Alinari; 23: Photo Scala, Florence, with kind
permission of the Ministry of Culture; 24: Interfoto/
Toni Schneiders; 25: Interfoto/Aisa; 26 B: Mattes/
mauritius images; 26: Interfoto/Aisa; 27: akg/British
Library; 28 and T: akg/Erich Lessing; 29 b: Interfoto/
Weltbild; 29 t: Decani Kloster, Kosovo, BAL; 30: akg/
Erich Lessing; 30 B and T: Altro - die Fotoagentur; 31:
ullstein – Archiv Gerstenberg; 32: Interfoto/Aisa;
33: Muzeum Narodowe, Warschau, BAL; 34 and T:
Basilica di San Marco, Venedig, Cameraphoto Arte
Venezia, BAL; 35 and T: Interfoto/Aisa; 36 B: Interfoto/
Klammet; 37: akg/Erich Lessing; 38: Interfoto/Photos12;
39: akg; 40, 41 t: Interfoto/Photos12; 41 b: Interfoto/
Aisa; 42 and T, 43, 44 B: akg/British Library; 44:
Interfoto/Alinari; 45: Interfoto/Photos12; 46: akg/
British Library; 47 and T: Interfoto/Zill; 48: Interfoto/
Photos12; 49: Centre Historique des Archives
Nationales, Paris, France, Lauros/Giraudon/BAL; 49 B:
Interfoto/Alinari; 50: Interfoto/Aisa; 51: Interfoto/IFPA;
52: Interfoto/Aisa; 52 B: Interfoto/Photos12; 53:
Interfoto/Aisa; 54: Nägele/mauritius images; 55: akg/
British Library; 56 and T: akg/British Library; 57 B and
T: Interfoto/Aisa; 57: bpk/Geheimes Staatsarchiv/
Al/Alfred Schwarz; 58 t: Tiroler Landesmuseum,
Innsbruck; 58 b, 60: akg; 61 Interfoto/Silvia; 62:
Camposanto e Museo dell' Opera, Piazza Duomo, Pisa,
BAL; 63: akg; 64: Interfoto/Baptiste; 65: akg;
66: akg/Erich Lessing; 67: prisma/F1 Online; 68 t: bpk/
Georg E. Hansen; 68 b and T, 69: akg; 70: Ashmolean
Museum, University of Oxford, UK, BAL; 72: mauritius-
images/age; 74 and T: RMN/Musée National de
Phnom-Penh/John Goldings/Bpk; 75: Interfoto/
Bildarchiv Hansmann; 75 B: Interfoto/Photos12; 76:
Bildagentur Huber/Picture Finders; 77 t: Jamie
Marshall/Alamy; 77 b: RMN/Paris, Musée National des
Arts Asiatiques Guimet/Thierry Ollivier/ Bpk; 77 B:
Interfoto/V&A images; 78 and T: Ali Kabas/ Alamy;
79: Interfoto/Aisa; 80: Interfoto/R. Brahm; 81: TAA/
Topkapi Museum, Istanbul/Dagli Orti; 82: Institute of
Oriental Studies, St. Petersburg, Russia, Giraudon, BAL;
83 B: Ashmolean Museum, University of Oxford, UK,
BAL; 83: Louvre, Paris, France, BAL; 84 and T: Stapleton
Collection, UK, BAL; 85: TAA/Private collection,
Paris/Dagli Orti; 86 and T: Interfoto/AAA; 86 B: Ei
Katsumata/Alamy; 87: Interfoto/V&A images; 88: The
Trustees of the British Museum; 89: Interfoto/ Aisa;
90 t: TAA/Tokyo National Museum/Laurie Platt
Winfrey; 90 b: Bpk/Paris, Musée National des Arts
Asiatiques Guimet/Daniel Arnaudet/Bpk; 91: TAA/
Imperial Household Collection Kyoto/Laurie Platt
Winfrey; 92: Interfoto/Photos12; 93, 94: akg; 95:
Interfoto/AAA; 96: Interfoto/Aisa; 96: Charles & Josette
Lenars/Corbis; 97: Bayerische Staatsbibliothek, Munich;
98 t: London British Museum, Photo Scala Florence/
HIP; 98 b: BAL; 99 and T: Interfoto/Aisa; 100 and T:
Interfoto/Aisa; 101 b: Interfoto/Weltbild; 101 t: The
Trustees of the British Museum; 103: Interfoto/Aisa;
104: Interfoto/Aisa; 105: Bibliotheque Nationale, Paris,
France, BAL; 105 B and T: National Palace Museum,

Taipei, Taiwan, BAL; 106 t: Interfoto/Aisa; 106 b: akg;
107 t: Interfoto/Alinari; 107 b: Interfoto/Fritz Pölking;
108, 109, 110 and T: Interfoto/AAA; 111: Novosti/BAL;
112: Völkerkunde Museum, Munich; 113 b: Interfoto/
Bildarchiv Hansmann; 113 t: TAA/Natural Science
Academy, Kiev/Dagli Orti; 114: TAA/Musée National
de Céramiques Sèvres/Dagli Orti; 114 B: mauritius-
images/age; 115: Roger Wood/Corbis; 116 and T:
British Museum, London, UK, BAL; 117: TAA/Genius
of China, Exhibition; 118: K.M. Westermann/Corbis;
119 tl: Interfoto/Photos12; 119 b: akg; 119 tr: Interfoto/
AAA; 119 c: ullstein/The Granger Collection; 120 b:
Archivo Iconografico, S.A/Corbis; 120 b: TAA/Dagli
Orti; 120 t: Interfoto/Aisa; 121 tr: Maher Attar/MGA
Production/Corbis; 121 c: akg; 121 tl: London, British
Museum, Photo Scala Florenz/HIP; 122: akg/Gérard
Degeorge; 122 t: akg; 122 b: Royal Ontario Museum/
Corbis; 123 b: akg/Werner Forman; 123 t: Interfoto/
AAA; 124 b: akg/Werner Forman; 124 t: Interfoto/
IFPA; 125 tl: ullstein/The Granger Collection; 125 tr:
Interfoto/Science & Society; 125 c: Bildagentur Huber/
S. Scattolin/Schapowalow; 126 b: Bpk/Museum für
islamische Kunst/Georg Niedermeiser; 126: BAL; 127 t:
akg/Werner Forman; 127 br: TAA/National Museum,
Cairo/Dagli Orti; 128: akg/Gilles Mermet; 130:
London, British Museum, Photo Scala Florence/HIP;
131 t: Photo Werner Forman Archive/Scala, Florenz; 131
b and T: Werner Forman/Corbis; 133 t: The Trustees of
the British Museum; 133 b: Paul Almasy/Corbis; 134 B:
Interfoto/Aisa; 134: Interfoto/AAA; 135 t and T:
Interfoto/Alinari; 135 b: Interfoto/AAA; 136 and T:
Photo Scala Florenz/HIP; 137: Fotoarchiv, Museum für
Völkerkunde, Munich; 138 t: ullstein bild/The Granger
Collection; 138 b: Fotoarchiv, Museum für Völkerkunde,
Munich; 139: TAA/Coptic Museum, Cairo/Dagli Orti;
140: Interfoto/Aisa; 141: Yann Arthus-Bertrand/Corbis;
142 and T: Interfoto/Aisa; 143: akg/Werner Forman;
144 B: Photononstop/mauritius images; 144, 145: Photo
Werner Forman Archive/Scala, Florence; 146 and T:
TAA/Antenna Gallery Dakar, Senegal/Dagli Orti;
147: Rapho/laif; 148: Photo Werner Forman Archive/
Scala, Florence; 148 B: D C Poole/Robert Harding;
149 b: David Klammer/VISUM; 149 t and T: Aura,
Schweiz; 150: Musee de l'Homme, Paris, Heini
Schneebeli; Bridgeman Giraudon; 151 and T: ullstein
bild/The Granger Collection; 152 b: Photo Scala,
Florence/HIP; 152 t: RMN/Musée du Louvre/Franck
Raux/Bpk; 153: Katja Krusebecker/F1 Online; 154:
ullstein - KPA; 155: Interfoto/Photos12; 156 t:
Interfoto/Aisa; 156 b and T: Chris Howes/Wild Places
Photography/Alamy; 157: Interfoto/Aisa; 158 b:
akg/Werner Forman; 158 t: Rapho/laif; 159 and T:
Private collection, Heini Schneebeli, BAL; 160: TAA/
Gabaldoni Collection, Lima/Dagli Orti; 162: TAA/
Archäologisches Museum, Lima/Mireille Vautier; 163 B:
TAA/Amano Museum, Lima/Album J. Enrique Molina;
163 and T: TAA/Museo del Oro, Lima/Dagli Orti; 164:
Birmingham Museum and Art Gallery/BAL; 165 B:
Keitel; 165 r and l: RMN/Musée du Quai Branly,
Paris/J. G. Berizzi/Bpk; 166 t: Bildarchiv Steffens/
H.Stierlin; 166 b and T: akg/Werner Forman; 167 B:
Keitel; 167 b: akg/Werner Forman; 167 r: Bonhams,
London/Bridgeman Giraudon; 168 b: ullstein-KPA/
HIP; 168 t: Christies Images/Corbis; 169 cl: akg/Werner
Forman; 169 cr: akg/Werner Forman; 170: University of
British Columbia/Bridgeman Giraudon; 170 B: milse/
mauritius images; 171: Peter Harholdt/Corbis; 172: akg/
Werner Forman; 173: TAA/Dagli Orti; 174: Interfoto/
Photos12; 174 B: TAA/Mexican National Library/
Mireille Vautier; 175 and T: TAA/Museo de Michoacan
Morelia, Mexico/Dagli Orti; 176, 177 t: TAA/Nicolas
Sapieha; 177 and T: TAA/Dagli Orti; 178, 180 B, 180:
The Trustees of the British Museum; 181: Interfoto/
Fritz Prenzel; 182: Interfoto/Science & Society; 183 and
T: Kunsthistorisches Museum, Vienna; 184 B: Douglas
Peeples Photography/Alamy; 184 and T: Patrick Ward/
CORBIS; 185: mauritius-images/Bibikow; 186 t: ullstein
bild/The Granger Collection; 186 b, 187 and T: The
Trustees of the British Museum.

Maps originated by Kartographic Müller & Richert
GbR, Gotha, Germany, and translated into English by
Alison Ewington.

The Illustrated History of the World:
THE AGE OF KINGS AND KHANS was published
by The Reader's Digest Association Ltd, London.

The Reader's Digest Association Ltd
11 Westferry Circus, Canary Wharf, London E14 4HE
www.readersdigest.co.uk

First English edition copyright © 2006

Reader's Digest English Edition
Series editor: Christine Noble
Volume editor/writer: Tony Allan
Translated from German by: Peter Lewis
Designer: Jane McKenna
Copy editor: Jill Steed
Proofreader: Ron Pankhurst
Indexer: Marie Lorimer
Product production manager: Claudette Bramble
Production controller: Katherine Bunn

Reader's Digest, General Books
Editorial director: Julian Browne
Art director: Nick Clark
Prepress account manager: Sandra Fuller

Colour proofing: Colour Systems Ltd, London
Printed and bound by: Arvato Iberia, Europe

We are committed to the quality of our products and the
service we provide to our customers. We value your
comments, so please feel free to contact us on 08705
113366, or via our website at: www.readersdigest.co.uk

If you have any comments or suggestions about the
content of our books, you can email us at:
gbeditorial@readersdigest.co.uk

First published as *Reader's Digest Illustrierte
Weltgeschichte: DAS ZEITALTER DER KÖNIGE
UND KHANE* © 2006 Reader's Digest – Deutschland,
Schweiz, Östereich
Verlag Das Beste GmbH – Stuttgart, Zürich, Vienna

Reader's Digest, German Edition
Writers: Karin Feuerstein-Praßer, Andrea Groß-
Schulte, Dr. Cornelia Lawrenz, Otto Schertler, Karin
Schneider-Ferber, Harry D. Schurdel, Dr. Holger
Sonnabend, Dr. Manfred Vasold, Dr. Roland Weis
Editing and design: Media Compact Service
Colour separations: Meyle + Müller GmbH + Co.,
Pforzheim.

CONCEPT CODE: GR 0081/G/S
BOOK CODE: 632-005-1
ISBN (10): 0 276 44121 4
ISBN (13): 978 0 276 44121 9
ORACLE CODE: 351600020H.00.24